PREFACE

PRIMAL SCREENS

We're far enough along in the desktop-publishing revolution that many of us have forgotten what the publishing industry was like 10 years ago. DTP changed the workplace in incredibly profound ways, affecting everyone from chief executives in Armani suits to clerks in fluorescent-lit cubicles—and even down to the folks in the boiler room with mops.

Before desktop publishing, everyone knew that graphic design was the province of experts. Clerical folks were asked to type, format, photocopy, mimeograph, and staple. Designers and art directors, often from outside the company, would make design decisions that were further carried out by highly specialized production people, some of whom spent years or decades working to become artists with an X-Acto knife and hot wax.

Desktop publishing changed all that, allowing CEOs and managers to produce horrific, typo-filled documents that have made their companies look ridiculous. On the other hand, it's also allowed tens—or possibly hundreds—of thousands of people who would formerly have been trapped at an IBM Selectric to learn enough about design and production to have a useful, creative job inside of dour companies.

The problem is that too often workers have come in one morning to find a scanner and its manual plunked down on their desk, and a note taped to the monitor: "Please get up to speed this week; you'll be producing our annual report."

This book is, in part, for you folks who found your job description changed, whether you fought for that change or read about it on your new business cards. It's also a primer if you're making the leap from older, conventional production methods involving photographic techniques—and even stripping film by hand—into mostly digital media. Finally, we hope to help those who've wrestled with the subject and have nearly pinned it to the ground, but who need some solid, focused techniques for producing consistent results that will take them to the next level in their work.

AS TIME GOES BY

The genesis of this book was *Real World PostScript*, a book that Steve wrote 10 years ago, and which was the first in what's become a series of *Real World* books from Peachpit Press. But where *Real World PostScript* focused on the hard-core programming involved with desktop publishing, it became clear that the world needed a book that helped the end user, one that talked more generally about the whole production process, including practical step-by-step advice that could be applied to any scanner, computer, printer, or imagesetter. So, with the collaboration of David Blatner and Glenn Fleishman, *Real World Scanning and Halftones* was born.

NEW OR IMPROVED

The first edition of *Real World Scanning and Halftones* appeared in 1993. Since then, however, desktop publishing has become professional to the point where a lot of elementary issues are no longer talked about—it's just assumed that everyone knows how to get a good scan and print it well. Paradoxically, it has also become harder to get good information about how to scan images and correct them effectively. Scanners have become better and much cheaper, and software has improved, but we still find ourselves answering the same scanning-related questions that we heard five years ago.

We decided to revise *Real World Scanning and Halftones* for three reasons. First, the original edition had fallen a little out of date, and we wanted to keep you all up to speed. Second, the world of com-

REAL WORLD SCANNING AND HALFTONES

The definitive guide to scanning and halftones from the desktop

2nd Edition

BY DAVID BLATNER, GLENN FLEISHMAN, AND STEVE ROTH

An Open House Book

Peachpit Press

For Cary Lu,
Mentor and friend

REAL WORLD SCANNING AND HALFTONES, 2ND EDITION

David Blatner, Glenn Fleishman, and Stephen F. Roth

Copyright ©1998 by David Blatner, Glenn Fleishman, and Stephen F. Roth

PEACHPIT PRESS

1249 Eighth St.
Berkeley, CA 94710
800/283-9444
510/524-2178
Fax: 510/524-2221

Find us on the World Wide Web at http://www.peachpit.com
Peachpit Press is a division of Addison Wesley Longman

Interior design and production: Glenn Fleishman
Cover illustrations: Cary Norsworthy
Cover design: Amy Changar
Copy editor/proofreader: Kris Fulsaas
Index: Jan Wright
Image credits, permissions, and other copyright notices appear on page 417.

ISBN 0-201-69683-5

Printed and bound in the United States of America

9 8 7 6 5 4 3 2

puter graphics has really changed since 1993, especially with the advent of the World Wide Web. In 1993, the Web barely existed, and, in fact, the first edition of the book barely mentions GIF or JPEG, the two most common image formats on the Internet.

Finally, back in 1993, our focus was on scanning and printing grayscale images—interest in color was still pretty low. Today, it's hard to find anyone not using entirely digital methods for scanning, correcting, and reproducing color images. In this edition, we discuss color and the Web in much more detail, and we've updated the grayscale information where necessary, too.

There are four new chapters covering subjects that weren't very real back then: color (correction and management), images for the Web, color output (as opposed to offset color printing), and stochastic screening. We also added a chapter in the Applications section to cover the major scanning applications for Hewlett-Packard, Linotype-Hell, Umax, and Agfa equipment as well as ScanTastic software, which can drive HP, Apple, and Epson scanners.

Note that this book is completely bi-platform—Macintosh and Windows—just as the first one was. We focus on Mac OS 8 and Windows 95/NT, but virtually every software package and trick we mention works in Macintosh System 7 and Windows 3.1 as well.

REAL WORLD SCANNING AND HALFTONES

Ultimately, there's simply no way we can provide you with the exact settings you need for every piece of hardware and software in every situation you'll find yourself in. So we've also done our best to give you the conceptual underpinnings you need in order to address your own publishing environment.

Because we want you to understand not only what button to push, but also why you should push it (or not), you'll find some lengthy conceptual explanations here. Hopefully we've presented them so that you can grasp them easily and without the pain that we've endured figuring this stuff out for ourselves.

Finally, while there are plenty of books out there on imaging theory, hundreds on printing, and thousands on application programs, almost nothing is informed by a real-world understanding of the whole production process—from scanning to imagesetting to offset printing. What none of these books brings to the party is the understanding of how all these pieces interrelate. And if there's one thing we've learned in the world of scanning and halftones, *everything* relates to everything else.

We didn't want this book to be yet another title that was really about Photoshop. We use Photoshop, as well as other programs, in our examples, but a few times we'll refer you to a title David co-wrote with Bruce Fraser: *Real World Photoshop 4*; it focuses on using Photoshop for real-world tasks like scanning, color correction, sharpening, and so on, as well as making selections, using color-management profiles, and creating images for multimedia.

HOW TO READ THIS BOOK

So how should you read this book? Since we wrote it, we think you should read it from cover to cover. In a single sitting. Twice.

We realize that's a bit unrealistic. Because all of this stuff is so interrelated, though, it's hard to give any other advice. In some ways, the topics in this book are like Steve's favorite obsession: sailboat racing. You just can't understand sail shape without a good knowledge of hull dynamics, or vice versa. Similarly, you can't understand scanning techniques if you don't know about printing presses, and so on.

There's no single chapter in this book that doesn't rely on information in some other chapter (or several other chapters). Everything depends on everything else. So when you read the book the first time, some things may appear somewhat mysterious. But when you read it again, the patterns and relationships will start to emerge, and techniques that at first appeared odd will begin to make more sense.

FIRST STEPS

Nonetheless, if you want to just dip into this book quickly, we suggest you begin with Chapters 3, 6, 7, 8, and 9; then jump to Chapters 15, 16, and 17. They'll give you a basic grounding in the essentials of scanning and halftones. From there you can wander through the other chapters, filling in the nooks and crannies of your expertise.

THE BOOK SITE

Like everything these days, there's a Web site for *Real World Scanning and Halftones*. Tune to *http://www.rwsh.com* for the latest links. We'll include the links to resources that appear in this book chapter by chapter; we opted not to include them in the book because many changed in the course of the few months it took to write the update, and will surely change again. We'll also provide links to other resources on the Internet and allow you to send questions directly to us.

WE HAD HELP

There's no way that any three people could have enough personal experience to address all the diverse areas that are encompassed in desktop scanning and halftones. So, while we'd love to take credit for the entire book project, we had help. Lots of it.

Here's a short list of the people who helped us create this book. What you find of value here probably came from one of them. What you find useless or just plain superfluous—well, that part we came up with ourselves.

Arlen Bartsch and Chris Dickman of i/us Corporation
Henry Bortman
Frank Braswell of Systems of Merritt
Jeff Cain of Linotype-Hell

Luis Camus
Cary Cartmill of Pacific Color
Bob Caspe of Sound Vision, Inc.
Rob Cook
John Cornicello and Lonnie Singer of Adobe Systems
Peter Fink of *Desktop to Press*
Bruce Fraser
Lance Gilbert and Keith Mowry of Second Glance Software
Jim Hamilton of Linotype-Hell
Michelle Hanson of Copithorne & Bellows for Hewlett-Packard
Peter Koons of High Resolution, Inc.
Tom Lane, organizer, Independent JPEG Group
The late (and great) Cary Lu
Paul McAfee and Joe Runde of Eastman Kodak Company
Christopher Mills of Ulead Systems
Michele Murphy-Crodeau of Corel Corporation
Tamis Nordling of *Adobe Magazine*
Herb Paynter of Image Express
Doug Peltonen of Luminous
Dave Pola of Equilibrium
Phil Rose formerly of the late, lamented Varityper
Pierre Sevé and Jon Phillips of Agfa
Joanna Sinwell of Hewlett-Packard
Steve Stankiewicz
Simon Tuckett
Imelda Valenzuela and Deborah Garcia of Umax
Greg Vander Houwen of Interact
Steve "dreams in PostScript" Werner
Pat Wood
"Wildman" Bill Woodruff, formerly of Adobe Systems

...AND A CAST OF THOUSANDS

Behind every great author stands a myriad of great supporters. We were very lucky to have a number of people who also helped in essential ways. The first and second editions of the book were supported greatly by all the folks at Steve's conference business, Thunder Lizard Productions, with whom we share space: old friends and former staffers Marci "Queen of Room Service" Eversole, John "DTP Forum" Cornicello, and Tim "TimBot" Cole, and current staffers (President) Steve "Hold Down Command, Option, Shift, Left Bracket, Escape, M" Broback, Toby "Stick Out Your Paw and Say 'Woof'" Malina, Sondra "Key Lime" Wells, Michele Dionne, Agen "If That Is Your Real Name" Schmitz, Krista Carreiro, Damian "Thuuuuuundeeerr Liizzzzzard Pro-DUC-tions" Prandini, Jessica Dale, and Lynn D. Warner.

We had the pleasure of working with several Peachpit Press staffers, including Roslyn Bullas, Nancy Davis, and Marjorie Baer on the editorial front; and Amy Changar and Cary Norsworthy, stalwart production folk who held our hand through the CTP process. Publisher Nancy Ruenzel's enthusiasm for a second edition motivated us to do it.

Scotty Carreiro at Point of Presence Company hosts our Web site and makes it possible for us to receive e-mail. Ole "Dreams in PostScript" Kvern is a wellspring of digital wisdom, even as he is enmeshed in his own busy and brilliant work. Don "Viva Zapata" Sellers we've seen less of at this writing, but he has gone to perfect the Microsoft work-for-hire-and-for-free model. Jan Wright did her usual outstanding indexing job. And our copy editor and proofreader Kris Fulsaas endured endless page proofs and corrections.

From Steve: "Special thanks, this time, to all the people who've taken the time to write, call, fax, and e-mail with their questions, comments, and suggestions for improvement. All your input—your questions especially—have been invaluable in bringing this second edition to be."

From David: "My sincere thanks go to Debbie Carlson, my family, and all my friends who suffered through months of my jabbering about the obscurities of digital imaging. Special thanks as well to everyone who has bought this book and my other Peachpit titles over the years, encouraging me to keep trying to explain this stuff better."

From Glenn: "My late friend and housemate Tara Hester convinced me through her deeds and words that life can be rich without working all the time. I wouldn't have written this book or been as happy without that advice. My deep thanks to my love, Lynn, for her unflagging support. And to my parents and grandparents who have supported all my life's precipitous actions. And I'd like to thank my foster cat, Earl Grey, for her supporting role in this book."

OVERVIEW

PART 1 SCANNED IMAGES

Part 2 Halftones

Part 3 Applications

CONTENTS

PART 2: HALFTONES

CHAPTER 23
BAND AID: FOUNTAINS, BLENDS, AND VIGNETTES 269

CHAPTER 24
WHEN GRIDS COLLIDE:
AVOIDING PATTERNS AND MOIRÉS 277

CHAPTER 25
ROSETTES AND MOIRÉS: BEAUTY AND THE BEAST 287

PART 3: APPLICATIONS

PART 1
SCANNED IMAGES

1 WALTZING THROUGH THE PROCESS

AN INTRODUCTION TO SCANNING

There was a time when we got excited about being able to use type in columns on a computer. Entire layouts that once required typesetting machines, chemical processing, paste-up artists, wax, X-Acto knives, layout boards, Rapidograph pens, and huge vacuum frames suddenly only needed a mouse and a keen eye. Oh, but images? Just leave a ruled rectangle of the right shape and we'll let the printer drop that in later, manually.

Not so efficient, really, but it took a few years after the advent of imagesetting and high-resolution output to start incorporating images—photographs, line art, and drawings—and type on a single electronic page and have confidence that the results would be predictable and of high quality.

Despite the years that have passed since that step, scanning a conventional photograph, slide, or film negative still seems like a black art to many people in the design community. Those who aren't formally designers, but are required to produce documents with images, may find themselves even farther out to sea, because they have fewer resources and colleagues to turn to.

These folks may rely on half-remembered oral lessons to scan images at the correct size or adjust them the right way. We still see people scanning images that take up two or four or even 10 times the storage they need to because someone they can't remember once told them to do it that way. And it pains us when we see anyone using Brightness and Contrast sliders to fix tonal balance.

We're here to tell you that there are simple, consistent, repeatable methods you can use to make sure that you scan, correct, and output the right way every time. We can give you advice about how to approach a new situation to establish your own rules to live by.

REAL WORLD SCANNING

Although we could talk all day about scanning, there are really only five basic considerations that you need to think about:

- ▶ Type of scanner

- ▶ Scanning mode

- ▶ Scanning resolution

- ▶ Adjusting the scanned image

- ▶ Printing the image

When scanning an image, you have to make decisions in each of these areas. What kind of scanner can I use? What resolution should I scan at? How am I going to output the image later on? The problem that most people have in scanning is that they don't understand the interconnectedness of each of these decisions. The scanning resolution depends on the output method; the type of scanner depends on what kind of art you have; the types of adjustments you do to the image depend on the manner in which you scan the image; and so on. (You'll see in Chapter 8, *Color*, just how interrelated each part is.)

Let's take a very brief look at each of these areas, outlining their key issues. We'll go into more detail in each of these areas in the subsequent chapters.

TYPE OF SCANNER

The type of scanner that you use is determined almost entirely by the image you wish to capture (and your budget, of course). If you're trying to scan someone's face without photographing it first, you have to use a device such as a video or digital camera. If you've got a color transparency, you'll have to use a scanner that takes transparent art, such as a slide or drum scanner. For reflective art, you can use a flatbed or drum scanner (of course, you can only use the latter if the reflective art can be taped around a cylinder).

The second consideration is the quality of the scan you're trying to achieve. A scan from a drum scanner often has much higher quality than a scan from a flatbed device (though this is changing with the high-end flatbeds). But a slide or transparency attachment on a flatbed scanner might be more than good enough for your intended output.

We'll take a look at the various types of scanners and what their strong and weak points are in Chapter 2, *Scanners*. This will help you in deciding what scanner to use for your purposes.

SCANNING MODE

One key to creating a good scan is picking the correct scanning mode. This means choosing among line-art, dithered, grayscale, and color. There's almost no reason to scan a black-and-white, line-art image in 24-bit color mode. Similarly, there's almost no reason to scan a beautiful photograph in high-contrast black and white.

What mode you use depends on what you're scanning, what you plan on doing with the scan on the computer, and what kind of output you're aiming for. If you're going to retouch an image in Adobe Photoshop, you'll avoid dithered images. If you're trying to scan type for later optical character recognition, you can choose to use a line-art scan.

If the words *dithered, grayscale,* or *line art* don't mean much to you, the next two chapters—Chapter 2, *Scanners,* and Chapter 3, *Scanned Images*—should be enlightening.

SCANNING RESOLUTION

If you have a scanner capable of 400 samples per inch (spi), you should always scan at 400 spi, right? Not quite. To pick the correct scanning resolution, you need to think about file size, output resolution (whether for imagesetting or color output), screen frequency (if it's a grayscale or color scan), and the size of the image—both the original image and the final image that you print. And all of these items interrelate. By the way, we'll discuss the difference between dots per inch (dpi) and samples per inch (spi) in the next chapter.

We talk about these issues in Chapter 5, *Image Resolution*, and Chapter 6, *Choosing Resolution.*

ADJUSTING THE SCANNED IMAGE

Once the artwork is scanned in, using a particular scanner in a particular mode and resolution, you have to save it as a file on a disk. And once it's on disk, you can change its tonal levels (highlights, midtones, and shadow detail) or color levels (hue and saturation), manipulate the picture (move a tree in the background, delete a person from the scene, and so on), and make it crisper or sharper. We'll talk about these issues in Chapter 4, *File Formats,* Chapter 7, *Tonal Correction*, Chapter 8, *Color,* and Chapter 9, *A Sharper Image.*

You can perform all of these functions—plus create lots of other effects—in programs like Adobe Photoshop, Equilibrium DeBabelizer, CorelPhoto-Paint, or Ulead PhotoImpact, which we cover in Chapter 30, *Image Applications.*

PRINTING THE IMAGE

The last area of scanning you need to think about is how you'll get the image out of the computer into some other form. This includes printing as halftones to black-and-white imagesetters (Chapter 21, *Who Does the Halftone?*), printing to a color device like a six-color printer or film recorder (Chapter 12, *Color Output*), or formatting for the World Wide Web (Chapter 11, *Images for the Web*).

But the issue is larger than just the final output medium; it also can include several factors, like screen frequency of halftones, file size, file format, and a host of other issues depending on the software that you're using (QuarkXPress versus CorelDraw versus Photoshop, and so on); we cover this in Part 3, *Applications*.

With all these items to think about for what seemed like a simple scan, it's amazing that anyone ever gets them right! Fortunately, the bark is worse than the bite; we're confident that after reading Part 1, *Scanned Images*, you'll have all the necessary information to create great scans.

2 SCANNERS

WHAT YOU NEED
AND WHAT YOU GET

Choice is good. We like having as many options as possible. But too much choice makes your head spin on its axis. Every day, it seems, a new scanner model or three appear—faster, stronger, and more powerful than the ones preceding it.

Every scanner does basically the same thing: it takes a picture of a physical image, like a photograph, and turns it into something your computer can use. All scanners even do it in pretty much the same way. But we're going to tell you how each part works so you can understand what's really going on at each step of the way.

We'll explain what different kinds of scanners can do—and what they can't do—as well as what makes a good scanner. You can use these guidelines in searching for a unit yourself or in reading product comparisons or marketing literature. We'll also talk a bit about digital cameras, which work almost identically to scanners but have a different purpose and different options.

SCANNING FACTORS

There are five major factors to consider in working with scanners: scanning, resolution, bit depth and dynamic range, software, and scanner type.

SCANNING RIGHT. We'll tell you over and over again in this book that you have to start with a scan done the right way. Most things you can fix later, but only at a cost in quality and time.

RESOLUTION. How many samples per inch (spi) can the scanner capture? This seems simple, but isn't always. There's optical resolution and interpolated resolution, and resolution needs vary depending on the size and kind of material you're scanning. (Resolution is explored in Chapter 5, *Image Resolution*, and Chapter 6, *Choosing Resolution.*)

BIT DEPTH AND DYNAMIC RANGE. How many bits per sample does the scanner capture and how well? Again, a simple number doesn't tell the whole story. All 30-bit scanners are not created equal—if they were, one wouldn't cost $150 and another $1,500. The real question is how wide a range of colors the scanner can capture and how well it can differentiate tones across that range and at the difficult extremes—whether grayscale or color. (We cover this in more depth in Chapter 3, *Scanned Images.*)

SOFTWARE. What capabilities are built into the scanning software? Does it just capture an image and drop it on disk, or can it apply tonal correction and sharpening as it scans? Does it allow you to correct in the scanner using deeper color than you can bring into the computer? Does the scanner only work with a standalone application, or can you access it via plug-in modules from within other programs? Does it work with the almost–industry-standard TWAIN format? (See Chapter 33, *Scanning Applications*, for more on this subject and a definition of TWAIN.)

SCANNER TYPE. Is the scanner a flatbed, slide scanner, or drum scanner? Does it use CCD, CMOS, or PMT to capture samples? Or is it a more specialized unit, like a video-capture system or sheetfed scanner? The type you use determines the types of images you can capture, and different types have different strengths and weaknesses in the four previous areas.

SCANNING RIGHT

For the first—but not last—time, we're telling you to get the scan right *before* making any changes to it. Taking precautions and experimenting a little can save you loads of time later—especially when you're trying to remove dust or smears from a scan, rather than from the scanner or photographic film you started with.

WARMING UP. Scanners take a few minutes to warm up. For better results, turn your scanner on 30 minutes before you make your first scan. Some scanners will automatically warn you when the scanner bulb hasn't reached the right temperature, and will perform warm-up routines until it's ready.

SHMUTZ AND FINGERPRINTS. As our grandmothers would say, shmutz is bad. Keep dirt and dust off scanners, film, and prints. Keep a can of compressed air (the non-ozone-layer-destroying kind) or a small compressor at hand to gently get rid of dust.

Don't use facial tissues, for heaven's sake. Facial tissues are made from wood pulp and can microscopically—but within a scanner's resolution—scratch the glass on a flatbed or put marks all over film and prints. You can get special, one-time-use cotton wipes for cleaning glass and gently removing dust from photographic materials.

Clean your flatbed's glass frequently. You can get a cleaner that doesn't streak; window cleaners are a bad idea for scanner glass.

Fingerprints on film can be unremovable. The skin's oils can chemically change film emulsion. You can get a cleaning solution that helps in some cases from a photographic store; never use water.

Try to keep a supply of white cotton disposable gloves around for handling film and other materials.

NEWTON RINGS. If you're scanning at very high resolutions, you can see a phenomenon called *Newton rings*, which are interference patterns resulting from the contact of film stock and glass. These are most commonly seen on drum scanners, where the film is taped up against a cylinder, but high-resolution flatbeds can demonstrate the same problem.

The solution is to use a special mounting oil between the film and the glass, which floats the film and removes the appearance of rings. You can get this oil from photographic stores, although they might not recognize the term; they know the problem, however.

SQUARING IT UP. It's easier and better to scan something square—with no rotation—than to use software to correct it later. When you use software, it reduces sharpness and degrades image quality.

CALIBRATION. If your scanner has some calibration software that can make adjustments to improve scans, use it. If you decide to use a color management system—see Chapter 8, *Color*—you might have to turn it off, however. Most scanners have some kind of calibration option that checks the light source and stepping motor, and you can run this once a day or so to keep yours in tune.

ITERATE. When you're making scans, don't be afraid to make some samples, be dissatisfied, and try it again. Experimentation is the root of success with scanning. Iteration doesn't have to be avoided. It can also help to build your visual acuity, when you make smaller and smaller changes to scanning settings, and then have to make a judgment about whether the resulting image is better or worse than the previous attempt.

Most scanners offer several options about how to perform a scan, from creating color scans in one pass or three passes, to color versus grayscale, to arbitrary settings that are listed as "good" and "better." We recommend performing the same scan a few times with different combinations of these settings until you get a result that you consider best—"best" based on the criteria we present in the rest of this book, of course! When you find the ideal combination of settings, write them down or save them in the software.

RESOLUTION

It seems like it should be easy to compare different scanners' maximum resolutions. One scans at 300 spi (samples per inch)—manufacturers like to say "dots per inch," but that's not really accurate—and another scans at 600 spi. So the 600-spi scanner is better, right?

Not necessarily. Manufacturers usually list both their scanners' *optical resolution* and *interpolated resolution* in their marketing materials. Optical resolution is the maximum number of samples the scanner takes per inch, but it's not always easy to find or clearly labeled. You can read Chapter 5, *Image Resolution*, to find out what interpolated resolution means, but we can tell you right here that it doesn't mean the scanner can actually capture more usable information than the optical resolution.

Keep in mind that you need a much higher resolution—more samples per inch—for slides and film than you do for reflective art because you're usually enlarging a 35 mm slide quite a bit more than 4-by-5-inch photo. We'll explain more about resolution in the next chapter, *Scanned Images*.

BIT DEPTH AND DYNAMIC RANGE

Bit depth is one measurement of the number of tones a scanner can differentiate; the depth is a measure of how many colors can be represented in each sample captured by the scanner. The more bits, the greater number of shades of gray or different colors that can be represented. (This is explained in greater depth in the next chapter, *Scanned Images*.) *Dynamic range* expresses how broad a range of tonal values a scanner can capture; this is similar to the photographic measure of *density*. And *tonal sensitivity* describes how well tones are differentiated.

BIT DEPTH. Bit depth is measured, naturally, in bits: single binary digits that represent either zero or one. An antiquated 1-bit-per-sample (or bilevel) scanner could only capture two colors: black and white. A hypothetical 4-bit scanner could capture 16 levels of gray (2 to the fourth power, or 2^4); 8-bit grayscale scanners grab 256 levels (2^8); and a 24-bit scanner can measure any of more than 16 million different colors (2^{24}). Some scanners capture 256, 4,096, or even 16 million times more levels than that.

DYNAMIC RANGE. Where bit depth counts the potential number of different colors a scanner can measure, dynamic range describes the actual limits of how many tones the scanner can really differentiate from light to dark. Our friend Bruce Fraser likes to compare bit depth and dynamic range to a staircase: the dynamic range describes the height of the staircase and the bit depth describes the number of steps from the bottom to the top. A scanner with an enormous dynamic range (able to capture information from the very light to the very dark) but only 256 steps doesn't do you any good; neither does a scanner with lots and lots of tiny steps (like a 36-bit scanner) that spans only a tiny dynamic range.

TONAL SENSITIVITY. Neither density nor bit depth tells you how *well* the scanner can do tonal sensitivity. That's the ability of a scanner to accurately represent similar, adjacent tonal values as distinct from each other. Some scanners are great in the lighter and darker areas of a scan, but muddy in the midtones, where most of the Caucasian flesh tones are found. The manufacturers don't report this, but the rule of thumb is—generally, but not always—the more expensive the scanner, the better the tonal sensitivity.

DENSITY

If you combine dynamic range and bit depth into a measure of the range and extent of tones that can be captured, you're pretty close to the photographic term *density*. The amount of light that film records is measured as density, using the symbol "D." Density is actually a measure of how opaque the film is, or how much light can shine through it (or reflect off it, in the case of prints). The more opaque or dense the film is, the more chemical that's been deposited on the film stock, and the greater tonal range the photographic emulsion can capture.

The lightest and darkest tones a particular film can capture—the minimum and maximum tonal values—are called the "D_{MIN}" and the "D_{MAX}". A film's entire tonal range is measured by subtracting the minimum from the maximum, like a D_{MAX} of 3.3 minus a D_{MIN}

of 0.3 means an overall density of 3.0D. Negative film is rated around 3.0D, while prints are usually less than 2.0D, and transparencies or slides are as high as 4.0D.

The densest areas of film and prints are hardest for scanners to capture. This is because scanners measure light in a straight line, while film records—and the human eye perceives—light as a sharply increasing logarithmic curve (see Figure 2-1).

FIGURE 2-1
Film density versus scanner exposure

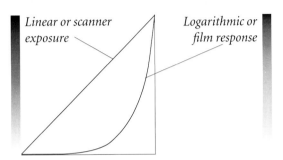

Linear or scanner exposure

Logarithmic or film response

The curve is steepest in the densest areas, which are also the darkest in film transparencies and reflective art; this is called the *shadow detail*. In film negatives, the densest areas represent the lightest tones or *highlight detail*, because the film is reversed out.

Bit depth and density are related concepts because of this problem of capturing enough information at the steepest part of the density curve. The greater the bit depth, the larger number of values that can be captured in the densest areas, which effectively increases the density value for the scanner (see Figure 2-2).

Most scanners have density ratings these days, which makes it easier to decide whether a given scanner can adequately capture the detail in the work you need scanned. If you're scanning mostly reflective art, a scanner with 2.8D is fine. If you're digitizing transparencies day in and day out, you'd better get a scanner with at least 3.3D, but maybe higher.

Unless you always use large-format transparencies and drum scanners, you'll always be making some compromises in your density. You have to sacrifice some tones at the upper or lower end of the scale. This might come when actually shooting the film—exposure time, aperture, and lighting affect density at that stage; or, it

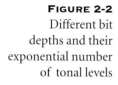
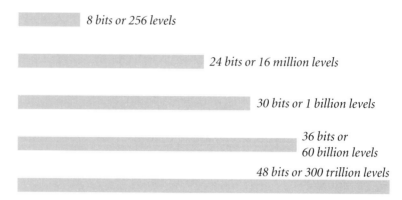

FIGURE 2-2
Different bit
depths and their
exponential number
of tonal levels

might happen when making the scan, where you use scanning software to capture more highlight or shadow detail, and give up some room on the opposite end of the scale.

SENSORS

A scanner's dynamic range, bit depth, and tonal sensitivity all depend on the hardware—specifically, two different pieces of hardware that act together: sensors that respond to the intensity of light hitting them, and the analog-to-digital converter that takes measurements from the sensors and turns them into numbers that the computer can understand.

Every scanner has sensors that measure the light *reflecting* off art or *transmitting* through film negatives and transparencies. There are three main kinds of sensors: CCD, CMOS, and PMT. CCD (charged-coupled devices) and CMOS (complementary metal-oxide semiconductor) sensors are found in flatbed scanners, digital cameras, and desktop film scanners, while PMTs (photomultiplier tubes) are exclusively the province of rotating drum scanners.

CCD AND CMOS. CCD and CMOS sensors work just like the light meter you have in a camera: light coming in is measured and then plotted on a scale. The more light that comes in, the higher the mark on the scale. (The scale itself has an arbitrary top mark based on the density of the scanner; see "Density," above.)

The difference between a camera's light meter and a scanner is that a scanner has several thousand sensors in a row (or *linear array*). Each sensor takes in a single sample of data (if there are 400 CCDs per inch on the linear array, you can say the scanner has a resolution of 400 spi). CCDs have been around for decades, and have improved in quality to the point where high-end CCD scanners rival drum scanning.

CMOS sensors first appeared in digital cameras in 1996, and started showing up in inexpensive flatbed and sheetfed scanners in late 1997 in the form of CISs (Contact Image Sensors). They're similar to CCDs, but have the advantage of being made using the same techniques that chipmakers use to create memory chips and processors; they benefit more quickly from improvements in that field. CCDs also have separate sensors, analog-to-digital converters (see "Quality of Measurement," below), and other electronics, while these are in a single package for CMOS sensors.

Sensors are bulk manufactured and aren't perfect; a few or even a few dozen won't work in any scanner you buy. However, the overall quantity of them is usually large enough that if an occasional one doesn't work or is out of whack, its neighbors pick up the slack. This happens in hardware or as the data's being read.

PMTs. Drum scanners use PMTs, which are one of the last incarnations of good old vacuum tubes. A PMT amplifies incoming light into a signal strong enough to be measured easily, so exposure time can be very short; CCD and CMOS sensors require a longer exposure time because they need to have more photons hit them before they can make an accurate reading. All PMTs used to have a much greater overall dynamic range than CCDs, but now CCDs have caught up to all but the high-end drum scanners.

QUALITY OF MEASUREMENT

Getting from a sensor's reading to a color or tone requires a bit of conversion. The scanner has to take the signal the sensor creates and turn it into a number. To do this, it uses an analog-to-digital (A/D) converter. The quality of your scanner is dependent on the A/D converter's ability to sample voltage output by a sensor and suppress or correct for noise.

An A/D converter works the same for CCD, CMOS, and PMT sensors. These sensors react to light by producing an *analog* electric signal; there are no bits or bytes or anything digital about it at all. The A/D converter fits in the scanning process as the mediator between the sensor and the scanner's onboard computer. (The scanner's computer is pretty primitive, and it mostly does just what the scanning software you're using on your own computer tells it do.) The converter has a bit depth that represents its precision: the number of digits to which it can accurately measure the analog signal coming from the sensor.

During a scan, sensors measure light and produce a voltage. The voltage varies directly in response to the intensity of the light being focused on the sensor; the light's intensity varies as a function of the spot on the image being scanned.

The sensors pass on this voltage to the A/D converter, which itself samples the values and produces a discrete number—a digital value representing the tone. Some scanners actually send the voltage through two or more different converters and average the results to try to correct for noise.

Noise is the introduction of random fluctuation into information. In the case of sensors and converters, noise shows up as values that are too high or low compared with the original image data that was sampled. Once the digital value's been created, noise doesn't play a part anymore in affecting the information. Noise might be attributable to ambient temperature, a subtle flaw in the sensor, a tiny change in the scanner's AC power, or even *nothing*—but that doesn't prevent noise from winding up in the final result anyway.

DISCERNING DETAIL

All scanner elements have a linear response to light; that is, there's a one-to-one ratio between the brightness of the light and the intensity of the outgoing signal. However, photographic film and the human eye both record light in a logarithmic fashion—we are actually more sensitive to detail in the deep shadows of an image (see Figure 2-1, earlier in the chapter).

The result is that two points that appear clearly different to us may appear the same (or only a tiny bit different) to a scanner. Detail in images is entirely a factor of pixels being different from each other; the more they differ, the more obvious the detail. The deeper the bit depth in a scanner, the better it can pick out detail.

The problem is that the tiny differences in pixel values that the scanner picks up are often completely overwhelmed by noise that naturally occurs when the scanner's A/D converter tries to interpret the very low electric signals that the sensors generate.

In Chapter 7, *Tonal Correction*, we discuss how you can emphasize the details in shadow areas with tonal correction—accentuating the differences between adjacent samples—and how you lose detail in the highlights in the process: either they wash out to white or they all become too similar to display much detail.

There are also a few methods to combat noisy shadows in scanner hardware and software. Each of these should be evaluated before you buy or use a scanner.

CAPTURE EXTRA BITS. While some low-end scanners only capture eight bits of data per channel (a single channel is either black, red, green, or blue), decent scanners on the market today capture at least 10 bits of data—or 30 bits overall. Some scanners can record as many as 48 bits per color sample.

When we wrote the first edition of this book in 1993, it was too expensive for anybody but a service bureau or dedicated department in a larger company to buy a 30-bit color scanner; at this writing, there's a 30-bit flatbed available for under $150. Of course, you still have to pay at least $500 for a professional DTP unit, and many are in the $1,200 to $1,500 range for the right combination of hardware and software to do a wide range of scanning in a managed and consistent environment.

A scanner that captures more than 24 bits per color sample reduces the image data down to just 24 bits per sample when the final scan is acquired in your computer software—the scanning program or plug-in removes extra data by averaging samples.

Photoshop added the ability to bring in scans with as many as 16 bits of data per channel, but not all scanning software supports this. This can be an advantage if you want to store the deeper scan and work on it later; Photoshop allows only minimal adjustment, such as tonal correction, at this color depth.

(We'll talk more about bit depth in Chapter 3, *Scanned Images*; more about scanning software support in Chapter 33, *Scanning Applications*; and more about deep tonal adjustment in Chapter 7, *Tonal Correction*, and Chapter 8, *Color*.)

ADJUSTING EXPOSURE TIME. Several CCD scanners (and almost all slide scanners) can adjust the amount of time that each scanning element is exposed to light. Most figure the exposure automatically, doing a prescan, then adjusting exposure based on the density of the image. By increasing the exposure time, you can push data lower on the density scale by letting more light pass through or reflect off your source image. This can blow out detail at the less dense end of the scale, but it is a way to spread detail in the densest area over a greater range. By doing this at scanning time, you capture better information, which you can balance in your image-editing software.

ADAPTIVE ANALOG-TO-DIGITAL CONVERTERS. Some scanners use adaptive analog-to-digital converters. If the image you're scanning concentrates most of its tonal values in a narrow band, adaptive A/D converters can use the CCD's full ability to discern tonal differences but apply it to a narrower range of values, resulting in better dynamic range. The hardware, in cooperation with the scanning software, handles this automatically; many scanners also allow you to do this manually using their software, as well. This automatic adaptation is less important with scanners that have a very high bit depth but is a great trick for a 24- or 30-bit scanner.

Software

Scanning software has improved to the point where you might do a variety of corrections in it before acquiring the scan into an image-editing program—we used to sniff at the very thought. But whether you buy the scanning software separately—like Second Glance's ScanTastic—or use what's bundled with the scanner, you should focus on tonal correction, sharpening, and plug-in modules. (We'll talk about another issue, calibration, in Chapter 8, *Color*; and about scanning software in Chapter 33, *Scanning Applications.*)

TONAL CORRECTION

If your scanning software allows you to apply tonal correction while you scan, you can save a lot of time when producing multiple scans. Without this capability, you need to scan, save, open the picture in an image-editing program, correct it, then save again.

The tonal correction that is offered, of course, has to be *good* tonal correction. As we point out later in Chapter 7, *Tonal Correction*, linear correction (usually consisting of contrast and brightness adjustments) is essentially worthless. You need good tools for nonlinear correction, and (perhaps) for closed-loop calibration.

Often the tonal correction is made on high-bit-depth data, so you can get a far better image than by acquiring and working on the image. Most scanners currently don't allow you to acquire full bit-depth scans—see "Discerning Detail," earlier in the chapter—so you really need to make the corrections before image acquisition.

SHARPENING

It's often nice to be able to sharpen the scans as you capture them, especially when you're under tight deadlines. Again, it avoids the "scan/save/open/adjust/save" routine. And, again, you need to be sure that the software's sharpening routine is up to snuff. Sharpening is the last manipulation you want to perform on a scan, however, so if you sharpen while scanning, you shouldn't make any further changes (like tonal correction, image editing, and so on). Run some tests to your final output device to make sure that the image quality with your scanning software's sharpening controls is equal to the sharpening available in image-manipulation packages. We devote Chapter 9, *A Sharper Image*, to this task.

ACCESS FROM OTHER PROGRAMS

Almost every scanner comes with a standalone application for controlling the scanner and capturing scans, but it's also convenient if you can scan images from within other applications. If your scanning application doesn't offer (good) tonal correction and sharpening, scanning directly into Photoshop or the like can partially short-circuit the multiple-save routine.

Most scanners come with either a Photoshop plug-in or a TWAIN module that lets you control the scanner and acquire a scan into a new, untitled window without leaving your image-editing program. Photoshop plug-ins work not only with Photoshop, but also with some other Adobe software, like PhotoDeluxe, and with some competitors' software, like DeBabelizer. TWAIN modules can be used with virtually every image-editing program for the Mac and Windows.

SCANNER TYPES

As we mentioned in Chapter 1, *Waltzing Through the Process*, the sort of scanner you need at any given time depends mostly on the sort of image you're trying to get into your computer. Different scanner types also perform differently in the areas discussed above: resolution, bit depth and dynamic range, and software. Let's take a quick overview of the various types of scanners, considering them for types of artwork that they support. We'll also take a dip into digital cameras, which work just like scanners, but require different considerations. Table 2-1 offers suggestions for the type of scanner you should consider for different kinds of output and resolution.

TABLE 2-1. Choosing the right scanner for the right output

If you need to scan ▶ when your final output is ◀	Reflective art or photos	Photographic film	In color	...for printing at a max. line screen (lpi) of ...	...then choose...
Just text, photos	FPO	No	Yes	n/a	Flatbed, 300 dpi, 24-bit color
stripped in	FPO	FPO	Yes	n/a	Flatbed, 300 dpi, 24-bit color with transparency attachment
	No	FPO	Yes	n/a	Film scanner, 2,000 dpi, 24-bit color
Newsprint, one-color	Yes	Yes	No	85	Flatbed, 300 dpi, 24-bit color with transparency attachment
Uncoated, one-color	Yes	No	No	133	Flatbed, 600 dpi, 30-bit color (10 bits for grayscale)
Quick print Color offset	Yes	No	Yes	133	Flatbed, 600 dpi, 30-bit color
High-quality color offset	Yes	No	Yes	200	Flatbed, 600 to 1,200 dpi, 36-bit color
	Yes	Yes	Yes	200	Flatbed, 600 to 1,200 dpi, 36-bit color for reflective *and* low-end drum, 4,000 dpi, 36- to 48-bit color for film *or* Flatbed with transparency attachment, 4,000 dpi for film, 600 to 1,200 dpi for reflective, 36- to 48-bit color
	No	Yes	Yes	200	Film scanner or low-end drum, 4,000 dpi, 36- to 48-bit color

[1]FPO = For Position Only for dummying images.

FLATBED SCANNERS

Flatbeds are cheap, good, and ubiquitous. They usually look like some weird cross between a photocopier and a packing carton for an alien computer. The idea behind flatbed scanners is that you can put flat artwork down on a sheet of glass, and a scanning mechanism moves under it, bouncing light off the material so the reflected light lands on the image sensors. Flatbed scanners are generally set up for *reflective* art (like photographic prints, printed pages, and so on), but they can often be fitted with *transparency* attachments that enable them to scan film (slides, negatives, or other transparent art). Many flatbeds are sold with the attachment as a bundle.

In the reflective mode, a light source is typically mounted below the glass on a motor-driven arm that sweeps by the material being scanned and it uses a series of mirrors to focus the reflection of the art onto the sensors. When doing transparencies, the light source usually looks more like a light box, and it's above the art in question. The light shines through onto mirrors that redirect the light onto the sensors.

WHY PAY MORE? Flatbed scanners can be incredibly cheap: $150 buys a 30-bit scanner in late 1997. But as with all computer equipment, you do get what you pay for, and a $750 Hewlett-Packard or $1,500 Agfa scanner will have some advantages in CCD quality, software adjustment, and lasting power over a lower-cost unit. Problems crop up with blurry or jittery scans when the scanning mechanism itself doesn't move smoothly or is on a shaky surface. And light sources wear out or become uneven over time.

HIGHER VERTICAL RESOLUTION. Some scanners have different horizontal and vertical optical resolutions, which they achieve by having a better "stepper" motor that moves the image sensors along the length of the bed of the scanner.

If that stepper motor moves in exactly the same increments as the density of sensors—for instance, if the scanner has 300 sensors per inch horizontally, and moves in $\frac{1}{300}$-inch increments vertically—the scanner has the same horizontal and vertical resolutions. If the stepper motor moves in $\frac{1}{600}$-inch increments, and the sensors are *still* the same size and *still* have the same amount of light shining on them, you're getting two different resolutions. Pay attention to the lower of the two.

Scanning software can also interpolate resolution on the fly, so while the manufacturer will say it's a 1,200-spi scanner, it might truly have only a 400-spi optical resolution. The lowest resolution the scanner manufacturer lists is the correct one to use.

That's not to say that higher vertical resolution can't help. In some scanners, especially those that have superior scanning software, like Linotype-Hell, the difference in resolution can actually help in the final scan. However, it's still not a good idea to assume that the higher resolution means much.

MULTIPLE OPTICAL RESOLUTIONS. When you get a transparency attachment for a flatbed scanner, it's important to check on what the highest optical resolution is for the scanner. The more expensive scanners have two sets of resolutions, and often two sets of optics (lenses). When scanning reflective art, the flatbed might do 600 or 1,200 spi over an 8.5-by-14-inch area. When you switch to transmissive film scanning, the scanner can swap in a different lens to do 2,400-spi or higher scanning by focusing a smaller area (usually 4 by 6 inches or smaller) onto the same sensors.

DENSITY. Reflective art, such as a photographic print, has a maximum possible density (D_{MAX}) of about 2.0D, while film captures a range as high as 4.0D or 100 times as many tones. Most flatbed scanners are geared toward reflective art; just putting a transparency unit on it won't improve the tonal differentiation. So when choosing a flatbed, check that its density is in the right range if you're planning to use a transparency attachment.

FILM SCANNERS

Film scanners are designed to scan photographic film. Flatbed scanners equipped with a transparency unit aren't always as good as film scanners because they interpose a sheet of glass between the sensors and the film, and the light is not usually as intense as in a dedicated film scanner. Further, because of the very short depth of field in flatbeds, you sometimes need to unmount transparencies from slide mounts to get the image in focus. A matter of millimeters can affect the sharpness of the scan.

What makes a film scanner different from a drum scanner? Film scanners are typically CMOS or CCD based, and they pass the film by the sensors rather than rotating around at high speeds.

FOCUS. Sometimes you have to adjust the focus manually on a film scanner, but often the scanning software uses some cues to auto-focus, just like a snapshot camera. One approach was used by Leaf Systems equipment: the scanner captures a short line of samples in a single location. It adjusts the focus in one direction in a large step, and then analyzes whether the contrast between adjacent pixels is higher or lower than in the first capture. Higher contrasts means that it's more in focus; if it were more out of focus, the samples would always be of lower contrast, or blurrier. It adjusts the focus in smaller and smaller steps until any subsequent adjustment is worse.

FORMAT. Typically, film scanners are geared around the 35 mm format, since it's the most popular. You can buy a variety of scanners that will handle larger formats, though the costs start to sky-rocket. Nikon has a low-end, 24-bit unit—the CoolScan II—that costs under $600 and does just 35 mm. On the other hand, you can pay $17,000 for the LeafScan 45 from Scitex—Glenn used the very first production model of this unit way back in 1992. The LeafScan 45 can take film formats up to 4 by 5 inches.

Film scanners generally have specialized mounts for each kind of film that allow it to be inserted, often using a standard film carrier for a photographic enlarger. If you're used to the 35 mm format, remember that professionals often shoot in 2-by-2-inch and 4-by-5-inch formats. Scanners have just started handling the newer Advanced Photo System (APS) format, which is around the size of 35 mm, as we go to press.

RESOLUTION, BIT DEPTH, AND DENSITY. Scanners dedicated to film start at around 2,400 spi, but 4,800 spi or higher may be necessary for reproducing 35 mm film to magazine-size resolutions. Don't accept less than 3.0D for a device you can't use for anything but film. Typically as well, the CCDs or other sensors are of a higher overall tolerance than you find in a flatbed scanner. It's rare to find a 24-bit film scanner—the Nikon CoolScan II aside; they're usually 30 bits or more per sample.

DRUM SCANNERS

Drum scanners rotate a cylinder at extremely high speeds while a sensor moves along the length of the drum. A high-intensity point-source light shines from inside the transparent drum, through film that's taped on the drum, onto the optics that carry the light to the sensors. The sensors take rapid-fire measurements, sampling the image at high speed as it rotates by, then stepping the optics in tiny increments down the drum.

The optics consist of a series of mirrors that reflect and then refract the light to three separate PMT sensors that record the red, green, and blue components of each sample.

Drum scanners can often do reflective scans as well by using an opaque drum and using a different light source to illuminate the art.

Drum scanners "traditionally" offered the very highest-quality scans. The scanners cost from $25,000 to millions, but the ones below a few hundred thousand dollars are being challenged in quality by the best of the CCD scanners—which can cost somewhat less, but still tens of thousands.

The key advantages of drum scanning—besides quality—are high resolution, wide density, large film format, and batch processing. Drum scanners can be tightly integrated with a complete imaging and color separation system, but with lower-priced units on the market, that's less commonly the case.

HIGH RESOLUTION AND DENSITY. Drum scanners are still the best way to make extremely high-resolution scans (exceeding 9,600 spi) with a wide density—as high 4.2D, or 10 to 15 times the number of tones of a good flatbed with an attachment. It's also one of the best ways to scan large-format film at high resolution, such as 8-by-10-inch artwork at 4,000 spi.

BATCH PROCESSING. Batch processing is just a tool of efficiency. Glenn worked with an Optronics ColorGetter on which he could load 50 35 mm images, select each and set different cropping and resolution, and then walk away for a few hours while each was acquired. Linotype-Hell's scanner software is the first package we've seen that offers sophisticated batch processing on a CCD flatbed scanner. Their package is bundled with all their scanners, from their low-end, $600 model to one that costs more than $40,000.

INTEGRATION. Drum scanners are often incorporated into complete image-scanning and processing systems (though some of them you can just plug into your computer). This makes it possible to get a great scan that can be corrected and output in a tightly calibrated environment. You might never touch the scan at all in those circumstances, but instead have the service bureau do the correction, and just give you a for-position-only placement link.

SPECIALIZED SCANNERS

For certain kinds of scanning, you might need to get something other than the standard flatbed or film scanner. For instance, using a sheetfed scanner is appropriate for massive text processing, whereas video-capture software is necessary when trying to "scan" something from a videotape.

SHEETFED SCANNERS. Sheetfed scanners are meant mostly for performing optical character recognition or OCR (see Chapter 13, *OCR*). These scanners will take a few sheets or a few thousand and process them automatically. They generally pull or push an image past a stationary scanning mechanism. The biggest problem is that they can only scan artwork that is flexible enough to be pulled through the pasta-making innards. That means pictures mounted on artboards and books are out. And, often, smaller images have to be mounted on a larger piece of paper before they can successfully navigate through the scanner. It's also extremely difficult to feed the art accurately so that horizontal and vertical lines end up horizontal and vertical. Some of them are meant for use with a desktop computer; others are $100,000 devices used by legal firms to turn acres of typewriting into computer text.

VIDEO. We didn't think that video scanning was a reasonable way to capture images (everything we'd seen looked terrible) until a friend of ours showed us the poster he produced that included 50 video captures. Now we know it's possible to get good images from a videotape or video camera; you just have to work hard to do it.

Video capture setups are typically in the form of a board or add-on that you plug into your computer; many Macs will do video capture just by adding an "AV" card that plugs into a special slot. You feed the video in through a cable, and then control the capture of a particular frame of the video through software.

Video resolution is typically low; it's measured in horizontal lines that sort of match up with vertical monitor-pixel depth. VHS has about 400 lines of resolution, while Hi-8 and professional Beta have 500 or more. This is still below the level of a small computer monitor.

There's another problem: *interlacing*. Televisions update their pictures 60 times a second. However, they only image half a frame at a time, alternating lines—or interlacing—each time. Video boards can typically grab two successive "frames" to make a full image capture, but this synchronization adds to the blurriness and jitter of videotape.

If you're going to capture video images from tape, consider using Hi-8 format and an SVHS cable—it's the best, cheapest solution.

DIGITAL CAMERAS

Digital cameras have had a couple of generations to mature, and they now come in all ranges of quality and cost. Our late colleague

Cary Lu did a roundup in *NetGuide* in mid-1997 of digital cameras under $1,000—and featured 14 of them from major manufacturers.

The cheapest digital cameras create images that aren't even as good as a video frame grab—the colors are blurred or washed out or the range of tones is highly compressed. On the other hand, the most expensive cameras rival or surpass what the best photographic film can capture.

Scanners and digital cameras are almost the same animal, with one important difference: cameras have lenses that focus over a range of distances; scanners mostly focus within just a few millimeters.

Digital camera software, storage, and capabilities vary widely. Some can store a few images on PC cards (removable hard drives or memory in a tiny package); others require a SCSI or parallel port connection to a computer in order to control the equipment.

Digital cameras come in two main flavors: *linear array* (or scanning back) and *area array* (or instant capture).

LINEAR ARRAY. The linear-array scanning-back camera works like a flatbed scanner: a single row of image sensors comprises the scanning element. The image elements in scanning backs are usually the most expensive that are made; even tiny defects in a few of the thousands of sensors are enough to reject it for use.

This kind of camera is primarily used to shoot still art in studio settings where lighting and vibration can be tightly controlled. The exposures can take minutes, because the device is usually doing long exposures.

If you're going to be shooting hundreds of products in controlled lighting for high-end catalogs, it's worth thinking about a scanning back. Sometimes these backs can be used as attachments to existing high-quality large-format cameras. Other backs are purchased as part of a custom-designed unit. They're always directly tethered to a PC so that the image is acquired directly into the computer, just as with a flatbed.

Scanning backs always do just a single pass, and even the fastest require absolute stability (tripods are a must). These shots often take place in specially designed studios that dampen all vibrations.

Because these cameras and backs are made entirely for studio purposes, they're all very high resolution, up to 7,000 samples in the linear array. (For reference, an image at 7,000 by 7,000 samples could reproduce at 23 by 23 inches at 200 lines per inch.) They range from just below $10,000 to more than $50,000.

AREA ARRAY. An area-array or instant-capture digital camera, on the other hand, has a two-dimensional matrix of image sensors in which all of them are exposed simultaneously to light. Some cameras have a single array with different elements painted with red, green, and blue to filter light. Others—though this is rare—have three separate arrays, each exposed at the same time through red, green, and blue filters.

Most of these cameras have three deficits for prepress use, but are fine for web and low-end catalog work: low resolution, low bit depth, and long exposure time. The cheapest area-array cameras do 640 by 480 to 800 by 600 samples at 24 bits, and require bright lighting and longish exposures. There are at least a dozen cameras like this for under $1,000 at this writing.

The more expensive cameras, running from a few thousand dollars up to $30,000, capture 30 or 36 bits of information at from about 1,000 by 1,500 up to 2,000 by 3,000 samples.

Both low- and high-end instant-capture cameras play various tricks in order to achieve that final resolution, often involving extensive interpolation that doesn't work as well on the cheaper models. In many cases, the sensor array has two green pixels for every red or blue pixel. Because the eye is more sensitive to green, capturing extra information in that color can provide better overall tonal information to make an image look smooth instead of having abrupt shifts in gradations.

Most of the cheaper cameras can simulate only about ASA 50 to 150—film speeds that require bright daylight or the equivalent to take clear pictures at exposures up to about $1/500$ second with a medium aperture setting. More expensive instant-capture cameras can do ASA 400 or 800, which are low-light indoor and outdoor film speeds.

Area-array cameras typically store several images on an internal hard drive or flash-memory cards. Some now use PC cards that simulate hard drives, so that they can be removed from the digital camera and plugged right into a Macintosh or PC that's equipped with a Type 3 PC Card slot. Hitachi makes a unit that can store up to 3,000 JPEGs at screen resolution—yup, 3,000—on that type of interchangeable memory card. Other units come with SCSI or parallel connectors to acquire the images off the digital camera into Photoshop or other software.

PUTTING BITS IN A BUCKET

Choosing what scanner to use can often be the most important part of setting up a workflow. Getting the right bit depth, the right resolution, the right kind of unit—whether it's a cheap digital camera or a $200,000 drum scanner—saves time and effort throughout the whole process. The more you can do at the time of the scan, the less you have to do later.

Nonetheless, we press on in the next chapter, *Scanned Images,* to define what makes up that scan you'll be using this equipment for.

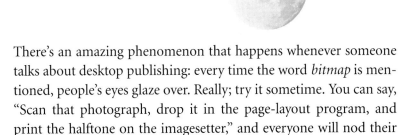

3 SCANNED IMAGES

ANATOMY OF A BITMAP

There's an amazing phenomenon that happens whenever someone talks about desktop publishing: every time the word *bitmap* is mentioned, people's eyes glaze over. Really; try it sometime. You can say, "Scan that photograph, drop it in the page-layout program, and print the halftone on the imagesetter," and everyone will nod their head and smile. Then say, "The resolution of the bitmapped graphic doubles when you reduce the image's size to 50 percent," and your audience will be asleep before you finish the sentence.

Bitmapped images do not make for exciting conversations. But it is a topic that is incredibly important to know about when working with scans. All scans are represented as bitmaps, and in the next few chapters we cover everything you need to know about how bitmapped images work and how to handle them. We promise it isn't as confusing—or as boring—as it sometimes seems.

The word *bitmap* is confusing only because its two constituents, "bit" and "map," both sound so technical. A bit is just the tiniest unit of computer storage, representing either a one or a zero. A map is jargon for a table, like a spreadsheet—the information is organized two-dimensionally, into rows and columns. A bitmap is a table that describes where bits are located—as in an image.

In this chapter we describe the characteristics of bitmapped graphics—the attributes that define them—and how those characteristics relate to file size.

WHAT IS A BITMAP?

A bitmap describes all the points in a rectangular grid of dots. In plain English, a bitmapped file might read, "The point at coordinates 1,1 is black; the point at coordinates 1,2 is white; the point at coordinate 1,3 is black," and so on.

SAMPLE POINTS

There's one other term we need to discuss here in relation to bitmaps. When we talk about points in a bitmapped graphic, we call them *samples* or *sample points*. We use this term because a scanner *samples* an image—checking what color or gray value it finds—every 1/300 inch, every 1/100 inch, or whatever. So we talk about the resolution of bitmaps in *samples per inch*, or spi.

Samples are not the same thing as dots (the things that laser printers and imagesetters make) or spots (the elements of a halftone) or pixels (the "picture elements" on a computer screen), so we prefer to use a distinct term for them.

CHARACTERISTICS OF BITMAPPED GRAPHICS

Every bitmapped graphic has four basic characteristics: dimension, resolution, bit depth, and color model. People use these terms all the time without really knowing what they mean, and then make poor decisions based on a faulty understanding. So let's look at what these words refer to, and why they're important.

DIMENSION

Bitmapped images are always big rectangular grids. Like checkerboards or chessboards or parquet floors in your kitchen, these big grids are made up of little squares. And the one thing you can always say about grids is that they have dimensions—specifically, two dimensions (see Figure 3-1). A chessboard is always eight

FIGURE 3-1
Dimensions of a
bitmapped image

*These dimensions
say nothing about
an image's size
or resolution.*

*62 samples
high*

170 samples wide

squares by eight squares. The grid of pixels that makes up your computer screen might be 800 by 600.

The dimensions of a grid—the number of squares tall and wide it is—are independent of the actual *size* of a grid. A chessboard can be a 6-inch square (the traveling set) or the size of an outdoor college campus quadrangle (the Renaissance fair set). The chessboard is still just eight squares by eight squares; it's independent of *resolution*.

However, increasing the dimensions of a bitmapped image increases file size geometrically. So if you double an image's dimensions, you increase file size by a factor of four. Increase to three times dimensions, and file size increases by a factor of nine.

RESOLUTION

The word *resolution* is so misunderstood and overused that we've devoted two chapters to it later in the book (Chapter 5, *Image Resolution*, and Chapter 6, *Choosing Resolution*). The resolution of a bitmapped image is the number of samples (or squares in the grid) in each unit of measurement. If we're talking in inches, then we talk about the number of samples per inch (spi).

If your bitmapped image has 72 samples per inch, and it's 72 samples long on each side, then you know that it's an inch long on each side. We can take the same bitmapped image and change it to 36 samples per inch (change its resolution without affecting the underlying grid dimensions), and suddenly the image is 2 inches on each side—same *number* of samples, but each one is twice as big; see Figure 3-2. Changing resolution of an existing scan doesn't change the file's size.

FIGURE 3-2
Changing bitmap
resolution

72 spi

36 spi

You can also look at bitmap resolution in another way: If you
know the size of an image and its resolution, you can figure out its
dimensions. When you scan a picture that is 3 inches on each side
at 100 samples per inch, you know that the bitmapped image has
300 samples on each side (100 per inch). If you scan it at 300 samples per inch, the dimensions shoot up to 900 dots on each side.
Because each sample takes up a little room on disk, the more samples, the larger the disk file is.

BIT DEPTH

In the previous chapter, *Scanners,* we explained what bit depth
meant when scanning samples. Each sample in a bitmapped image
can be black, white, gray, or a color; the key is the number of bits
used to describe it. A sample that is defined using one bit of information can only be black or white—zero or one. If you have two
bits of information describing a sample, there are four possible
combinations (00, 01, 10, and 11), hence four possible colors or
gray levels (see Figure 3-3). Eight bits of information gives you 256

FIGURE 3-3
Bits per sample

1 bit;
2 colors

2 bits;
4 colors

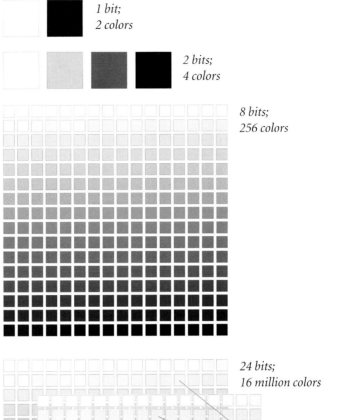

8 bits;
256 colors

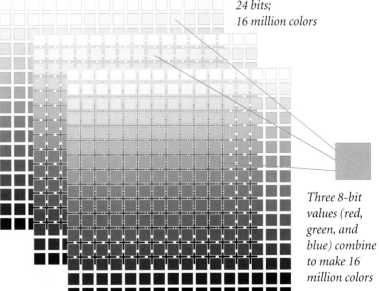

24 bits;
16 million colors

Three 8-bit
values (red,
green, and
blue) combine
to make 16
million colors

levels of gray; 24 bits of information results in over 16 million possible colors (with 24-bit images, each sample actually has three 8-bit values—one each for red, green, and blue).

The number of bits is called the image's *bit depth.* We call a 1-bit image a *flat* bitmap, also called a bilevel image. A *deep* bitmap is any image that has more than one bit describing each sample (see Figure 3-4).

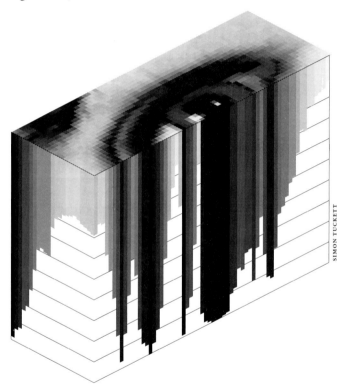

Bit depth also affects the image's file size. An 8-bit image is eight times the size of a similar 1-bit image: it uses eight bits to describe each dot instead of one. A 24-bit image is 24 times as big, and so on. Increasing bit depth increases file size arithmetically.

COLOR MODEL

The final attribute of a bitmapped image is the color model, which really only applies to color images. The most common color model is RGB (red, green, and blue), in which each color is represented by an 8-bit value for a total of 24 bits.

Some bitmaps are described using the CMYK color model, defining values for each of the four process printing colors: cyan, magenta, yellow, and black. While this results in 32 bits per sample, it doesn't add more colors; it's just a different method of describing the colors—a method that's required for most offset printing and many color printers. For more on CMYK bitmaps, see the discussions of the TIFF and EPS formats in Chapter 4, *File Formats.*

We use RGB because monitors display color by striking red, green, and blue phosphors with an electronic beam; monitors use RGB because those three emitted colors can be mixed to create most of the visible spectrum. CMY without K is the reflective equivalent of RGB; when white light strikes cyan, the ink absorbs all the other colors, and so on. To make red on a monitor, you excite just red phosphors; to do this on paper, you print magenta and yellow ink, which together absorb everything but red light. CMY add up to black, but impurities in the ink and limitations on how much ink paper can hold require the use of black.

DEVICE-INDEPENDENT (CIE) COLOR. This class of color model emerged to work with the color management systems now available that improve color correspondence between your screen, color printouts, and final printed output. These *device-independent* or *perceptually based* models don't describe a color by the components that make it up (RGB or CMYK, for instance). They describe *what a color looks like.* All of them are based, more or less, on the standards defined by the Commission Internationale de l'Eclairage (CIE) in 1931.

The problem with RGB and CMYK color models is that a given RGB (or CMYK) specification doesn't really describe a color. A color specified using RGB may look totally different on your monitor than it does on color-printer output. Perceptually based color definitions describe what a color looks like; it's up to your color-management software to decide what RGB or CMYK values are needed to create that color on a given device.

Color-management systems and their associated color models are starting to reach maturity, and we'll discuss the solutions in Chapter 8, *Color*.

INDEXED COLOR. Indexed color is a method for producing 8-bit, 256-color files. Indexed-color bitmaps use a table of 256 colors, chosen from the full 24-bit RGB palette. A given sample's color is defined by reference to the table: "this sample is color number 123, this sample is color number 81," and so on.

While indexed color can save disk space (it only requires eight bits per sample point, rather than the full 24), it only gives you 256 colors (although they can be optimized for that image), and sometimes the tables don't match between platforms, or too many colors are being displayed on the screen at the same time, so you get weird color changes. You might want to convert indexed-color bitmaps to true RGB, though you won't improve the image any in the process—you're still only getting 256 colors.

Indexed color is used primarily in GIF files, which is the standard—though imperfect—image format used on the World Wide Web. (See Chapter 11, *Images for the Web*.)

Unlike resolution and bit depth, the color model of a bitmapped image doesn't necessarily have a direct bearing on file size. However, if you change the color model, the computer might need to change the image's bit depth, which will change file size. For example, if you convert a CMYK image to a grayscale image, the computer changes the bit depth from 32 bits (eight bits for each of the four channels) to eight bits. This cuts the file size by 75 percent. Similarly, if you change a flat, bilevel bitmap into an RGB bitmap, the computer has to add 23 bits to each pixel, making the file size 24 times as large.

BITMAPS AND FILE SIZE

You've no doubt noticed that throughout this chapter we've commented on how different bitmap attributes affect file size. We've done so because it's a really important topic. Big files are hard to work with, hard to print, and hard to transfer. So it's well worth reducing file size when you can.

To encapsulate what we've said above, here's a rundown of the characteristics of bitmapped images that affect file size.

DIMENSIONS AND RESOLUTION. Increasing the number of samples in a bitmap by increasing the dimensions raises file size geometrically: 200-spi bitmaps are four times as big as 100-spi bitmaps, and 300-spi images are nine times larger. Resolution is independent of dimensions; it's the measurement of samples against a scale, like 300 samples per inch.

BIT DEPTH. Increasing bit depth increases file size arithmetically. A 24-bit image is three times as large as an 8-bit image.

COLOR MODEL. Color model doesn't necessarily increase file size, but going from RGB (24-bit) to CMYK (32-bit) color models does because it alters bit depth.

FIGURING FILE SIZE

Now that you know the factors that affect the size of bitmaps, it's a simple matter to calculate file size using the following formula.

$$\text{Resolution}^2 \times \text{Width} \times \text{Height} \times \text{Bits per sample} \div 8,192 = \text{File size (in kilobytes)}$$

This formula works because 8,192 is the number of bits in a kilobyte. For example, if you have a 4-by-5-inch 1-bit image at 300 spi, you know that the file size is 220 K. You multiply 300 squared (or 90,000) by 4 by 5 by 1; divide by 8,192 and you get right about 220. A 24-bit image of the same size would be 5,273 K (which is just about 5 Mb).

FILE FORMAT

One other factor—file format—can also affect the file size of bitmapped image files (we discuss these in detail in Chapter 4, *File*

Formats). Storing an image as a TIFF file creates a file size different from one stored as a JPEG or EPS file, even if the dimensions and bit depth are the same. Why? Because the EPS file typically includes a preview image over and above the image stored in the file. JPEG and TIFF files can include built-in compression (see Chapter 10, *Compression*), making files smaller. And other file formats include similar additions or compression methods to suit different needs.

Plus, when you're saving bitmapped images in EPS format, there's one other consideration: binary versus ASCII encoding. Binary-encoded bitmaps are half the size of ASCII-encoded bitmaps. ASCII encoding is sometimes necessary for passing data over old networks or ancient modems.

IMPLICATIONS OF FILE SIZE

This section describes the problems posed by large bitmapped image files. For advice on reducing file size, see Chapter 6, *Choosing Resolution*.

STORAGE AND TRANSMISSION. Hard disks come incredibly cheap these days—$\frac{1}{10}$ or less of the cost for the same storage four years ago—but they're still not free (we can't imagine why!). Smaller files save you money because you don't have to buy new hardware. And if you want to give images to a colleague or service bureau, you have to fit them on some kind of disk or tape or send them over a phone line or Internet connection. As David's grandmother always says, "Smaller is better."

MEMORY. You often don't need a lot of RAM to open an image (and you can usually place images on pages regardless of how much RAM you have), but speed suffers radically. If you can fit a whole image in memory, you can manipulate it between five and 50 times faster than if you have to work off a disk.

Some scanning and image-manipulation packages *require* that the whole image fit in memory. With these packages, your only choices are to reduce file size or buy RAM. At this writing, it's hard to buy a machine with less than 16 Mb of RAM; but we say start at 32 Mb and work your way up from there.

PRINTING. The biggest problem with big files is printing. You have to transmit the files over some kind of cable or network (serial, parallel, Ethernet, ISDN, whatever), and the printer or imagesetter has to digest all the information. At best, big files make you wait for output. At worst, you incur additional imagesetting charges for slow output—or the files won't print at all. Keep files small to avoid all these problems.

WHAT'S IN A BITMAP?

Now that we've covered the attributes that define what's in a bitmap, in the next chapter, *File Formats*, we move on to discuss the different containers available for saving that information to disk and passing it between programs.

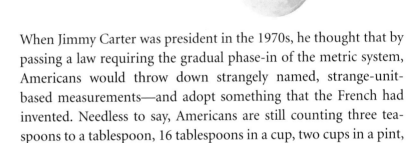

4 FILE FORMATS

WHICH ONE AND WHY

When Jimmy Carter was president in the 1970s, he thought that by passing a law requiring the gradual phase-in of the metric system, Americans would throw down strangely named, strange-unit-based measurements—and adopt something that the French had invented. Needless to say, Americans are still counting three tea-spoons to a tablespoon, 16 tablespoons in a cup, two cups in a pint, and so on. Everyone agrees that metric makes more sense, but Americans just can't seem to get their brains wrapped around it.

In the computer industry, we have even stranger standards—things like GIF, TIFF, JPEG, and PNG. These are used not because they make sense to most people, but because they work. In this chapter, we explain what these formats are, why they work, and how you should use them. Without this knowledge, you'll be a lame-duck publisher, adrift among a sea of acronyms.

PLACING, PRINTING, AND EDITING

When we talk about file formats, we're referring to how the graphic image is stored on a disk. How it's stored determines what programs can open ("read") the graphic, and what you can do with it once it's opened. If you say a program can read a given format, you may mean one of two things. It may be able to place the image on a

45

page and print it (and perhaps apply some overall tonal adjustments), or it may be able to open the file and actually edit it.

Some file formats are industry standards (used by many different programs), and others are particular to a given program, like Adobe Photoshop's native file format, which is used almost exclusively by Photoshop itself. Proprietary formats have the advantage of being specialized for given programs, so they can store those programs' information completely and efficiently. Their disadvantage is that other programs sometimes can't read the information (for placing, printing, *or* editing) without using an intermediary like Equilibrium's DeBabelizer.

EPS and TIFF are the two primary formats of interest to desktop publishers, while JPEG, GIF, and PNG affect those working most of the time on the Web or in multimedia. Adobe's PDF format has applications for both audiences.

OBJECTS AND BITMAPS

The first and most important distinction to understand with file formats is the difference between object-oriented and bitmapped graphics. Let's take a look at these first.

BITMAPPED GRAPHICS. Bitmapped images are just big grids of pixels, as we explained in the previous few chapters. To do something useful with a bitmap, the file format needs to contain information on dimensions, resolution, bit depth, color model, and compression. (We covered the first four in Chapter 3, *Scanned Images*; compression is covered in Chapter 10, *Compression.*)

Bitmaps come from three primary sources: scanners, painting and image-processing programs (such as Photoshop, Picture Publisher, DeBabelizer and so on), and screen-capture programs (HyperSnap, SnagIt, Exposure Pro, and a host of others). If you create a graphic with any of these tools, it's a bitmap.

OBJECT-ORIENTED GRAPHICS. Object-oriented files are typically more complex. Instead of describing a rectangle with a bunch of dots, object-oriented graphics just say, "Draw a rectangle this big and put it at such-and-such place on the page." These images can include lines, boxes, circles, curves, polygons, and text blocks, and all those items can have a variety of attributes—line weight, type formatting, fill color, graduated fills, *et al., ad nauseam.*

You can scale object-oriented graphics to almost any size, large or small, without distorting their appearance. The interpreter that understands the object language always draws the details of the object down to the resolution of the printer it's outputting to. There's no bitmap that can get more or less fuzzy at different sizes—just shapes that don't have a particular size, although you usually design them to fit certain dimensions.

There is no universally editable object-oriented file format that is robust enough to describe all of those different sorts of objects (see "Exchanging Objects" later in this chapter). You can almost always place an object-oriented graphic on your page and print it, but it's not always certain that you'll also be able to edit it.

Object-oriented graphics come from two primary sources: drawing programs (Macromedia FreeHand, CorelDraw, and Adobe Illustrator, to name the big ones) and computer-aided design (CAD) programs. You also might export object-oriented graphics from a graphing program or a spreadsheet with a graphing module.

BITMAPS QUA OBJECTS. As it turns out, the distinction between bitmaps and objects is slightly fuzzy, because object-oriented files can include bitmaps as objects in their own right; they just usually don't allow you to make any changes to them. If you're creating an illustration in Illustrator, for instance, you can include a TIFF or other bitmapped image as one of the objects in the illustration. The bitmapped image actually acts like an object on the page, much like a rectangle or oval.

If you include a bitmap as an object in an illustration, you can almost never edit that bitmap. You can place it, rotate it, or twist it around, but you can't actually go into the image and change it. Some programs, however, such as Deneba Canvas, have object-oriented *and* bitmapped layers, allowing you to jump back and forth between models.

BITMAP-ONLY OBJECT-ORIENTED FILES. An object-oriented file can also include a bitmap as its *only* object. In this situation, the file is essentially a bitmapped graphic file, and depending on the file format, you may be able to open the bitmap for editing in a painting or image-processing application. (Photoshop's EPS files are the best example of this.)

SCREENING INSTRUCTIONS

Half of this book is about halftoning, so we can't neglect to talk about screening with different file formats. Remember, halftoning isn't just for scanned images; it's necessary for anything gray—lines, boxes, type, or whatever. So you may want to specify screening instructions (frequency, angle, spot shape) within a file, whether it's bitmapped or object-oriented. If that's the case, you need to save the file in EPS format—the only format that can include screening instructions. (For more on how these internally specified screen settings interact with other programs' settings, see Chapter 27, *Controlling Halftone Screens,* and Chapter 31, *Illustration Applications.*)

TONAL ADJUSTMENTS

Another important consideration in choosing file formats is where tonal adjustment happens in the workflow. If you're planning to place a scanned image on a page and then use the tools in your page-layout software to adjust tonal levels, you can't use EPS. The tonal values in an EPS file are fixed, and can't be altered or tweaked unless the image is opened for editing by an image-processing program.

If you want to use a page-layout program's tonal controls on a scanned image, you need to save the image as a TIFF. Of course, you're probably better off managing your tonal control in an image-processing program rather than relying on the lesser controls in layout software. See Chapter 7, *Tonal Correction,* and Chapter 8, *Color,* for more on tonal adjustments.

BITMAPPED FILE FORMATS

When the first edition of this book appeared, folks were still arguing over which bitmapped file formats to use. In 1998, the disputes are over: TIFF, EPS, GIF, and JPEG rule the day. The formats each have a specialty, making them distinct from each other. All four formats have compression options, but each treats color and tonal fidelity differently. In Table 4-1, we compare some basic features of each format; if you don't understand all the terms listed there, don't worry—by the end of the chapter, you will. (We include PNG, FlashPix, and Photo CD for comparison; Photo CD has its own chapter: 14.)

TAGGED IMAGE FILE FORMAT (TIFF)

The Tagged Image File Format (TIFF) is the most widely used, industry-standard bitmapped file format. A TIFF bitmap can be of any dimensions and any resolution (at least we haven't heard of any limits). It can have theoretically unlimited bit depth, but most software reads or writes some standard sizes: 1 to 8, 24, 32 (for CMYK), or 48 (for RGB) bits per sample. TIFF can encode grayscale, RGB, indexed-color, or CMYK color models. It can be saved in compressed and uncompressed formats. Almost every program that works with bitmaps can handle TIFF files—whether for placing, printing, correcting, or editing the bitmap.

TIFF sounds like the ideal bitmapped file format, and it's pretty close. A few years ago, there were problems in converting files between different programs and different platforms, but those issues have disappeared when you're working with any major desktop-publishing program. There are rare times when you have to open a TIFF—usually an older one—in an intermediary program and then save it from that program in order to make it fully compatible with other programs.

Here's some background on the choices you face when saving files in most programs; this can also help you debug problems you might encounter with archived files from the depths of time (late '80s and early '90s).

Format	Compression	Displays in browser	Bit depths	Color	Interlacing	Labels/text[1]	Transparency
TIFF	Lossless	No	1–8, 24 32, 48	Indexed, gray, RGB, CMYK	No	Yes	Alpha channel
EPS	Lossless or lossy	No	same as TIFF	Gray, RGB, CMYK	No	Yes	Only in bilevel mode
GIF	Lossless	Yes	1–8	Indexed	Yes	Yes	One color
JPEG	Lossy	Yes	8, 24, 32	Gray, RGB, CMYK	Yes[2]	No[3]	None
PNG	Lossless	Yes[4]	1–8,16,24, 32, 48	Indexed, Gray, RGB	Yes	Yes	One color or alpha channel
FlashPix	Lossy and/ or lossless[5]	Yes[6]	8, 24	Gray, RGB, PhotoYCC[7]	No	Yes	Alpha channel
Photo CD	Lossy	Yes[6]	24	PhotoYCC[7]	No	Yes	None

TABLE 4-1
Major bitmap formats compared as implemented

[1]Stores information in text form about the image in a way that image-editing programs can read and/or modify. [2]Multiple settings for interlacing. [3]Photoshop supports this, but the basic image data format used for JPEG doesn't. [4]Requires third-party plug-in for older browsers at this writing. [5]Each 64-sample-square chunk can have separate compression choice applied. [6]Requires third-party plug-in for all browsers at this writing. [7]PhotoYCC is a Kodak-only colorspace that's similar to LAB in how it stores color.

GULLIVER'S SAMPLES. Computer files are just sequences of bytes, and all modern computers agree that a byte is eight bits. This lets you move files from machine to machine without jumbling the contents. But for computers to manipulate image (and other) data in an efficient way, they assemble bytes into larger units. Just as letters make up a word, computers call groups of bytes "words."

With European languages, you read words left to right, whereas you do the reverse direction for Hebrew and Arabic. Computers also have a left/right split in which the bytes that make up a word are read from one direction or the other. Nerds call the left-to-right byte ordering "big-endian" (because the big end, or digits representing higher units, are read first); right-to-left byte ordering is "little-endian" (the lower-unit digits are read first). Motorola processors that power the Macintosh prefer big-endian, while Intel PCs running Windows, OS/2, and Linux are little-endian.

The terminology comes from Jonathan Swift's *Gulliver's Travels* in which the Lilliputians war absurdly over what end to eat a soft-boiled egg from, and is another example of why programmers need more sun. (A programmer who nicely vetted this chapter for us suggested that computer-book authors just need a better sense of the absurd.)

Nowadays, the Lilliputians' wars are forgotten and virtually every major image-editing program that can open and save TIFFs can read either kind of byte ordering without a hitch; the TIFFs actually have a key at the beginning of the file that tells an application what order they're stored in. Other image formats hide this ordering from users, and they just cope without a word. (You can also see some low-level information about this later in Table 4-2.)

When you choose IBM PC or Macintosh from Photoshop's Save As dialog for TIFFs (see Figure 4-1), you're choosing the byte order. If you ever encounter a problem image, open the file on the platform it was created on and save it with the setting for the platform you're moving the file to.

FIGURE 4-1
Photoshop's Save As
dialog for TIFF files

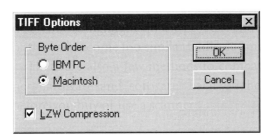

COLOR MODELS. TIFF's specification allows for CMYK color as well as RGB. This means you can separate an image into the four process colors, and save that preseparated image in a TIFF file. (If that last part was meaningless to you, see Chapter 8, *Color.*) When you place that file in a page-layout program or the like, no further separation is required. The program can simply pull the cyan channel when it's printing the cyan plate, the magenta channel when it's printing the magenta plate, and so on.

TIFF can also store indexed-color bitmaps, but almost no one ever uses it for this; we prefer to use GIF for indexed-color images. (The PNG format offers the same choice of indexed or deep color with its own unique advantages, which we describe below.)

COMPRESSION. You can save TIFFs with LZW compression (we'll discuss what LZW is and why it can be a good thing in Chapter 10, *Compression*), but you don't have to use it. Fortunately, LZW compression is lossless, meaning that the image data doesn't degrade when you save the file.

POSTSCRIPT EXTRAS. There is no facility for including screening instructions in a TIFF file. Screening is controlled by the program from which the TIFF is printed. If you want to save a bitmap with screening instructions, use EPS.

TIFFs can handle a clipping path, however; both QuarkXPress and PageMaker can read it and properly trim out a background. See "EPS" later in this chapter for a description of clipping paths.

PRONUNCIATION. TIFF is pronounced *tiff.* That wasn't hard, was it?

GRAPHICS INTERCHANGE FORMAT (GIF)

We barely mentioned GIF in the first edition because in 1993 it was used almost exclusively by CompuServe users to send low-quality images to each other. Now, almost everyone on the planet knows that GIF is one of the World Wide Web's standard graphic formats.

The GIF file format was originally developed in 1987 ("GIF87a") and revised in 1989 ("GIF89a")—unfortunately, not every program upgraded its support to the later version. The main visible difference is that GIF89a added a transparency color (see "Transparency" in Chapter 11, *Images for the Web*). In fact, Adobe didn't even update Photoshop until 1996 (via the "GIF89a Export" plug-in).

Don't use the GIF format for any kind of high-resolution color output for printing; the color fidelity is too poor and the images almost always appear posterized.

COLOR MODEL. GIF files can contain a maximum of 256 different colors, which are stored in a palette that is part of the GIF file itself (see Figure 4-2). It's called an indexed color palette because the colors in the image data aren't directly represented by RGB values. Instead, the image data comprises single-byte values that corre-

FIGURE 4-2

A sample GIF color-map in Photoshop (which calls it Color Table)

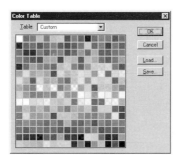

spond to entries in a color palette, just like entries in a two-column spreadsheet. The single-byte value is paired with a full, 24-bit (3-byte) RGB value in the palette. This saves a lot of space but still allows you to specify an actual color for samples to be translated back into when the file is displayed.

GIF image data and the indexed color palette are editable in virtually every image-manipulation program. You don't have to use all 256 colors: GIF palettes can represent anywhere from one to 256 colors using from one to eight bits for the index value. And the fewer colors in the palette (or *colormap*), the better the built-in compression works and the more consistent the display across different browsers and platforms. (Again, see Chapter 11, *Images for the Web*, for details on reducing the color palette and other GIF-related issues. Also, see the color pages for examples.)

COMPRESSION. GIF uses lossless compression that can't be turned off (you wouldn't want to), and that can substantially reduce file size. Compression depends entirely on image content; images with mostly flat colors—solid fields of color—can be reduced to one-tenth (or even one-hundredth) the size, while natural images (scans of photographs) often compress very poorly. (We talk about this compression more in Chapter 10, *Compression.*)

PRONUNCIATION. Discussions on how to pronounce GIF have resulted in fistfights. The guy who actually wrote the format, Steve Wilhite, apparently said the "g" as "j" as in "jihad," and often uttered the line, "Choosy programmers choose jiff" (if you're not up on American television advertising from 20 years ago, just smile and nod appreciatively). However, many well-meaning and gifted professionals say the "g" like in "gift." We tend to just say, "Ummm …you know…*that* format."

JPEG

The JPEG file format—known as the Joint Photographic Experts Group standard by those wishing to be excessively obscure—has risen to prominence as the compressed file format of choice for both print and Web publishing.

JPEGs lose quality each time they're saved, due to the format's lossy compression scheme (we'll explain why in Chapter 10, *Compression*). Because of this, you don't want to save multiple generations of the image. Typically, you should only save an image in the JPEG format as the last stage in a production process.

JPEG is useful as a method of getting a file small enough to fit on a disk or send over a modem line because you can compress natural, scanned images significantly (often to less than 5 percent of the original size). This is why JPEG images are used so often on the Internet. JPEGs are also often made for proofing purposes so that someone can look at a final illustration on screen without requiring large source files, though the PDF file format is quickly replacing this function. (PDFs, in fact, allow JPEG compression as one of many methods of shrinking images.)

IMAGE FORMAT. An image saved in the JPEG file format is, strangely enough, actually an amalgam of two different formats: the JPEG spec itself, which defines the image's compression and is wrapped inside an image data format which defines the color model and resolution. Photoshop—and virtually every other program that reads and writes JPEGs—stores the image data in JFIF (JPEG File Interchange Format) or something just like JFIF. JFIF is just a simple method to wrap an image format around JPEG compression; it doesn't have any bells or whistles.

COLOR MODELS. JPEG allows bitmaps eight, 24, and 32 bits deep to be stored with variable compression (from high compression and lousy quality, to low compression and high quality). The original JFIF spec only allows 8-bit grayscale and 24-bit RGB images, but Adobe "hacked" the format to handle 32-bit CMYK data as well. Unfortunately, most page-layout programs can't actually separate CMYK JPEG images, so it's sort of meaningless.

PRONUNCIATION. Say "jay-peg" and you're set.

PORTABLE NETWORK GRAPHICS (PNG)

The genesis of the PNG file format was the controversy over the LZW compression algorithm used to compress GIF images. In 1995, when the patent holder, Unisys, belatedly started to demand its (rightful) dues, software developers started balking at this extra cost. This camp stated that, had they known that GIF would require licensing fees, they would have developed their own, free format.

They put their money—or principles, rather—where their mouths were and developed a specification that could describe rich, deep, complex images better than GIF. These folks came up with the PNG file format.

PNG has key features that make it akin to GIF: it uses lossless compression, can interlace images, is displayable in browser windows, and can use an indexed color palette up of to 256 colors. However, PNG has incredibly powerful features found together in no other image format, meant for the Web or not. (See Chapter 11, *Images for the Web*, for the Web-related features.)

We hate to predict the future—it's so easy to be wrong where technology is concerned. (Glenn even thought that the Iomega ZIP drive was going to be a dud.) So we're not going to say whether we think PNG is the next sliced bread—or eight-track tape. But we will say that it's at least worth paying attention to.

COLOR MODELS. PNG can store either deep bitmaps (from one to 16 bits for grayscale and 24 or 48 for RGB) or an indexed color map. You have to choose one or the other, but you get the best of either JPEG-like deep color without compression, or GIF-like indexing to control how colors display on low-bit-depth monitors.

The format was designed for the Web, so there's no support in the specification for CMYK.

SUPPORT. The biggest problem with PNG files today is that the majority of surfers are using browsers that can't display PNG files. Microsoft introduced built-in PNG support with the release of 4.0 for Windows—Mac users weren't fortunate enough to get PNG support in that platform's 4.0 release—and Netscape added it with its micro-update 4.0.4 for Macintosh and Windows. (Neither supports PNG transparency or gamma controls; see Chapter 11, *Images for the Web*, for details.)

You can get free plug-ins for other browsers and older Internet Explorers and Navigators. As we write this paragraph, you can use a PNG image and count on it displaying for about 25 percent of all Web surfers. Since there's a trend for users to update to get security fixes, new features, and crash preventers in new releases, that number will rapidly climb.

PRONUNCIATION. The folks who developed PNG weren't going to lead people down the same path as GIF, so the PNG specification spells it out for you: "PNG is pronounced 'ping.'"

FLASHPIX

FlashPix stores an image at multiple resolutions in the same file so that you can access any resolution without loading the entire image. It can store cumulative sets of corrections in the file without affecting image data; it can use JPEG compression or not; it can add rich-text tags or other objects inside the same file, which actually has its own internal directory structure.

At first glance, it sounds like it shares some features with Photo CD, which also stores several resolutions in the same file. But unlike Photo CD, it's optimized for rapid access and doesn't throw away nearly as much color data; it can also be entirely lossless (see Chapter 10, *Compression*, for more on lossless and lossy compression).

FlashPix appeared in 1996, but didn't get its momentum until a Seybold Publishing Conference announcement in October 1997. It was developed by Kodak, Hewlett-Packard, Live Picture, and Microsoft—we'd hate to see the bed they all shared—and virtually every other company that develops imaging software or digital photography hardware had signed on by the time of the Seybold announcement. This includes Apple, Adobe, Canon, Corel, Fuji, Intel, IBM, Polaroid, and about a dozen others. (Note that Quark and Netscape weren't among them.)

This level of broad industry support makes us wonder if this just might not catch on. That opinion is buoyed by the fact that both Macintosh and Windows Photoshop and Netscape plug-ins are available (for free) at this writing. Unlike PNG, which is a grassroots movement gaining support, FlashPix is a top-down, executive-style file format that's almost mandated to be widely used. We'll see if that's the case if you're reading this in the year 2000 and laughing; but you'll certainly encounter images in this format and need to make decisions about whether to use FlashPix yourself.

IMAGE STORAGE. FlashPix starts with an image of any resolution and then downsamples it repeatedly by half until it gets a final image less than 64 samples wide in the widest direction. Let's say we start with a 1,000-by-2,000-sample image. That original image is stored along with versions at 500 by 1,000, 250 by 500, 125 by 250, 62.5 by 125 (yes, it uses pixel fractions!), and 31.25 by 62.5 samples (see Figure 4-3). It also stores a separate 96-sample-square preview image.

The actual image data at each of these resolutions is further chunked into blocks 64 samples square, which are stored in order in the file. Other graphic file formats store the data in series of lines of samples the entire width of the image; to get just a part of the file, all the lines making up the area you're viewing have to be read in to

FIGURE 4-3
FlashPix's multiple resolutions

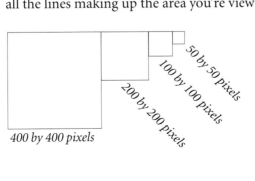

400 by 400 pixels

FlashPix stores the original image plus a series of images, each of which is half the size of the previous image in the series until you reach a size smaller than 64 pixels in each dimension.

the computer, the software has to discard the bits it doesn't need, and the rest is displayed. FlashPix can select just the blocks it needs to display or manipulate, requiring less memory and time since it's not reading as much data and then just throwing it away.

COMPRESSION. Compression comes in three flavors: JPEG, none, and single-color. JPEG we discuss in depth between this chapter and Chapter 10, *Compression.* None is just none. We exchanged some e-mail with one of the software developers, who noted that future versions might incorporate a lossless method like LZW in the future.

Single-color compression is unique, in our experience. If every sample in a 64-sample square is identical, it represents the square with a single piece of data, achieving 4,096:1 compression. Single-color compression would work well for computer-generated (artifical) images that have large, flat color fields.

Each 64-sample square can have its own compression method, meaning you can choose some areas of the image to have perfect fidelity and others to be highly compressed using JPEG.

COLORSPACE. FlashPix supports two kinds of colorspaces that are device-independent: NIFRGB and PhotoYCC. The former is supported (as far as we can tell) only by this product and it's intended for accurate on-screen display; it's calibrated for display on a reference monitor, and can transform the color to your particular display. PhotoYCC is part of the Photo CD spec, and it's similar to and easily convertable into LAB, which Photoshop supports. Both formats will be supported in color management systems: an easy solution, since the companies supporting FlashPix develop and maintain the various color management systems! Both 8-bit grayscale and regular 24-bit RGB color are supported as well. (See Chapter 8, *Color,* for background on all these subjects.)

SUPPORT. Even this early in the adoption process, the FlashPix format can be read and written by Photoshop (using free Mac and Windows plug-ins available from the LivePicture Web site), Microsoft Picture-It, and most of the other image-editing software. Not surprising, since most application developers have signed on to the (all lowercase) digital imaging group—or (all-caps acronym) DIG—which is the defender of the FlashPix flame.

Free Mac and Windows Netscape plug-ins are also available; only the Windows version works with Internet Explorer, too. Netscape hasn't signed on to DIG at this writing, but Microsoft is a co-developer and a prime advocate. The format even uses some of Microsoft's OLE (Object Linking and Embedding) technology, helping it to spread more of its software tools and formats.

WHY USE IT? Why start FlashPix instead of TIFF, JPEG, or EPS? We can think of a few reasons relating mostly to workflow and the Web—not any inherent advantage in the file format. TIFF is still the best way to store single-resolution, device-targeted (i.e., corrected for particular output), lossless color bitmaps.

▶ *Stored corrections.* If you're using software like LivePicture, FlashPix can store any corrections you make to a file as a series of steps without changing the original image data. You can even store *different* sets of corrections in the same file. This makes it possible to use a single file to target different purposes and still maintain your untouched originals.

▶ *High-res editing on low-end systems.* FlashPix loads only what it needs at the resolution you're viewing. For editing big files on machines without a lot of memory or resources—like a regular old Windows box with 32 Mb of RAM—this is a godsend, and it comes without the price tag or learning curve of something like LivePicture. A low-end program from Microsoft called Picture-It! already can handle enormous images because of this feature. But even high-end users could appreciate the reduction in display time. The more memory that's free, the faster everything works.

▶ *High-res images for the Web.* It's a way to include high-resolution images on the Web without requiring a user to download the whole thing or click separately to view a larger version. A single version of the file can be stored on the Web server, and the Web page can be coded to show just a low-resolution version;

on-screen controls let the user zoom in or pan—and the format just quickly requests just the 64-sample-square chunks needed to display the zoomed-in pieces.

OBJECT-ORIENTED FILE FORMATS

As we mentioned earlier, object-oriented file formats need to store a much wider variety of information than bitmapped formats. Given that variety, it's not surprising that there isn't a good industry standard object-oriented file format that can be edited by a wide variety of programs and printed to any printer.

Bear in mind that you can use some of these object-oriented file formats as bitmap-only formats. This means that a painting or image-processing application can open the file for editing.

EXCHANGING OBJECTS

While there's no universal format for exchanging object-oriented files, Adobe Acrobat Portable Document Format (PDF) does allow an interesting workaround for this problem. Adobe Illustrator includes a PDF reader plug-in that allows Illustrator to turn any PDF file into an editable Illustrator file.

This means that you could build a page in QuarkXPress, print a PostScript file to disk, run the PostScript file through the Acrobat Distiller—a separate program that creates PDF files—and then open the results in Illustrator. Voilá—an editable object file.

This isn't to say that it's a two-way road. At the time of this writing, Quark has announced its intention of being able to import PDF files for manipulation, but no one has yet seen what this means. Currently, it's a one-way street. (You can't edit files in Illustrator, save as PDF, and then have QuarkXPress read the file.) But in many cases, it might allow the transfer of objects that would otherwise be impossible. For instance, you can rescue illustrations in orphaned EPS files for which the source file is no longer available by doing the above steps to convert to PDF and import into Illustrator.

You can also use this method to create complex graphics in whichever program you prefer, and then touch them up and edit them elsewhere. We like to use QuarkXPress for certain kinds of tables, for instance, but we'd rather do the final work in Illustrator.

Illustrator 1.1 used to be the *lingua franca* of object-oriented programs; every program would save and open in that format for interchanging files. Most still do, and in a pinch, it's a great choice; but these programs will also save and open more advanced versions. Illustrator and FreeHand are always in close parity, being able to import or just plain open and save each other's files up to the near-current version.

ENCAPSULATED POSTSCRIPT (EPS)

Encapsulated PostScript is absolutely the best format for storing graphics of any kind. That's a big statement, but it's true—as long as you have a PostScript printer and you don't want to edit the graphics, even to adjust their tonal values. With some exceptions, you can't print EPS files on non-PostScript printers, and you can't open them for editing except through the PDF workaround discussed above. We describe other exceptions below.

If you're like lots of people, you're wondering what encapsulated PostScript is, and why it has such a funny name. Let's start by talking about what PostScript is.

PostScript is a page-description language. It's like Basic or C or any other programming language, except that it's optimized for putting type and graphics on paper. When you're working with a PostScript printer and you tell your word processor (or any other program) to print a page, the computer writes a program in PostScript that describes the page, and sends that program to the printer. The printer—which actually has a full-blown computer and PostScript interpreter inside it—executes that program, draws the picture on a virtual page in memory, and then dumps it out to paper.

If you don't have a PostScript printer, it's hard to print an EPS graphic. However, almost all Adobe software since 1996 has some kind of PostScript interpreter built in, so you can open or place an EPS graphic in Photoshop or PageMaker and do some tricks to make it output. (We cover this in Part 3, *Applications.*)

So at its lowest level, a PostScript file is just a bunch of text commands that a PostScript interpreter understands. EPS is a refined form of PostScript, and it comes in several varieties, including with and without preview, Illustrator 1.1 format, and bitmap-only EPS.

BINARY VERSUS ASCII. Binary encoding uses all eight bits in a single byte, while ASCII encoding requires two to do the same job. ASCII sends an identical data stream, just recorded in a less efficient way. The reason for this choice—which most programs still let you make—was to avoid problems that cropped up when transferring images over serial cables, onto network file servers, or to a commercial online service. Sometimes binary encoding would get garbled or cause wacky file-server behavior. These problems are long gone in contemporary systems, but older computers and servers abound. Use binary unless you have odd problems crop up; then try ASCII. Then call a nerd.

EPS WITHOUT PREVIEW IMAGE. In their simplest form, EPS files are just made up of PostScript code that conforms to a few document-structuring conventions defined by Adobe (creator of PostScript)—certain commands can't be used, and there are some comments in the file specifying the file name, creator, and so on.

If you get one of these files and place it on a page in non-Adobe software, you probably won't see the graphic; you'll just see a gray box and some of the comments. For example, if you transfer an EPS image from a Unix workstation to your PC and then place it on your QuarkXPress page, you may only see a gray box where the picture should appear. When you print to a PostScript printer, however, the graphic will appear in all its glory.

Also, as we noted above, most Adobe software will render a preview using built-in mini-interpreters. This is another way for it to support its PostScript franchise by making it easier to transfer files around.

EPS WITH PREVIEW IMAGE. The most common form of EPS has a low-resolution screen-preview image built in. We call these viewable EPS files. When you place one of these files on a page, the computer shows you the low-res image, and when you print it, the computer uses the PostScript code. (If you don't have a PostScript printer, what prints out is the low-res preview—not terribly useful except for simple proofing.)

Photoshop has the richest set of preview options. On the Macintosh, it can save an EPS with one of three Macintosh previews (1-bit, 8-bit, or JPEG); on both Mac and Windows it can include either a 1-bit or 8-bit TIFF preview. (In other image-editing programs, like Ulead PhotoImpact, the options for previews aren't quite as varied; see Figure 4-4.) If you know your EPS will be moved from a Macintosh to a PC, use the TIFF preview; otherwise, the PICT preview will get stripped away when transferring the document.

FIGURE 4-4
Photoshop and
PhotoImpact's
approaches to EPS
previews saved with
files

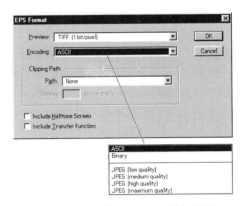

PhotoImpact offers a single TIFF preview option, a settable clipping path, and an ASCII or binary encoding option.

Photoshop can include a 1- or 8-bit TIFF preview and a clipping path for which you set flatness; it also has a menu of encoding options, including four JPEG choices.

CLIPPING PATH. Often, you'd like to mask the edge of an image so that you're not printing a rectangle. EPS has the ability to use a *clipping path* that's just a PostScript outline that defines the image; the rest of the image is transparent. This can cause problems when you've defined too complex a path, or are printing on an old laser printer or imagesetter RIP. The clipping path can be calculated at the full resolution of the output device—which can be thousands of dots per inch—and the "decision" has to be made about which pixels fall inside and which fall outside the path. The printer also has to handle the interface between the edge of the path and the image or text underneath.

However, by setting *flatness*, a measure of how closely to calculate a curve against the output resolution, you can eliminate almost all problems that result from too complex a path. Flatness is an option that appears in almost all DTP programs that do PostScript paths. Some, like Macromedia FreeHand, let you set flatness per object; others have a setting in the Page Setup or Print dialog boxes nested a level or two deep. David prefers to set flatness to 3 or 4—it sacrifices a little bit of smoothness in curves, but it dramatically reduces processing time on older machines and it's almost unnoticeable.

DESKTOP COLOR SEPARATION (DCS). The DCS specification was developed by Quark, Inc., for use in process-color work, though PageMaker can handle it, too. A DCS image is an EPS format that consists of five parts: a low-resolution screen preview, plus cyan, magenta, yellow, and black layers.

DCS version 1.0 is made up of five files—the low-resolution version that you place on a page, which contains pointers to four data files. These are sometimes called five-file DCS or EPS-5 files. DCS version 2.0 format can contain all the information in a single file. Plus, DCS 2.0 files can contain more than just four process colors; you can have a number of spot colors included as well, or even High-Fidelity or Hi-Fi color separations (see Chapter 22, *Stochastic Screening*, and Chapter 25, *Rosettes and Moirés*, for more on Hi-Fi).

ACROBAT PORTABLE DOCUMENT FORMAT

PDF is a both child of and big brother to EPS. Adobe introduced it as a paperless document file that could be created from PostScript output and pretty much exactly reproduce the original document. If you wanted to distribute over the Web a document—say, a modem specification sheet—that was as close as possible to the original, PDF is the easiest way.

It has built-in compression (JPEG, TIFF's LZW, and CCITT fax-style), preserves the look of the original document, can be searched and indexed, and—with a simple plug-in—can even be viewed inside a Web browser window. The reader software that displays PDFs is free.

PDFs can be multiple pages, in which each page can have different dimensions and be printed separately. This is a big advantage over EPS files, which can only represent a single page and can't be printed out by themselves. (It's also a big advantage over PostScript files, which store multiple pages, but aren't good at letting them be printed separately.)

Making a PDF requires either the Adobe Acrobat package (which puts together a bunch of separate components: Capture, Catalog, Exchange, and Distiller) or the PDFWriter, which is shipped free with lots of Adobe software. (Photoshop and Illustrator can also save directly in PDF format, though in both cases you can only create a single page and you'll need Acrobat Exchange to do anything with it.) We don't suggest using PDFWriter for anything with lots of images, though, because PDFWriter doesn't have options you can set for compression, and it can't handle much complexity.

Files created through Acrobat Distiller using the Portable Printer Description (PPD) file called, eponymously, Acrobat Distiller, are always smaller and more accurate to the original. If you choose the right options in Distiller—or do a Save As from the Acrobat Exchange editor later—the file can be optimized for "page-at-a-time" download over the Internet. The PDF Web plug-in lets you view PDF files directly in major Web browsers, and an optimized PDF stores the text first, followed by graphics, and then the fonts (if needed). This way, you can read the text long before images arrive. Acrobat uses Adobe's Multiple Master fonts to fake the text display without necessarily having the original fonts.

Acrobat can be used in prepress, too. Distiller has an option to leave CMYK images in their original form; you can convert them to RGB if you're creating just an on-screen version. We talked to several people using PDF as a way to deliver an electronic proof to a client and then deliver it as a final output file for film or plate output. Ad agencies that do placements in magazines and newspapers are starting to use PDF instead of EPS or other file formats; PDF is more reliable, compresses extremely well, and can be used without having anything like the original application around. It's also, needless to say, totally compatible with imagesetter PostScript interpreters; PostScript 3 even allows direct output of PDFs without any intermediate step.

FUHGETTABOUT 'EM

We don't want to let you down and not mention golden-oldie file formats that are now deprecated—meaning, don't use 'em, don't accept 'em, forget about 'em entirely. (David and co-author Bruce Fraser refer to them as "unreasonable formats" in *Real World Photoshop 4*.)

WINDOWS WIPEOUTS

In the bad old days—which continue til today for users of older programs and operating systems—PCX and BMP were what you used in Windows for bitmaps, and CGM (Computer Graphics Metafile) and WMF (Windows Metafile) for objects. None of these four formats is really used except by older programs, ones that create files for use only in Windows, or some built-in software that comes with Windows.

The best thing you do with any outdated Windows file format is convert it immediately to a modern file format, like GIF, TIFF, JPEG, or EPS.

ODDBALL MACINTOSH FORMATS

The Mac has its share of items peculiar to it, and graphic file formats aren't an exception. Two of the most popular have been around as long as the Macintosh itself, though their use is rightly minimal for most purposes these days.

PICT. The PICT format is the original Mac-standard object-oriented file format. A PICT graphic can contain a bitmap as one of the objects in the file, or as its only object ("bitmap-only-PICTs"). Bitmap-only PICTs can be any size, resolution, and bit depth. Object-oriented PICTs, which have mostly disappeared from view, had strange problems with line widths and other irregularities when printing. We don't recommend using PICT these days unless you're creating desktop backgrounds on a Macintosh or doing certain kinds of Mac-only multimedia work. PICTs are awfully difficult to open on other platforms, which is why we deprecate their use.

MacPaint. The MacPaint format is ultimately the most basic of all graphic formats on the Macintosh. Paint files (more rarely called PNTG, or "pee-en-tee-gee," files) are black and white (one bit per sample), 72 samples per inch, 8 by 10 inches (576 by 720 dots). That's it. No more and no less.

BAD IDEAS

Some vendors thoughts that developing their own, distinct file format was a good idea, despite growing industry consensus on other formats. RIFF (Raster Image File Format) was a TIFF competitor primarily supported by the company formerly known as Fractal Design software, which created Painter and ColorStudio—the world's greatest orphaned program. QuarkXPress used to place RIFF files, but since we haven't seen a RIFF file since 1993, we don't know if it still does.

FILE TYPES, EXTENSIONS, AND MAGIC NUMBERS

The Macintosh, Windows, and Unix operating systems "see" files differently. Mac OS uses file types and file creators to track what program to open a given file in and what format the file uses. Windows still uses filename extensions—even though Windows 95 introduced long file names—and a Registry that records what these extensions mean. And Unix uses "magic numbers" to identify a file type. (Why talk about Unix? Because you may have to upload files to a Unix Web or file transfer server; and you can use this magic to help identify and recover image files.)

MACINTOSH

Every Macintosh file has several attributes attached to it, including file type and creator. These are mysterious four-letter labels that tell the Mac OS what sort of file it is and what program generated it. For example, when you double-click on a file, the Mac looks at the file's creator to see what application to start up. You often get blank document icons when the original program disappeared—the icons get removed from the system along with the application!

If you move an image from some other platform to the Macintosh, you may not be able to open or place it, because it has a file type of TEXT or DATA or some such, when the opening application is looking for EPSF or TIFF or the like. You can view and change a file's type using Apple's free ResEdit, and various other commercial, public-domain, and shareware programs (we really like the shareware FileBuddy). If you really dig this kind of detail, check out Robin Williams and Steve Broback's *Beyond the Little Mac Book*.

WINDOWS

In the Windows world, everything is different. Although Windows 95 added "long filename support," every Windows (or DOS) file is still identified by a simple three-letter extension. Before Windows 95, the format was called "eight-dot-three" for the maximum filename length of eight characters, a period, and then three more characters. Now it would be "252-dot-three."

The Windows Registry maintains a list of extensions and what programs they are mapped to. Unfortunately, until recently (and we believe this still goes on), many programs named their specific files with the same extensions, like ".doc". Newer programs tend to be better behaved and not overlap existing extensions.

The Registry is a nightmare to figure out, and books have been written on the subject (and millions of hours of sleep lost, too). But there's a simple way in Windows 95 and later versions to see a list of the extensions your particular system knows about. Double-click on "My Computer" on the desktop. Select the View menu, and then the Options menu item. Click on the File Types tab. You'll see a scrollable list of extensions and what programs they belong to (see Figure 4-5). This is a lifesaver when you're trying to sort out what's going wrong.

FIGURE 4-5
The list of extensions in the Windows 95 My Computer Options dialog box

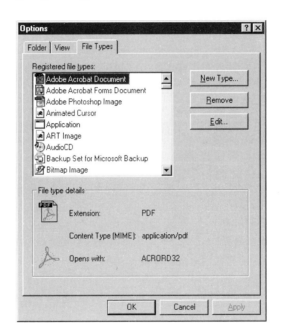

UNIX

Where do we get off bringing in Unix in a desktop-publishing book? It's only important because of the World Wide Web. When Glenn worked at Amazon.com Books, one of the programs he wrote for automating catalog operations took images transferred from a Macintosh and batch converted them using odd-but-scriptable freeware Unix graphics tools.

Hopefully, you'll never have to deal with this, but Unix does have some oddities when it comes to images. Unix doesn't look at extensions or file types when it comes to identifying what a file is. Unix looks at the first several bytes of data in a file, which is called, in the bearded-guru land of workstations, the file's "magic number." These bytes usually contain enough information for the Unix system to guess what it is, and most image file formats are designed to have this kind of identification in place. Hardly efficient, but it works. (This can also be a kind of help in figuring out corrupted files with a disk file editor; see Table 4-2.)

In general, as long as you've transferred the file as binary or what's listed as Raw Data in some programs and with the right capitalization on the name, Unix shouldn't intervene. (See Chapter 11, *Images for the Web*, for the full range of transfer tips.)

The other reason to mention this is that it looks like this is a trick Photoshop pulls on Mac and Windows boxes as well. Photoshop can identify most image files when you open them with the Open As file menu item even if they lack an extension or file type. It looks like Photoshop has a little "magic" in it, too.

TABLE 4-2
Image format magic numbers

Format	# of bytes	Start of file[1]	ASCII[2]
GIF87a	6	47 49 46 38 37 61	GIF87a
GIF89a	6	47 49 46 38 39 61	GIF89a
JPEG	3	ff d8 ff[3]	...
PNG	8	89 50 4e 47 0d 0a 1a 0a	.PNG....
TIFF (big-endian[4])	4	4d 4d 00 2a	MM..
TIFF (little-endian[4])	4	49 49 2a 00	II..

[1] In hexadecimal, or base-16, numbering.
[2] The characters that the start of file represents, with periods for control characters.
[3] Some Mac-created JPEGs have headers before this pattern that must be discarded in order to open the file.
[4] See "TIFF," earlier in the chapter, for an explanation!

WORKING WITH FILES

Without a solid grounding in what kind of graphic files you're working with, it's almost impossible to be efficient in desktop publishing—you're forever banging into barriers. Why can't I import this image into my illustration program? Why can't I edit this photograph in this program? Why can't I move this file format over to the Macintosh? Why can't I use tonal correction on this file? And so on.

However, now that you know something about bitmapped versus object-oriented images, and TIFFs versus EPS files, you'll be able to really start to fly. Our next few chapters go into more detail in the area of bitmapped images, particularly scanned images.

5 IMAGE RESOLUTION

SCANNING, SCALING, AND RESAMPLING

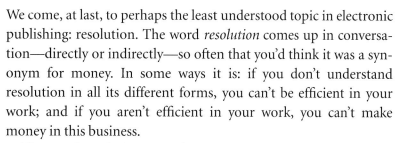

We come, at last, to perhaps the least understood topic in electronic publishing: resolution. The word *resolution* comes up in conversation—directly or indirectly—so often that you'd think it was a synonym for money. In some ways it is: if you don't understand resolution in all its different forms, you can't be efficient in your work; and if you aren't efficient in your work, you can't make money in this business.

The word *resolution* is used in so many different contexts that people quickly get confused about what it means. There's the resolution of an image, of an imagesetter, of a scanner, and so on. In this chapter we want to solidify your understanding of scanned image resolution in all its incarnations. Just remember what we keep saying: It's not as hard as it sometimes seems.

THEY'RE ALL JUST DOTS

Whenever someone talks about resolution, they're talking about a grid of dots that are assigned or mapped to a given space (typically measured in inches or centimeters). It's as simple as that. The complicated part is getting it clear in your head which dots belong to which grid, and what those dots are doing.

Most people use the word *dot* to mean many things: a printer dot, an on-screen pixel, a value for an area created by a scanner, and so forth. We've defined our terminology for dot, spot, pixel, and sample to make it simpler to understand exactly what we're talking about.

▶ *Dots.* Printer resolution is measured in dots per inch (dpi). These are actual dots created by a laser printer or imagesetter.

▶ *Samples.* For scanned images or bitmapped images, we talk about samples per inch (spi). A sample is a measurement of tone or color at a given place. Many people will insist that image resolution should be specified in dpi rather than spi, but you can look them right in the eye and say, "There are no dots in an image; just samples."

▶ *Pixels.* For display resolution, it's pixels per inch (ppi). A pixel (or "picture element") is a single x,y coordinate on a monitor that can represent any one of from one to 16 million different values. Adobe Photoshop uses ppi instead of spi for image resolution, and although Photoshop is the standard in image-editing tools, we aren't bowing to its terminology.

▶ *Spots and lines.* We talk about halftones themselves by using the term *spot*: the shape made up of printer dots that creates the halftone value. (We examine this in much greater detail throughout Part 2, *Halftones,* but look specifically at Chapter 15, *Dots, Spots, and Halftones.*) Halftone are measured in lines per inch (lpi).

▶ *Res.* Some service bureaus may use the term *res* (pronounced rez) to refer to the resolution of a scanned image. Res is another word for samples per millimeter. Scanner operators often scan at "res 12," meaning 12 samples per millimeter or 304 spi (25.4 mm to the inch).

By using these separate terms, each of which has a specific meaning, you'll always know when we're talking about a monitor display or a scanned image.

SCANNING VERSUS IMAGE RESOLUTION

If there's one distinction we'd like you to leave this chapter with, it's the difference between *scanning resolution* and *image resolution.* They're not always the same. Just because a scanner scans an image at 200 spi doesn't mean that the resolution of the image that finally gets printed will be 200 spi. The resolution can be affected by scaling and resampling.

SCALING

First and foremost, when you place a scanned image on a page and scale it, you change the image resolution (see Figure 5-1). As we noted in Chapter 3, *Scanned Images,* the grid's dimensions stay the same. Let's say you have a 2-by-2-inch, 100-spi image. Reduce it to 50 percent, and you have a 1-by-1-inch, 200-spi image—the same number of samples packed into half the space.

If you specify a scaling percentage in the Print dialog box, you're further affecting resolution. If you enlarge to 200 percent, for instance, you're reducing the resolution by a factor of two.

RESAMPLING

You can resize a bitmap without affecting resolution, however. Or you can change a bitmap's resolution without changing its size. This process is called *resampling,* and it's accomplished by using an image-editing program.

The best way to explain this is to show you Photoshop's Image Size dialog box (Figure 5-2). With Resample Image checked, when you enter new values for Width and Height under Pixel Dimensions, the file size changes but Print Size stays constant.

When you reduce the resolution of a bitmap, it's called *downsampling.* When you increase the resolution, it's called *interpolation.* In either case, there are smart and not-so-smart methods.

Interpolation is the process of generating a sample point in a bitmap where there wasn't one before. Downsampling is similar,

FIGURE 5-1
Scaling and
resolution

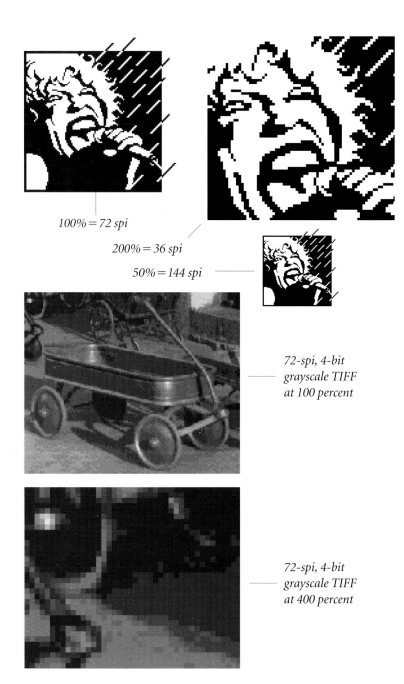

100% = 72 spi

200% = 36 spi

50% = 144 spi

*72-spi, 4-bit
grayscale TIFF
at 100 percent*

*72-spi, 4-bit
grayscale TIFF
at 400 percent*

FIGURE 5-2

Photoshop's Image
Size dialog box

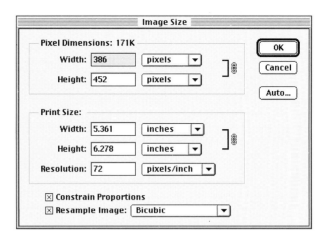

but it removes sample points throughout the image. Most resampling processes are very basic. A scanning or image-editing program might add a sample point and, to figure out what color it should be, just look at the value of the sample next to the new one (*nearest neighbor*). If the software is slightly smarter, it'll look at the samples on either side and average between the two (*bilinear*). Sometimes this process gives you a good image, and sometimes it doesn't. The best kind of interpolation is *bicubic*, which looks at all four surrounding samples and applies their average value to the new sample point. This takes the longest, but yields the best quality. Photoshop offers all three methods.

THE LIMITS OF INTERPOLATION

Unlike downsampling, which simply removes existing information (using more or less intelligent methods), interpolation is more problematic, because it's attempting to add information that doesn't exist in the original image (see Figure 5-3). While it can help reduce the aliasing (a.k.a. *the jaggies*) in some situations, it can't add detail to an image if the detail isn't already there.

FIGURE 5-3
Interpolation

*When you double the reso-
lution, interpolation creates
extra gray samples.*

FIRM RESOLUTIONS

With any luck, now that we've laid out the essentials of resolution, next time someone comes shaking their scan at you, you'll be able to fix their problem and send them on their way. Plus, to really get you on your way, in the next chapter we get into some specific advice on what resolution settings to use for different types of images.

6 CHOOSING RESOLUTION

WHEN ENOUGH IS ENOUGH

Remember the good ol' days when cars had a choke knob? In the cool early morning you could help your car start by pulling the knob out a little and then perhaps pumping the gas pedal a bit to prime the engine. If you did too little, your car wouldn't start properly. If you pulled the knob out too far and pumped too hard, your engine would flood with gasoline and you'd sit there, frustrated, in the fumes. Unfortunately, cars not being digital, figuring out just how much to pull and pump was more an art than a science.

Enter scanning, stage left. If scanning is like an old car, then scanning resolution is like the choke knob. How do you know what resolution you should scan at? The highest resolution possible, right? No! You'll too often flood the engine (your computer) with too much information. The image file size gets too big, it takes too long to process or print (if it prints at all), and everything gets bogged down. Okay, so how about scanning at a really low resolution? Images look pixelated and computeresque—fine if that's your design goal, but problematic for most work.

Fortunately, although there is an art to scanning, much of your work can be figured out by science. Simple formulas can help you decide how much resolution you need for different types of images.

Remember: The resolution we're talking about here is *image resolution*—after an image has been placed on a page and scaled to fit (see Chapter 5, *Image Resolution*, for more on this difference).

LINE ART

Back in Chapter 3, *Scanned Images,* we talked about line-art images. These are always black and white; each sample point in the image is described with one bit of information. Bilevel scans are great for reproducing straightforward line drawings, and even images as complex as the finely etched pictures in those old-fashioned Dover clip-art books.

To achieve line-art quality approaching that of photographic reproduction, and to avoid the jaggy look (Figure 6-1), you need two things: very high resolution and sharpening. We discuss sharpening in Chapter 9, *A Sharper Image* (but we will say here that sharpening improves line-art scans *dramatically*). We'll cover the details of line-art resolution here.

When printing line-art scans, you never need image resolution higher than your output resolution (a 300-spi image looks about the same as a 600-spi image if they're both printed on a 300-dpi printer), but if you're printing on an imagesetter, plan on using an image resolution of *at least* 800 spi—preferably 1,000 spi or more. Yes, you heard us right. Line art with an image resolution of less than 800 spi shows jaggies, even to casual observers at normal viewing distances. Note that if you're printing to a toner-based laser printer or onto porous paper such as newsprint, you can often get away with lower-resolution scans (perhaps 400 to 600 spi).

But how do you create an 800-spi image if you've only got a 300-spi scanner? There are two answers, which you can use independently or in combination.

LARGE ORIGINALS. The simple solution is to use large original art. Scan at your scanner's maximum resolution, then scale the image down on pages, increasing the resolution (or, if your scanning software lets you, scale the image down and raise the resolution in one fell swoop at scan time). If your original art isn't big enough, you can enlarge it photographically (even using a high-quality photocopier), with minimal loss of quality. (Photocopiers generally use lenses to enlarge art, which avoids jaggies you'd get digitally.)

200 spi   *400 spi*   *800 spi*   *1,200 spi*

FIGURE 6-1
Jaggy edges
in line art

COOL GRAYSCALE-TO-LINE-ART WORKAROUND. Here's a technique that you'd never think would work, but it does. This method uses the extra information captured in a grayscale scan, and converts that information into higher-resolution line art. You can actually increase your line-art resolution by a factor of two over your scanner's true optical resolution by using this technique. Here's the step-by-step; thanks to Rob Cook for explaining this technique. See Figure 6-3 for the settings and controls to use in Photoshop.

1. Scan the image in grayscale mode, at the maximum optical resolution your scanner supports; we assume 300 spi for this example.

2. Resample the image, doubling the resolution—in this case, to 600 spi. (You may be able to do this in the scanning software, but it's safer to do it in an image-editing program.) Bring up your program's image sizing controls, and enter 600 for dpi.

3. Sharpen the image using your image program's unsharp mask filter, setting Amount to 500 percent, Radius to 1 for Photoshop and 2 for most other programs, and Threshold to 5. (See Chapter 9, *A Sharper Image,* if you haven't used unsharp mask before, and Chapter 30, *Image Applications,* if you're not using Photoshop.)

4. Use the threshold control to adjust the level where gray pixels jump to white or black. This control will make the lines thinner and thicker in the process.

5. Convert the image to black and white by with the 50-percent threshold option selected, if your image-editing program offers it. You've already turned everything into 0 or 100 percent.

FIGURE 6-3
Cool grayscale-to-
line-art workaround
for Photoshop

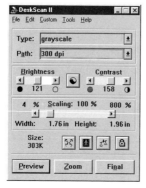

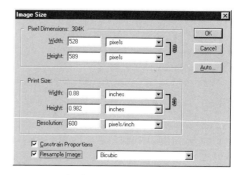

1. Scan your image in at
300 dpi in grayscale.

2. Resample the image to 600 dpi
(pixels/inch in Photoshop lingo).

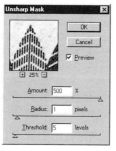

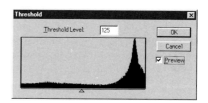

3. Apply unsharp masking
with the above settings.

4. Use the Threshold control to
reduce tones to just black or white.

5. Under Mode, select Bitmap, and
choose 50% Threshold.

You've now got a 600-spi line-art scan, created with a 300-spi scanner! Note that some scanning software packages can perform this whole process automatically; we'll talk about that in Chapter 33, *Scanning Applications.*

HIGH-RES LINE-ART OUTPUT

Printing high-resolution line art formerly overworked the PostScript RIPs (Raster Image Processors) that had to take the art and redraw it against the resolution grid of the imagesetter the RIP was outputting to. Grayscale images of 300–400 spi were processed and spat right out, while line art at 1,000 spi could take minutes.

However, times have changed, even though you might hear the old cavils. Modern RIPs are damned powerful and can handle the task with great ease. But given our conservative nature, we'd rather spend the time *once* in an image-editing program getting it right first so that we don't have to process it again and again through a RIP. Also, there are plenty of older, less powerful RIPs still in use.

So try to size line art to the imagesetter resolution or a half, quarter, or eighth of it. If you're outputting at 2,540 dpi, in the above grayscale-to-line-art workaround, you'd want to use 635 or 1,270 dpi as your final size.

GRAYSCALE AND COLOR

As with line art, there's a relatively straightforward formula for deciding how much resolution you need for grayscale and color bitmaps: It should never be more than two times the output screen frequency (see Figure 6-4).

For example, if you're printing a halftone at 133 lpi, the image resolution shouldn't be more than 266 spi. Any higher resolution is just wasted information. Contrary to what you might think, it doesn't improve image quality at all (if you're looking for a solution to blurry-looking scans, increased resolution isn't it; sharpening is). And since increasing resolution increases file size geometrically (see Chapter 3, *Scanned Images*), it's well worth limiting the dimensions.

FIGURE 6-4
Grayscale images
at 133 lpi

72 spi

133 spi

186 spi

266 spi

In fact, the 2x rule has become so common that people have forgotten (or never learned) that you can almost always use lower resolutions. We typically recommend a multiplier of 1.5, based on the theory that the square root of two—1.414...—is the most apt multiplier. For images without much clear detail, 1.2 often suffices.

Ultimately, only images that have very fine detail—like rigging on a sailboat, or a baby's hair—need resolution higher than 1.5 times lpi. In these cases, you can lose image detail at lower resolutions, and run into two other quality problems: aliasing and mottling.

ALIASING. Hard diagonal edges in lower-resolution images often display aliasing, or jaggies. A sailing ship's rigging in front of a bright sky, for instance, can often look quite "stair-steppy" at lower resolutions. This effect is accentuated by sharpening. If hard diagonal edges or fine lines, like those found in a baby's hair, make up important elements in the image, you should consider using a higher resolution.

MOTTLING. Lower-resolution scans can sometimes display mottling in areas of smooth gradation. In people's faces, it looks like a poor complexion. This is mainly a problem with scans from lower-quality scanners that have a lot of noise—samples in uniform gray areas that don't match their surroundings. Since sharpening works by accentuating the differences between adjacent light and dark pixels, it increases the mottled effect.

AUTOMATIC DOWNSAMPLING IN PAGEMAKER AND QUARKXPRESS

Both PageMaker and QuarkXPress can automatically downsample images at print time, lowering their resolutions to two times screen frequency. In PageMaker 6.5, this is accomplished in the Print dialog box by clicking Options and then selecting Optimized Subsampling from the Send Image Data popup menu—this is the default option (see Figure 6-5). In QuarkXPress 4, you can turn this off through the Print dialog box's Options tab, through the Full Resolution TIFF Output dialog box; it's checked by default (see Figure 6-6).

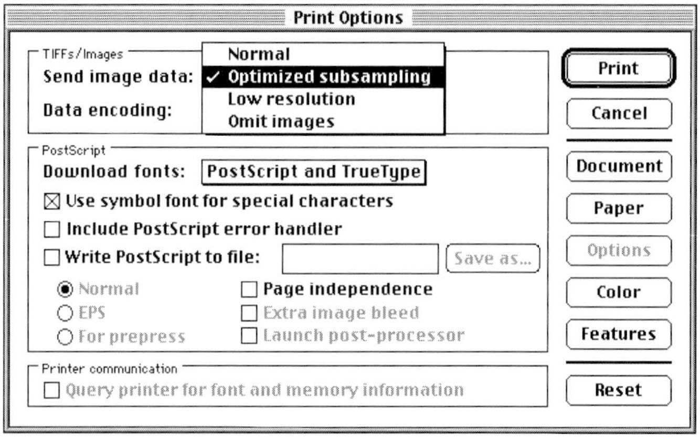

FIGURE 6-5
PageMaker's Print
Options dialog box

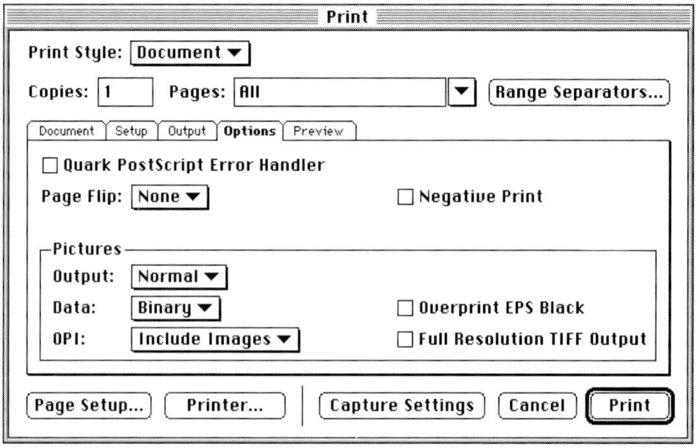

FIGURE 6-6
QuarkXPress 4's
Options tab in the
Print dialog box

In either case, there's rarely a reason to hand off the downsampling to a page-layout program. Adjust the size and resolution of images below twice screen frequency in an image-editing program before importing them into PageMaker or QuarkXPress. Then neither program will touch the images. The one case we've found where this downsampling is useful is in proofing documents to laser printers: you can dramatically reduce the amount of data the laser printer has to process, and you're not relying on the laser proofs for a final quality check, anyway.

RESOLUTION AND QUALITY

We hope this chapter has convinced you to drive your computer like you'd drive your old beater car. It's hard to go wrong; just pay attention to the signs and don't try to throw too much information at the computer by flooding it with scans at too high a resolution.

In the next couple of chapters we look at some ways that you can enhance the quality of your scanned images: image correction—both tonal and color—and sharpening. These two topics are in many ways the keys to getting great-looking images out of your desktop computer.

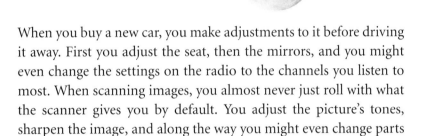

7 TONAL CORRECTION

GETTING GREAT GRAYS

When you buy a new car, you make adjustments to it before driving it away. First you adjust the seat, then the mirrors, and you might even change the settings on the radio to the channels you listen to most. When scanning images, you almost never just roll with what the scanner gives you by default. You adjust the picture's tones, sharpen the image, and along the way you might even change parts of the picture to suit your needs.

In this chapter, we discuss one of the first things you want to adjust in your image: *tone.* You can think of tone as how the colors or gray levels throughout a picture relate to one another.

As we pointed out in Chapter 2, *Scanners,* many scanners have difficulty picking up detail in the darkest areas of prints and film. That means most of the desktop-created scans you see are either too dark, with no detail at all in shadow areas, or blown out, with white representing all the lighter tones, like light reflecting off a face.

In this chapter we concentrate on dealing with that central problem—increasing detail at the trouble end of the scale (and lightening the image overall) without washing out or filling in the other end.

HISTOGRAMS

Histograms are an extremely useful tool for looking at how gray levels are spread out through an image. A *histogram* is simply a chart of how many samples in the bitmapped image are set to each gray level (see Figure 7-1). For example, a histogram can tell us that there are 10 sample points that are totally black, 34 sample points that have a gray level of 1 (out of 255 levels of gray), 40 sample points that have a gray level of 2, and so on.

FIGURE 7-1
Histogram

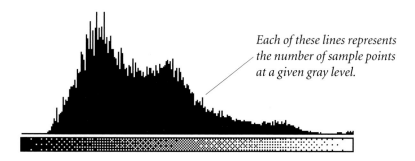

Each of these lines represents the number of sample points at a given gray level.

By looking at the histogram of an image, you can quickly tell where the information in the image is concentrated—in shadow areas, in highlights, or in the midtones (see Figure 7-2).

GRAY-MAP CURVES

In order to change the tonal balance of an image, you need to adjust its gray levels. Different programs let you do this in different ways, but typically the mechanism is through a *contrast* or *gray-map curve* (see Figure 7-3). It *maps* grays to different gray values.

Perhaps the easiest way to understand a gray-map curve is to think about coffee or tea filters. When you pour water through a fil-

FIGURE 7-2
Various histograms

Original image

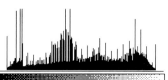

FIGURE 7-2
Histograms,
continued

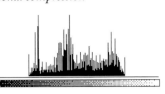

*Low contrast;
tonal compression*

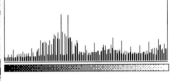

*High contrast;
expanded tonal range*

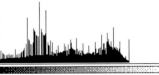

*Darkened; histogram
moves to the left*

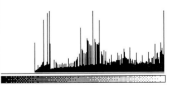

*Lightened; histogram
moves to the right*

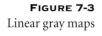

FIGURE 7-3

Linear gray maps

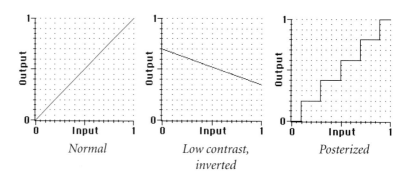

Normal　　*Low contrast, inverted*　　*Posterized*

ter with coffee or tea in it, the water becomes flavored. You can use filters with images, too. And a gray-map curve is a type of filter that you can pour an image through.

By looking at the gray map, you can actually figure out what will happen to an image when you apply that filter to it. Typically, the horizontal axis of the chart describes the levels of gray—from white to black—of the input image (the image that you start out with). The vertical axis describes the levels of gray of the output image (what you'll end up with). A map with a straight 45-degree line in it like the one shown in Figure 7-3 on the left is called a *normal* contrast curve. It doesn't change anything. After applying this filter, the pixels in the input image that are black stay black; the pixels that are 50-percent gray stay that tint, and so on.

LINEAR CORRECTION

The most basic method of tonal correction is altering the slope of the line, while keeping it straight. Because the gray map is still a straight line, we call this *linear correction.* When you use run-of-the-mill brightness and contrast controls in a program, you are making linear corrections (even if you can't see the graph in your application, that's what's happening behind the scenes).

As you'll see in the next few paragraphs, linear correction throws away data in a not-terribly-intelligent manner. We consider linear correction—brightness and contrast controls—to be essentially worthless; but we'll explain how it works so you can agree with us.

You can effect linear correction in two ways: by moving the line up and down, and by changing the slope of the line.

BRIGHTNESS

The first linear correction we'll look at is adjusting brightness. If you move the line straight up, you lighten the image (see Figure 7-4; remember that some curves have the input and output levels reversed and looks just the opposite—it depends on how the application's interface is designed). That's because all the sample points are made brighter. For example, let's look at a sample point that is 50-percent gray in our input image. When we pass it through this filter, that sample point gets converted into a lighter value—let's say 30-percent gray. Lowering the line has the opposite effect: it darkens the image. That same 50-percent sample point gets changed to a darker value when it is passed through the filter.

As you can see in the histograms in Figure 7-4, brightness controls just shift all the values in the image up. While brightening can make shadow detail easier to see, it doesn't increase the differentiation between subtly different values (which is what *really* increases detail in an image). And—this is the worst thing about linear brightness adjustment—all the information at the highlight end of the histogram simply disappears. Subtle tonal differences in highlights—the details—wash out to white.

CONTRAST

While changing the position of the line changes brightness, changing the slope of the line alters the image's contrast. If you make the slope of the line steeper, you increase the contrast of the image (see Figure 7-5). Gray levels that are nearly white get pushed to white, and those that are nearly black get pushed to black. And all the grays in between are spread apart, increasing the contrast between samples. If you make the slope of the line less steep than the 45-degree normal curve, you decrease the contrast of the image. This is also called tone compression, because you're compressing the whole range of 256 gray levels into a smaller number of gray levels.

FIGURE 7-4
Linear brightness
adjustment

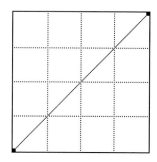

Before linear correction

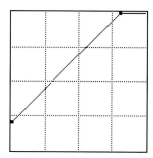

Line pushed up lightens the image

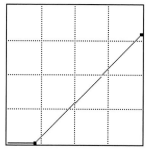

Line pushed down darkens the image

Linear contrast adjustment is just as problematic as linear brightness adjustment, but in a different way. Increasing contrast does increase the difference between adjacent gray levels—improving detail in the midtones—but it lops off detail in both highlights

FIGURE 7-5
Linear contrast
adjustment

Steeper slope, higher contrast

*All these grays are
pushed to black.*

Shallower slope, less contrast

and shadows. Decreasing contrast is almost never a very useful technique, unless you're seeking to limit the range of highlights and shadows for reproduction reasons (see Chapter 18, *Reproducing Halftones*).

NONLINEAR CORRECTION

To achieve the kind of tonal correction you really need—increasing shadow detail and brightening images without washing out highlight areas—you need to use *nonlinear correction* (sometimes called *gamma correction*).

Nonlinear correction is not a panacea, however. It loses data just as linear correction does, but in a much more sensible manner.

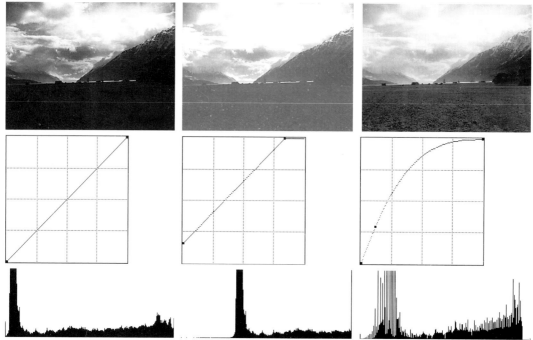

Uncorrected. As scanned, the image is very dark overall. There is no visible detail in the shadow areas—or well into the midtones, for that matter. (We chose this image because of its huge tonal range, with lots of subtle detail in both highlights and shadows.)

Linear brightness adjustment. This method simply pushes all the values up (the whole histogram is just shifted to the right), without increasing the differentiation between samples. All detail in the highlights is gone—pushed to white—but shadow detail is not enhanced much.

Nonlinear adjustment. The bars in the histogram are spread out, increasing the difference between samples. This increases visible detail in the shadows and midtones, with only minor loss of highlight detail.

FIGURE 7-6
Nonlinear tonal
correction

When you use nonlinear correction to bring out shadow detail, you do lose some detail in the highlights. Because the curve is flatter in the highlight area, samples that did have different values have the same values after correction. Since the biggest problem with desktop scans is bringing out shadow detail, however, the trade-off is well worth it.

Another problem to watch for with nonlinear correction is posterization in deep shadow areas. If the angle of the curve in shadow areas gets too steep, you start seeing distinct jumps from one gray level to another—especially in areas of smooth tonal gradation.

METHODS OF NONLINEAR CORRECTION

Different programs offer different methods for nonlinear correction—from drawing a curve to moving sliders.

DRAWING CURVES. A common, but not terribly useful, approach is the simple pencil-and-graph tools in programs such as QuarkXPress (see Figure 7-7). The lack of numerical readouts and inability to interact with a histogram make it difficult or impossible to predict or repeat results with any precision. It's also quite difficult to draw a decent curve with the little pencil (though the option offered in some programs to smooth your coarsely drawn line can help solve this problem). We recommend you walk, or run, away from this method.

FIGURE 7-7
Pencil-like curve tools

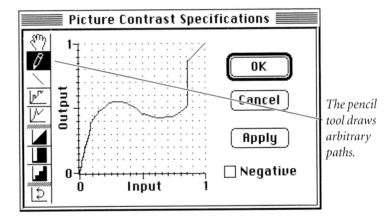

The pencil tool draws arbitrary paths.

ADJUSTING CURVES' CONTROL POINTS. Most programs, whether page layout or image editing, let you move control points on a curve that represents input and output values. It's more like working in a drawing program than a painting program. In the better-implemented of these techniques—Photoshop's, for instance—you can see the numeric values associated with control points as you move them (see Figure 7-8).

ADJUSTING INPUT AND OUTPUT SLIDERS. Photoshop used to be one of the few image-editing programs that displayed a histogram—a visual representation of the number of pixels at each tonal value—

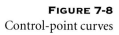

FIGURE 7-8
Control-point curves

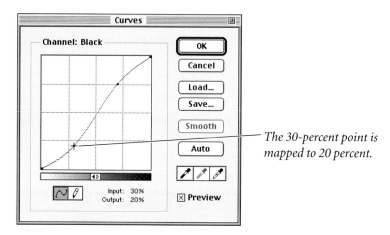

The 30-percent point is mapped to 20 percent.

and let you drag sliders to modify it. Virtually all image-editing programs now offer this feature, although some call it Image or Histogram Equalization. Some programs go a step further and show an overlay with the before and after histograms, or a sidebar with the resulting gray map you created with the sliders.

Whatever the program, and whatever it's called, we like this technique the best. It's fast, it's easy, and it does exactly what you need.

In all of the programs that use this histogram approach, you have two or three sliders, which represent the black point, midtone point, and white point of the image data. (Some programs label these shadow, midtone, and highlight.)

Most programs also allow you to clip the upper and lower output levels, but some require values to be entered manually; others use a separate image-control dialog box.

We like to make changes with preview set to on, or preferences set to show a live update; the setting depends on the program. In Photoshop, you should check the Video LUT Animation box in Display & Cursors Preferences (see Figure 7-9). Bring up the Levels dialog box (Command- or Control-L—memorize this immediately) and check the Preview box.

Here's how we adjust grayscale and color scans in Photoshop (see Figure 7-10), but these same tips apply to CorelPhoto-Paint, Picture Publisher, and others. (See Chapter 30, *Image Applications*, for a program-by-program analysis of tonal correction tools.)

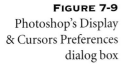

FIGURE 7-9

Photoshop's Display
& Cursors Preferences
dialog box

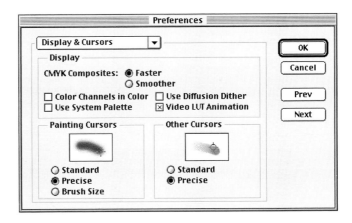

1. Encompass the majority of the data on the histogram with the left and right input sliders. (See "Tone Clipping," below, for a useful technique for adjusting these sliders.)

2. Adjust the output levels so that the resulting image doesn't include highlight or shadow dots that can't be reproduced on press (see Chapter 18, *Reproducing Halftones*). Table 7-1 shows typical ranges for three classes of printing paper. The third column does the arithmetic for you; it tells you what output levels you should specify in the Levels dialog box, though the principle applies to any scanning or image-editing software. (These values are just rules of thumb; talk to your printer to determine the best settings for your printing method and paper choice.)

TABLE 7-1

Output level settings

Printing Stock	Percent Range	Output Levels
Newsprint	12–88	30–225
Uncoated stock	10–90	25–230
Coated stock	5–95	12–243

3. Move the center or midtone input slider to the left until the image looks about right on screen. We usually bump this up to at least 1.5. Once it looks just about right, bump it up a little more. Scans look lighter on monitors (which are actually projecting light) than they do on paper (which relies on reflected light). You'll almost never make an image too light with this method (see "Bit Depth and Dynamic Range" in Chapter 2, *Scanners*). Watch out for posterization in the deep shadow areas, however.

FIGURE 7-10
Using Photoshop's
Levels dialog box

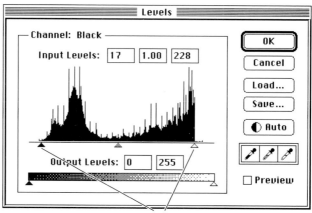

*Hold down
Option (Mac)
or Alt
(Windows)
to see clip-
ping while
moving the
left and right
Input sliders.*

*Move the left and right sliders to encompass the bulk
of the information in the scan.*

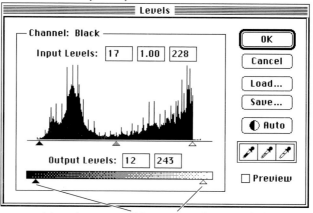

*Move the output sliders to the values specified in
Table 7-1 (or type in the values).*

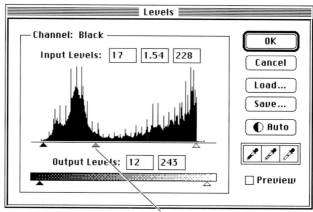

*Move the center input slider to the left to brighten
the image and bring out shadow detail.*

EQUALIZE. You'll often find an equalize or auto-balance setting in image-editing programs, sometimes in the same dialog box where you find the histogram and input sliders. These typically just evenly spread tonal values across the entire range. We find this almost totally useless. The point of nonlinear controls in the first place is to make a value judgment about where the upper, middle, and lower levels belong.

TONE CLIPPING

One of the most useful tools for tonal adjustment we've seen is the tone-clipping display in Photoshop (see Figure 7-11). This tool shows you which samples in an image are getting clipped to the tonal edges—going all black or all white.

Using the tone-clipping display, you can make sensible judgments about what information is being lost, and how important it is. For example, your thinking might go like this: "Well, that shiny

FIGURE 7-11
Photoshop's tone clipping display

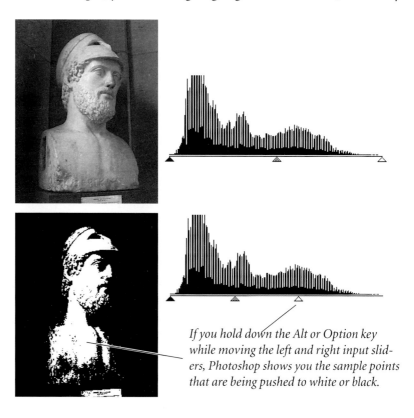

If you hold down the Alt or Option key while moving the left and right input sliders, Photoshop shows you the sample points that are being pushed to white or black.

area over there is getting clipped to white, but it doesn't matter much because it's not central to the photo. I'll bring the slider in a bit more because I don't care if I lose detail there, and I can bring out more shadow detail by losing the information in that unimportant highlight area."

To use Photoshop's tone clipping display, hold down Option (Macintosh) or Alt (PC) while dragging the left and right input sliders in the Levels dialog box. (For more on clipping, see "Color Management Systems" in the next chapter, *Color.*)

CUMULATIVE CORRECTIONS

As we said earlier, making tonal corrections always involves some data loss in your picture. Sample points that were originally a range of different colors may become the same color after tonal correction; therefore, you lose detail in the image. With linear adjustment, you lose detail in highlights and shadows (they go all white or all black). With nonlinear adjustment, you lose detail mainly in the highlights, because the curve is flatter in that area. Samples that are different before correction are the same (or more similar) after.

Whatever correction method you use, remember that multiple corrections multiply the data loss. So if you use your scanning software's adjustment tools to correct an image, then use Photoshop's Levels dialog box to further adjust it, you lose data twice.

Some programs (LivePicture, for instance) address this problem by "remembering" each of your corrections. They don't actually apply the corrections to the file when you make them; they just show their effects on screen. Then when you're finished correcting the image, they concatenate all the corrections into a single gray- or color-mapping operation, and perform the actual correction only once. This is the best method of correction; Photoshop sort of lets you do this via its Adjustment Layers feature. We now do almost all our tonal manipulations in adjustment layers, and hardly ever use Levels or Curves directly on the image itself.

KEEPING IN TONE

Almost every image that you scan in will need to be adjusted in a number of ways, including tonal correction. Without this, your scans will almost always be too dark and too muddy. Of course, as we've said repeatedly throughout this chapter, you want to keep as much image data as you can while you're correcting (an image's data is its *sine qua non;* when you lose the data, you've just got a pile of dirt left).

In the next chapter, we talk about applying these lessons to color images, as well as setting up your system to do color corrections. And we address color management, which is increasingly the solution to many woes in the workflow.

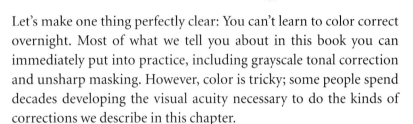

8 COLOR

Painting by
the Numbers

Let's make one thing perfectly clear: You can't learn to color correct overnight. Most of what we tell you about in this book you can immediately put into practice, including grayscale tonal correction and unsharp masking. However, color is tricky; some people spend decades developing the visual acuity necessary to do the kinds of corrections we describe in this chapter.

Just as typesetting was brought to the desktop, color correction has been brought within most people's fingertips—especially with cheap 24-bit color cards. But you have to earn your pips, and the only way to get it right is to do it over and over again until you train your brain to make the distinctions.

There's a way to shortcut this process—you knew there had to be one. You can learn what the ideal numbers are that represent color values, and adjust your images while keeping your eye on the digits. We recommend leaving the Info palette open in Photoshop at all times so you can get familiar with the numbers you want to have in your corrected output. Adjusting by numbers is a time-honored art; the analog drum scanner operators had to learn to tune by numbers long before we had onscreen color correction.

Author Dan Margolis performs an impressive demonstration in which he loads up an uncorrected color image, switches the monitor to grayscale, does his color correction by the numbers, and switches back to color. And the correction is great. Dan thinks everyone can do this, but we're a little more skeptical; the learning curve is high enough that it might not be worthwhile for everyone to learn.

Now you know why we like color management so much and are happy it continues to improve. With color management, you don't have to rely on numbers so much, nor do you have to have the most expensive equipment to ensure consistent color.

We also want to point out that each of the areas covered in this chapter have entire sections or chapters devoted to them in *Real World Photoshop 4*, a book by David and his colleague Bruce Fraser. Because of their focus on Photoshop, image data, and color—though grayscale images aren't avoided—they devote several chapters to issues surrounding color correction and color management.

DECLARING (IN)DEPENDENCE

When you work with digital color, you have to discard the notion that what you *see* is what you *get*—wysiwyg. Unless you're using a very expensive monitor combined with a color-managed system, what you see on screen is a *device-dependent* view into the colors that make up an image.

It's easy to get an example of this. Walk into any consumer electronics store and look at the wall of televisions showing the same program. No two the same, eh? Computer monitors are better calibrated and more consistent than television sets, but the principle is the same: Each TV displays the same data in different ways.

But you can store color in a way that is independent of a specific device; this image data represents absolute color, like that you can measure with a colorimeter. We call this *device-independent* color. Device-independent color is converted to device-dependent color by building a table that represents the differences between the specific device's method of representing a set of colors, and this absolute, independent model of color.

But image data has to represent some physical properties, because images are displayed or printed or scanned in the physical world. This representation is called *modeling*, and the color model pinpoints each value in image data to a specific place in the *colorspace*. The colorspace is a way to visualize three components that combine to make a given color.

The big difference in color models is between RGB and CMYK, which model physical properties of light but don't truly identify what a color is, and LAB, which describes a color objectively but doesn't identify how to represent it on a specific monitor or printer. HSB (or HSL or similar models) are yet more ways to represent color more intuitively; they have neither a one-to-one relationship with how the information is stored nor a perceptual basis.

RGB

All monitors use a combination of red, green, and blue phosphors or LCD filters to show color. It seems a natural consequence of this that we should store image data in RGB format as well, using three channels, one for each of those colors with a value from 0 to 255 (or to 65,535 for 48-bit RGB) representing a point on each color axis which combine to form a color (see Color Page N).

But the problem that you can demonstrate with the TV-store test is that RGB values are not objective. They describe a particular location in a colorspace, but not what that color should "really" look like. Every device, whether input, display, or output, has a different representation of RGB values. Sometimes this is just a small shift; other times, it's an entirely different view. It's highly dependent on the kind of materials used to create colors. In a monitor, different phosphors make slightly different colors; with a printer, inks can vary widely from device to device, creating huge color shifts between two similar ink-jet printers made by different companies.

CMYK

CMYK color is used in a one-to-one correspondence to represent the inks, dyes, and waxes used to create color in offset printing and digital color printing. Unfortunately, every device uses different colorants, meaning that the CMYK on one printer won't look the same as the CMYK on another. In fact, two different kinds of ink used on the same printing press will produce different results.

Because of this, we recommend rarely working in CMYK on screen. When you convert from any colorspace to another, you lose information, and CMYK is really a targeted, highly device-dependent final transformation. (Of course, if someone gives you a CMYK and doesn't have the original, you can do your best.)

Working in RGB and saving a final-stage image in that mode lets you retarget your images to different presses, color printers, and alternative output devices. Another downside is that some of the tools for color correction we describe below are disabled in Photoshop and other programs when working in CMYK.

LAB

Another way of looking at color is the LAB colorspace, which many image-editing programs support. LAB stores color in three channels, as does RGB. But whereas you have three color channels in RGB, in LAB you have a single channel for luminance or tonal values (L) and two channels of color information (A and B). The color channels correspond to a scale, rather than a single color. A is a continuum from green to red, while B is a range from blue to yellow. The midpoint values for A and B correspond to neutral grays. (See Color Page N.)

The idea behind LAB is that every step—an increase in a single channel's numeric value—represents the same perceptual distance as every other step. RGB colors are all bunched around, so a single number (or step) difference in the red channel might be imperceptible; but the same difference in the luminosity channel of LAB is identifiable. LAB is tied to measurable, physical properties, so that it can be used as an independent reference by which deviation from objective reality can be measured.

LAB might appear to be a perfect environment in which to work, but, unfortunately, it's not. LAB is really a space to move colors through to correct for device-dependency. For instance, Linotype-Hell's LinoColor scanner software allows you to scan and save files in LAB space—but it's really doing the scan in RGB. LinoColor has built-in color correction that fixes the scan against either its idealized notion of what that model of scanner is capable of, or a more specific target you generate yourself (see "Color Management Systems" later in this chapter). It uses that correction to transform the raw RGB data into LAB data for export and editing.

If you're doing a lot of Photo CD work, you can acquire Photo CD images directly as LAB images from Kodak's similar YCC color model (see Chapter 14, *Photo CD*). And FlashPix images can be stored in either YCC or NEFRGB, a reference RGB colorspace, to avoid device-dependency in the file (see Chapter 4, *File Formats*). TIFF can also store images in LAB format.

HSB

The Hue-Saturation-Brightness model (sometimes called HSL, with L for Lightness) is a method of breaking up color into three separate visual components. Hue is the actual color on a spectrum. Saturation is the intensity of that color from 100-percent white to 100-percent of the hue. And brightness or lightness is a measure of how much black is added to the color, from 0 to 100 percent.

You can visualize this model as a cylinder. The perimeter represents 100-percent saturated hues; the spectrum is wrapped around the cylinder; and the core is pure white. Moving outward from the center to the edge increases saturation. Moving up and down changes the amount of black. Walking around the core on a single slice of the cylinder changes the point on the spectrum or the hue.

HSB in practice isn't a perfect cylinder; there are combinations of HSB that can't be mapped to RGB. But it's a good tool for thinking about which aspect of color to change (see Color Page N).

CORRECTIONS

Now that you know the limitations of colorspaces and visual perspicacity, here's some advice about reasonable changes you can make to color images to dramatically improve their quality.

GOALS

The goals in color correction need to be defined up front. Are you trying to make the image match as close as possible to a reference print? Or do you have a predefined idea of what the color composition should like? You might also be trying to match the balance, cast, and saturation in images supplied to you from other sources, or the color scheme of an existing layout or book.

Note that we're not talking about special effects here. Most image-editing programs come with so many filters and effects now that we have to lie down after reviewing the menus. Color correction isn't about making an image look unlike the original, but about targeting your specific need and keeping it realistic.

Here are the primary goals to pursue with color correction.

REMOVE COLOR CASTS. A *neutral* color is one that contains equal components from all RGB color channels, or a little more cyan than equal amounts of yellow and magenta in CMYK. Where these values are out of balance, you have a *color cast*; where you should have a straight gray, a disproportionate amount of one or more colors tints that part of the tonal range or the entire image. Try scanning the same black-and-white image twice—once as grayscale and again in color. Check the Info palette for each and you'll probably see a slight color shift that can occur when trying to achieve these neutrals.

Sometimes it will be hard to find neutrals in an image, especially pictures with high color saturation—they may not exist at all. Our suggestion is to always scan a neutral gray wedge so that you can use one of the techniques described in "Methods," below, to help you find a neutral at many different tonal levels.

You don't always need to remove all color casts. Some are effects introduced by photographers through lighting or choice of film; different films have different color properties. It's best if you have a print of an image you're working on so you know what's supposed to be neutral and what's not. If that's not possible, look for flesh tones, green grass, blue sky, or brown wood: these *memory colors* can help you make corrections in the absence of other information.

CHANGE SATURATION. Scanners do a great job of capturing a larger range of color than any color output device can render. When you *desaturate* an image, you're reducing the intensity of particular hues in the image. (See "HSB," above.) Sometimes, however, an image is washed out—the hues are blanched and need to be boosted. Reducing saturation can make an image reproducible; increasing it can sometimes make it "pop" and appear vibrant.

SETUP

Before doing color correction, you need to do some setup of whatever program you're using. We approach this from the Photoshop perspective because it's most closely aligned with the coming color management system (CMS) solutions. Hopefully, when standards finalize, you'll be able to make these same adjustments in every DTP and prepress program without learning new methods for each.

Photoshop ships with a Gamma plug-in for the Macintosh (see Figure 8-1), which is nearly identical to the Photoshop-specific Gamma adjustments available under Windows by clicking the Calibration button in the Monitor Setup dialog box that is available under Photoshop's Color Settings popout menu. (The control panel isn't installed on the Mac by default; you'll find it in the Photoshop Extras folder. Drag it into the System Folder's Control Panels folder and restart the Macintosh.)

FIGURE 8-1
Gamma control panel
for the Macintosh

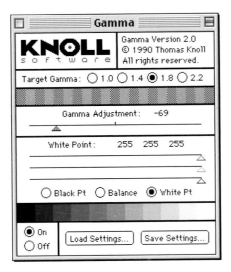

Gamma adjustment affects the way in which the entire tonal range is mapped to display on your particular monitor (or any device, really). You need to set Gamma/Calibration and Monitor Setup before doing any color correction in order to match Photoshop to your monitor's particular display.

Also under the Color Settings popout menu, you'll see Printing Inks and Separation settings. You have to set these two if you're planning to create or preview CMYK separations. Printing Inks tells Photoshop about the colorants used to make up CMYK on a particular device or press; Separation gives you control over how you create or preview CMYK separations.

Again, note that *Real World Photoshop 4* goes into much more depth about these settings and procedures.

GAMMA. After accessing Gamma or Calibration as we described above, you'll want to do some small adjustment. We recommend turning on calibration and setting it to 1.8 for prepress work; use 2.2 if your final destination is on screen. Click the On button on the Macintosh, or click Preview under Windows. Now adjust your monitor's brightness, contrast, and other color settings until you have a good match. Finally, drag the Gamma Adjustment slider until the gray boxes and the black-and-white crosshatches appear to have the same tonal value. These changes put you in the ballpark.

If you're using a monitor calibration utility, don't use the Gamma control panel. The CMS or monitor calibrator should be the only part of the system in charge of this adjustment.

MONITOR. Monitor Setup lets you select a predefined profile for a set of monitors most often used for desktop prepress (see Figure 8-2). If your monitor isn't listed there, consult your owner's manual or the manufacturer's Web site to get the characteristics of your monitor. You can even define the phosphor values for your monitor, but that might involve more specifics than are reasonably available. The more specific you are with this setting, the better your monitor's display will match the source art or scan's appearance.

FIGURE 8-2

Monitor Setup

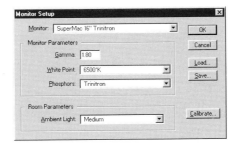

FIGURE 8-2

Monitor Setup

PRINTING INKS. If you're aiming for CMYK output or separation, you can choose a target device under Printing Inks Setup to use a pre-built table that describes the color characteristics of the printer or press you're heading to (see Figure 8-3). Even without a CMS, it's possible to create your own tables by taking measurements and entering values by selecting Custom from the Ink Colors popup menu. You can import a file with these values supplied by an output device manufacturer or a printer for their particular press. Typically, we select SWOP for coated, uncoated, or newsprint stocks unless we know otherwise.

FIGURE 8-3

Printing Inks Setup

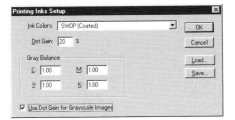

SEPARATION. Separation Setup lets you choose the method by which black is added into the process-color equation and CMY are subtracted to replace neutral grays or areas where cyan, magenta, and yellow add up to black in an ideal world (see Figure 8-4). These two methods are called gray component replacement (GCR) and undercolor removal (UCR), and we explain them in additional depth in Chapter 18, *Reproducing Halftones*.

METHODS

Many programs supply dozens of methods of adjusting color images, but we suggest you look at just four categories. Levels and curves we discussed in the last chapter, *Tonal Correction*. The same

FIGURE 8-4
Separation Setup

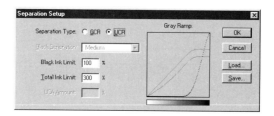

lessons apply for color. We haven't really mentioned the eyedropper tool until now; it's a method of choosing samples in an image to help you target your results. Hue and saturation are nonlinear corrections, but they can help you make global changes that can put an image back into the right gamut for your output device. And the replace and selective color options allow you to tweak individual colors and ranges while leaving the rest of the gamut alone.

For best results, work in RGB if that's where your source image came from—and always save your original, uncorrected data as a separate file that you can return to later. But if you're heading for four-color output, and if you've set everything up as we discussed above, you can select CMYK Preview from View in Photoshop to give yourself some predictive ability as to the final separations. The image is still stored as RGB values, but the CMYK changes are looked up and displayed as you make them.

Another option is to make sure that the Photoshop Info palette is displayed with one of the panels showing CMYK values. If you learn to read the numbers, as we mentioned earlier in this chapter, you can sample values to make sure your changes are providing the right color shifts without going out of range.

There are other tools that appear in Photoshop when you're editing a color image, like Color Balance, Variations, and Desaturate. However, none of these tools provide you with anything but arbitrary sliders. Typically, we avoid using these tools unless we have a specifically tricky image or special effect.

LEVELS AND CURVES. In the last chapter, we covered how levels and curves are edited to create nonlinear corrections to grayscale images. Fortunately, both options are available for color correction as well. Levels and curves apply corrections on RGB data, which means that you are simultaneously changing hue, saturation, and brightness. In both levels and curves, you can edit by channel or a master setting for all three. (Most image-editing applications handle this the same way.)

In Photoshop, the midtone slider in Levels and the point adjustments in Curves give you tools to remove slight color casts. In Levels, you can adjust an entire cast away by moving the midtone slider in a particular channel. In Curves, you can drag individual points in separate tonal ranges on individual channels to remove casts that might appear on just part of the scale.

EYEDROPPERS. The eyedropper tool appears in many image-editing programs' nonlinear corrections, allowing you to select values directly from an image. You can use curves, points, and sliders to adjust these values after you've sampled them, but it allows you the flexibility of making visual decisions about where you're correcting.

CorelPhoto-Paint's Sample/Target Balance dialog box is the most intuitive we've seen, as it displays the starting points, target samples, and histograms in the same window (see Figure 8-5). Photoshop's Levels and Curves dialog boxes offers the eyedroppers, but there's no representation of input and output samples.

If you've done what we suggest under "Goals," above, and scanned a gray wedge along with your image, you can use the midtone eyedropper to find a midtone-point gray with a single click.

FIGURE 8-5
CorelPhoto-Paint's
Sample/Target
Balance dialog box

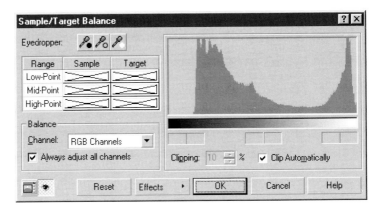

In Photoshop, the gray eyedropper allows you to select a value without affecting the tone or brightness, just the hue and saturation. As we suggested earlier, leave your information palette open while working on color; you can then hover over areas with the eyedropper to examine the values in each color channel and choose which ones to sample.

HUE/SATURATION. Because the tonal correction tools move a color around on the lightness scale, the Hue/Saturation control—found in most image-editing programs—allows you to make moves by hue or overall in any combination of hue, saturation, and lightness (see Figure 8-6).

FIGURE 8-6
Hue/Saturation in
Photoshop

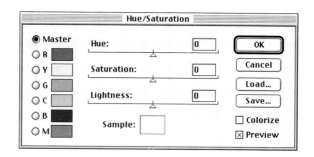

Hue/Saturation in Photoshop offers the three primary emitted colors and their reflective counterparts, plus black. You can drag the sliders to make small or large adjustments from the color's starting point. It's a great way to increase or decrease saturation by hue, or to fix an overall color shift without changing tone or saturation.

REPLACE AND SELECTIVE COLOR. Replace and selective color allow you to do a kind of search-and-replace function in an image. You can use replace color to select specific colors wherever they appear in an image—or more than one depending on the way the control is implemented—and make adjustments of the kind found in the Hue/Saturation control (see Figure 8-7).

Selective color lets you make shifts from any point on the color wheel towards or away from any of the reflective color comple-

FIGURE 8-7
Replace Color

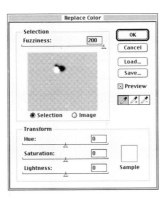

FIGURE 8-7
Replace Color

ments (cyan, magenta, and yellow) and black. This is the subtlest tool for making changes in overall hue. It's recommended for making changes in CMYK separations, but it's a finely graduated tool for doing small color changes in RGB, as well (see Figure 8-8).

COLOR MANAGEMENT SYSTEMS

At the outset of this chapter, we talked about how hard it is to have color travel along a production workflow—from scanner to screen to proofer to offset press—and keep it consistent throughout because each device perceives colors differently. Color management systems offer a solution by providing an objective frame of reference against which all devices can be measured.

WHAT'S IN A CMS

A color management system (CMS) comprises three parts: a reference colorspace, a set of profiles that describe each device, and an

FIGURE 8-8
Selective Color

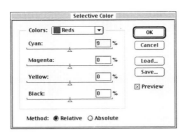

engine that applies these profiles against image data at each step of the workflow. Most CMSs also have components that let you build new profiles.

REFERENCE COLORSPACE. The reference colorspace is typically something defined by CIE, which we described in Chapter 3, *Scanned Images*. The LAB colorspace is one of these, and we discuss it earlier in this chapter. The CIE or CIE-derived colorspaces are all references based on an objective notion of color; they're all device-independent. The LAB and similar colorspaces are perceptual in nature, but it's not necessary to have a reference colorspace that has that property to use it as a reference.

ENGINE. The CMS engine uses CMS profiles to correctly adjust images when they're scanned, displayed, or printed.

PROFILES. Profiles are descriptions of how a given device varies from the reference colorspace. Some profiles are generic and describe the general characteristics of a specific device (like "all Radius monitors act like this"). Others are generated specifically for a given device (like "this Radius monitor on your desk acts like this"), which we describe a little later. The more specific your profile, the better chance that a CMS will work well for you, especially with less-expensive equipment not manufactured to as precise tolerances as the pricey gear. The Linotype-Hell scanners, for instance, come with prebuilt profiles, but they also ship with software that lets you build a specific target for your individual scanner.

GAMUT MAPPING

Part of the problem in using color on different devices is that each device has a certain range of colors it can represent. This range is called the *gamut*. A CMS has to take colors that are part of the gamut of one device—typically an input device, like a scanner—but outside the range of colors of another, like a CMYK proofer.

The technique of moving these out-of-gamut colors around is called *gamut mapping*, and it's typically done in one of four ways. The first two, clipping and compression, are used to map out-of-gamut colors without regard to a specific tone, hue, or saturation. The second two, desaturation and extra saturation, preserve one or more of those factors while adjusting the rest. (Some CMS systems don't provide saturation options, while others only desaturate or have limited controls.)

CLIPPING. You can preview gamut clipping in Photoshop, which will allow you to see what source colors fall outside the gamut of a target device. With gamut clipping, those source colors are just replaced with the nearest value in the target's gamut. This method involves no changes to the source values that fall inside the gamut, but may show posterization on the out-of-range colors.

COMPRESSION. Gamut compression takes the entire tonal range in the source image and squeezes it to fit in the target device's gamut. The relationship between colors and tones is preserved relatively, but the fidelity can be off. However, it makes the image have much the same feel as the original (remember that our eyes are very forgiving, and we value the relativity of colors more than "absolute" color), and is often used for photographic images.

DESATURATION. Colors that are outside of the maximum saturation or intensity of the target gamut can be desaturated to preserve the hue and tonal value.

EXTRA SATURATION. Colors can be pushed to their maximum saturation. Out-of-gamut colors are clipped to the same color, while in-gamut colors have their intensity increased. This causes tonal and saturation shifts, but the hue remains the same. There is limited practical use for this kind of mapping outside of creating presentation graphics that you make into slides.

CALIBRATING THE SYSTEM

When you put your whites into a washing machine, you hope that when they come out of the dryer, they're still white. But everyone knows that scanning a white piece of paper and then printing it will result in something unexpected: usually gray. Different systems have different methods, but we can outline what you can do to improve and calibrate color inside and outside a CMS for each part of the workflow.

MONITOR. The typical method of calibrating a monitor is to use a *colorimeter*—a device that measures color—that attaches with a suction cup onto a target on the monitor. These have been around for years, and it wasn't until you could insert this calibration into a CMS workflow that it made complete sense. You were calibrating the monitor—but not in conjunction with other devices.

With the Gamma control panel (Macintosh) or Monitor Settings Calibration button in Photoshop (Windows), you can adjust the overall tone mapping of a monitor. You need to adjust brightness and contrast on your monitor and choose a gamma before doing any color calibration. A gamma of 1.8 is typical for prepress work, while 2.2 works well for multimedia or other on-screen image displays. (As we note in Chapter 11, *Images for the Web*, default gamma differs substantially between Mac and Windows displays.)

Monitors have temperature characteristics that affect how colors get displayed. Temperature is a measure of the color of emitted light from red to blue (corresponding to the colors emitted by objects heated to different temperatures). Temperature is a fixed characteristic of a monitor; it can be compensated for, but not changed. (It's measured in Kelvin and abbreviated as K—not to be confused with K standing for kilobyte used to measure memory or hard disk storage.)

You can improve the usefulness of a monitor as a soft-proofing device by using incandescent or fluorescent lights of the same temperature—you can find temperature-specific bulbs pretty easily. You can also reduce ambient light in your working environment.

Glenn worked in a facility where all monitors, lights, and viewing stands were tuned to 5,500 K, and blackout shades and monitor hoods kept out extraneous light of other colors.

SCANNER. Scanners have a particular problem with CMS targeting, which Bruce Fraser, David's co-writer on *Real World Photoshop 4*, has pointed out quite vociferously. Scanner profiles do transformations on 24 bits of data maximum, while most modern scanners of worth capture 30 to 48 bits per sample.

Bruce notes that using these profiles might improve your workflow, but that you're in the position of tossing away some of your best tonal information. He argues for scanner profiles that would work in the acquire phase or with high-bit (greater than 24 bit) data before the images hit the computer and are reduced in depth.

Different systems have different methods of measuring scanner information, but the typical process is to place a target on the scanner, capture it with all adjustments (such as sharpening or tonal correction) turned off, and read it into a package that "knows" what the correct values should be.

The target is generally an industry-standard IT8.7, which has several hundred color and tonal values on it. Kodak's version is the Q60, which also includes a photographic image as part of the target.

Many scanners now have a calibration pass they perform before each scan; this is sometimes configurable, but we recommend leaving it on for all serious scans. These scanners have a small area outside of the scanner bed that you need to keep clean. It performs a self-test in that area.

COLOR PRINTING. Color printers usually come with generic profiles. But individual color output devices can vary considerably, in part because of operating conditions, age of the device, and flexibility in manufacturer; and in part because of changes over time in colorant formulations by the manufacturers that aren't identified. These small changes can throw profiles way out of whack.

You can buy software for most systems that will allow you to print out a standard sample, scan it in through an already calibrated scanner, and build a custom profile for your specific device. If you're using a color printer for proofing or for final prints, it's probably worth going through this process to make full use of the CMS.

PRESSES AND PROOFING. Offset printers have never liked desktop color separation because only they really know the characteristics of their printing presses and digital and film-based proofers. However, with an output test of a target and a colorimeter, you can create a profile for a specific press and set of conditions. Bruce and David did this for *Real World Photoshop 4*, actually getting a four-color test run off in order to match colors. They were relatively pleased with the result, but you should anticipate this extra step and cost if you plan to introduce it into your workflow.

COLOR ME CORRECTED

As you can see, you have to keep a close eye on any scanned image as you walk it ever closer to the press or output bin. But the corrections we suggest in this chapter should give you practical tools to produce scans every bit as good as those formerly available for $50 to $200 apiece at color houses. And you avoid all that nasty stripping tape as well.

In the next chapter we go back to black and white—with some tips on color—to look at the other major image adjustment besides tonal correction that you'll need to make in almost every scan: sharpening. Using these two corrections, you can create halftones that rival those from almost any high-end system.

9 A SHARPER IMAGE

GETTING RID OF THE BLURRIES

How do we know when we see an edge? Our brain has specialized parts that process optical data, and one set is devoted to identifying adjacent areas of high contrast. Perhaps this was once a survival mechanism, especially in foggy climates, but today it just keeps most of us from walking into doors.

A good photographic print *pops* when you look at it: there are depth and contrast to a print that make it seem real. Images reproduced directly off a scanner without correction look flat and blurry. You have to take the scanned image and increase contrast at edges so that you see it as sharply and crisply as a photographic print—and the world around us. Fortunately, computers are good at recognizing edges: pixels next to each other that have a tonal difference.

Scans almost always require sharpening because of something we discussed at length in Chapter 2, *Scanners*. Because scanners can't easily distinguish the darkest (or densest) tones, the contrast and sharpness at edges can be lost. There's also some averaging that affects an image: a scanner might capture a sample that's part of an edge and is half black and half white; the sample gets averaged to 50 percent, not captured as a sharp edge.

When you fix an image as we described in Chapter 7, *Tonal Correction*, you improve the overall appearance and make it possible to reproduce it on an offset press the way you see it on screen. However, you also further reduce the range of tones and make it less likely that an image will pop. Scanning at higher resolution doesn't help: more data of the same kind won't increase clarity, and usually it's just wasted information. (In fact, we show you in this chapter how lower resolution can help in sharpening an image for reproduction.)

Almost all image-editing software, like Photoshop, has simple and complex software sharpening filters that do edge detection and increase contrast. The simple ones are called Sharpen, Sharpen More, or Sharpen Edges. These don't allow you the kind of control that's needed for doing professional work; for that, you need unsharp masking.

All sharpening tools do one thing: emphasize difference, which helps our eyes pick out detail. Sharpening increases differences where they count (see Figure 9-1).

Unsharp Masking

The method of choice for sharpening scanned photographs is called (somewhat oxymoronically) *unsharp masking* (USM). With its roots in the darkroom and its genesis in high-end prepress systems, unsharp masking provides controls that let you adjust sharpening for particular situations.

Unsharp masking works by combining a slightly blurry (unsharp) version of an image with the original. This combination results in sharp details in high-contrast areas (the edges, where adjacent light and dark samples are markedly different), without accenting tonal shifts in low-contrast areas (areas of smooth gradation, where rapid tonal shifts would destroy the subtle transitions).

Since it increases the contrast in many areas of an image, unsharp masking also tends to increase the overall appearance of contrast.

HOW UNSHARP MASKING WORKS

How does combining a blurry version with the original make for a sharper image? We knew you'd ask that, so we prepared ourselves. Here's the skinny on how unsharp masking works.

FIGURE 9-1
How sharpening
works

Unsharpened   *Sharpened*

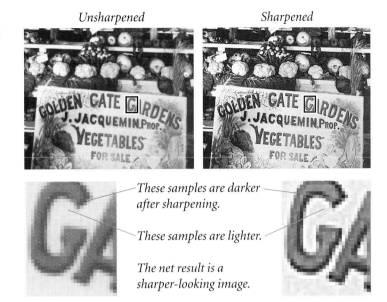

*These samples are darker
after sharpening.*

These samples are lighter.

*The net result is a
sharper-looking image.*

Figure 9-2 shows a simple situation—a jump in tonal value from 40 to 60 percent. The accompanying graph depicts this value jump.

When you apply a blurring filter to the image (in our example, we've used a Gaussian blur filter), you get what you see in Figure 9-3. The values ramp up from 40 to 60 percent in a smooth transition. Note that this is an intentionally low-resolution bitmap we're working with, so that it shows the effects clearly.

The USM filter does some clever if/then calculations. If the sample in the blurred image is darker than the same sample in the orig-

FIGURE 9-2
40- to 60-percent
tonal jump

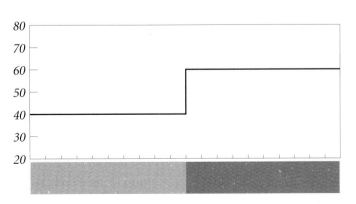

FIGURE 9-3
After Gaussian blur

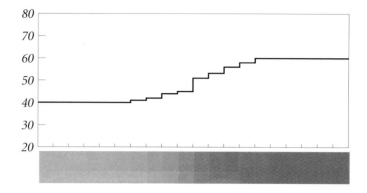

inal, it makes that sample lighter by an amount equal to the difference. If the sample in the blurred version is lighter, it does the opposite. The result is an image like the one in Figure 9-4.

FIGURE 9-4
After unsharp
masking

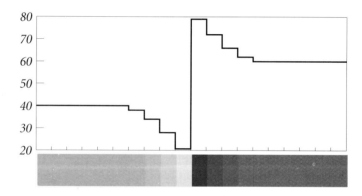

The key thing to notice in this figure is the "blips" on either side of the tonal shift. By accentuating the adjacent light and dark areas, unsharp masking gives the impression of sharpness. Figure 9-5 shows a photograph with intentionally exaggerated unsharp masking, to show the "halo" effect that unsharp masking creates.

This halo effect is both the secret of sharpening and its most potent Achilles' heel—depending on the size and intensity of the halo, and where in an image it appears. In the next section we discuss some of the problems that arise with sharpening; then we get into the details of Photoshop's Unsharp Mask filter, and discuss settings that optimize sharpening while avoiding sharpening problems.

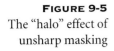

FIGURE 9-5
The "halo" effect of
unsharp masking

Unsharpened   *Oversharpened*

*Note that the size of the halo is especially notice-
able—not just the amount of tonal difference.*

PROBLEMS WITH UNSHARP MASKING

When used improperly or excessively, unsharp masking can make
an image look artificial or bizarre, and it can accentuate problems
in the original image or the scan.

HALOS. The blips that appear on either side of tonal shifts with
unsharp masking can turn into a too-obvious halo, giving the image
an artificial look. In excess, it can make an image look blurrier as
well. This is especially a problem when the halo is too wide, though
it's also a problem if the blips are too light or too dark—if they're too
different from their surroundings. Figure 9-6 shows an image that is
sharpened excessively (though not as badly as Figure 9-5).

ALIASING. Hard diagonal edges—like a dark building against a
light sky—often display aliasing (the *jaggies*) after unsharp masking
has been applied (see Figure 9-7). Aliasing is a more significant
problem with lower-resolution scans—those that are less than two
times the screen frequency (the lower the resolution, the more
potential aliasing).

FIGURE 9-6
Artificial look due
to halos from
unsharp masking

SPECKLING AND MOTTLING. Scanned images often contain a few random sample points that don't match their surroundings. This may be due to a noisy scan, irregularities in the original image, or simply the content of the image. At the outer limits, it can even be caused by the scanner picking up the grain of the film. (This is mainly a problem when you scan high-speed, coarsely grained film on high-resolution drum and slide scanners; or, when you scale an image up significantly.) Sharpening can accentuate those irregularities, resulting in a number of problems—especially with lower-resolution scans.

The most immediately noticeable problem is speckling—usually light pixels in otherwise dark areas. This is especially a problem with low-quality scans that have a lot of noise. You can get rid of speckling to some extent by running a despeckle filter before sharpening.

A less obvious but equally problematic result of sharpening is mottling—often causing people to look like they have bad complexions. It can also destroy the impression of smooth gradations; for instance, in a photograph of a sand dune.

CONTENT-RELATED PROBLEMS. There are many other sharpening problems that are content-related, and that you need to watch for on an image-by-image basis. For example, sharpening can accentuate the "highlights" in someone's hair, giving them a case of

FIGURE 9-7
Resolution,
sharpening,
and aliasing

300 dpi, unsharpened

300 dpi, sharpened

200 dpi, sharpened

150 dpi, sharpened

Higher resolution does little to improve sharpness (though it can improve detail; note the lettering on the ships' bows). Lower resolutions with sharpening applied produce much better results, but aliasing is a danger at lower resolutions, as is visible in the ships' rigging.

premature gray. And, in heavy doses, it can give the impression of buck teeth. Watch out for embarrassing accentuation; it's the stuff that caricatures are made of.

UNSHARP MASKING IN PHOTOSHOP

Okay, let's get to the juice of the chapter: how Photoshop's Unsharp Mask filter works, and how best to use it. Photoshop offers the most complete unsharp masking controls we've seen on the desktop, so by explaining those controls, we can give detailed suggestions on how to control the sharpening process.

Some other programs offer similar, sometimes identical controls, so you can apply these lessons to those. (See Chapter 30, *Image Applications*, for how other major image-editing programs handle unsharp masking.)

Photoshop's Unsharp Mask filter has three variables: Amount, Radius, and Threshold (see Figure 9-8). Each increases or decreases sharpening in different areas and situations. As you're reading through this section, refer to Figure 9-9 at the end of the chapter, which shows the same image sharpened with many different combinations of settings.

RADIUS. The first step in properly using unsharp masking is figuring out the Radius value. Once you've set Radius, you can go on to adjust the other settings relative to that.

The Radius setting controls how many samples wide the blips are on each side of an edge. Large values make for wide blips (big halos, lots of sample points involved); small values make smaller blips. The size of the sharpening-induced halo affects how sharp an image looks (larger radius means more sharpening). And in excess, it causes most sharpening-related problems.

A Radius value of 1.0 results in blips one sample wide (two samples total, for the whole light-and-dark cycle). A value of 2.0 gives you two samples on either side of the blip, and so on. So what Radius value should you set? Resolution divided by 200. For a 200-spi scan, use a Radius setting of 1.0. For a 300-spi scan, use a Radius setting of 1.5. This results in a halo of $1/50$ inch—$1/100$ inch for each blip. It's big enough to provide the sharpening effect, but not so big as to look artificial.

Overly large Radius settings are the prime culprits in producing the ugly oversharpened look that stands out so markedly, so watch

FIGURE 9-8

Photoshop's Unsharp
Mask dialog box

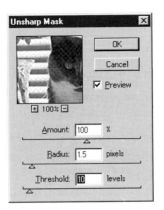

out if you increase this setting much. The images with a Radius of 2.0 in Figure 9-9 make this clear.

The one situation where you might want to use a larger Radius setting is for large images that people will never look at up close—billboards and (some) posters. In this case, you may need a larger Radius to make the sharpness really pop at the intended viewing distance ($^1/_{100}$ inch ain't much at 100 feet). In that case, try this formula to determine an appropriate Radius setting:

Viewing Distance (") × Resolution (spi) × .0004 = Radius setting

This formula is based on some theories about the eye's sensitivity to cycles of amplitude modulation over a given viewing arc (we love throwing around big words like that). We haven't had the chance to test this on a billboard, so we suggest you use it as a starting point, and with a pinch (if not a bag) of salt. You might try a small (tabloid-sized) area first, and place it far away to see how it looks.

AMOUNT. We like to think of the Amount setting as the volume, or amplitude, control. It adjusts how intense the blips are on each side of a tonal shift—how much the tonal differences are accentuated. Large values make for big blips (large tonal differences where edges meet); small values make for less significant blips. We're not talking about the width of the halos here—just the *amount* of tonal difference between adjacent samples.

Although we can't tell you the math behind Amount, we can tell what values work well. If you use the settings described above for

Radius, an Amount setting of 200 percent is a good choice, or at least a good starting point. If the Amount value is set too high, you can get the kind of artificial look we talked about above. It's not much of a problem if you keep the Radius setting low, but if you increase both Radius *and* Amount, images go weird very quickly.

Also be aware that as you increase the Amount setting, you start to reach a point of diminishing returns. The blips around big tonal shifts end up going all the way to white and to black (a problem in itself, because the white blips in particular show up as noticeable artifacts), so increasing the amount has no further effect in those areas. Since those areas of large tonal shifts are the ones you most want to accentuate to give the effect of sharpness, and since you can't accentuate them beyond black and white, increasing the Amount setting beyond a certain point is fruitless.

Large values in the Amount field can also accentuate the problems with noise and mottling that we mentioned earlier, but you can avoid these problems by using the Threshold value, which we discuss next.

THRESHOLD. The Threshold value specifies how many tonal steps apart, on a scale of 0 to 255, that adjacent samples have to be before the filter does anything to them. If Threshold is set to 3, for instance, and adjacent sample points are of values 122 and 124 (a difference of two), they're unaffected by sharpening. So low-contrast areas—those with smooth gradations—aren't affected; the gradations stay smooth.

The Threshold setting is the key to avoiding mottling, speckling, and artifact-related problems that sharpening can cause. It causes the filter to ignore those slightly-out-of-place pixels, rather than accentuating them. This is especially important for smooth natural tones as in a image that has a solid blue sky in the background.

Low Threshold values result in an overall sharper-looking image (because fewer areas are excluded). High values result in less sharpening. We recommend a setting of 3 or 4 for most images. Settings of 10 and above aren't advisable, because they exclude so many areas as to reduce sharpening to near-invisibility.

COLOR SHARPENING

While it's easy enough to play with the values and settings we suggested above, we have three additional concrete tips that will dramatically improve your ability to use unsharp masking.

LUMINANCE

The eye perceives differences in luminance—tonal values—much more readily than differences in chrominence—color variation. In RGB colorspace, these values are all lumped together. However, Photoshop and several other programs support the LAB colorspace, which stores a color image as a channel of luminance (L) and two channels of color information (A and B); see the previous chapter, *Color*, for a full explanation.

In LAB mode, it's easy to just sharpen just the tonal information without disturbing color details. One reason to do this is to avoid oversaturating color images. When you increase the contrast in a color image, you increase the saturation in colors that are on the "high" side of an edge (see Color Page B).

You have to avoid going back and forth between RGB and LAB, because values are lost and compressed during the conversion. But if you're doing sharpening as the last step before CMYK conversion, you won't lose much information going from RGB to LAB, sharpening, and then converting to CMYK.

SELECTIONS

As with any filter, you don't have to arbitrarily select the whole image. You can manually select an area—or use one of many tools to select by color or tone—and sharpen just that bit. This is sometimes used to sharpen the eyes in a face without disturbing flatter facial tones; it's also used to sharpen faces in a crowd.

If you have an image with a relatively flat or even-colored background, you would normally just set the Threshold value at 2 or 3 to avoid mottling in the flat colors. However, you might simultaneously have a subject in the foreground that needs a Threshold of 0 or 1. The solution is to select the background you want to preserve using the Magic Wand in Photoshop, invert the selection and just sharpen your foreground subject (see Color Page C).

FACIAL CARE

We scrutinize faces, even in photographs, more carefully than anything else—it's an automatic reaction. So if you sharpen photographs with people in them, especially close-ups of faces or mug shots, it's a good idea to increase the Threshold value. The plane of a face will have many subtle transitions, and a low Threshold will create artifacts all over a face. Set the Threshold high and the Radius small, and you'll get the best results (see Color Page A). If you combine this with selections in particularly difficult images, you can get much better results over an entire image.

RUNNING THE NUMBERS

We used to be incredibly frustrated by the documentation of Photoshop's Unsharp Mask filter, which used to say things like "If you'd like to enter 1 in the Radius field, enter 1." The manuals have improved to the point that they explain each setting and suggest how to approximate your needs. But we slogged through endless trial and error—on screen and on output—to develop simple formulas we can use for sharpening. It makes our lives much simpler; we hope it will do the same for you.

FIGURE 9-9
Various settings
for Photoshop's
Unsharp Mask filter

200-spi image
133-lpi screen

Unsharpened

Optimal sharpening:
Amount: 200 Radius: 1 Threshold: 3

FIGURE 9-9
Various settings
for Photoshop's
Unsharp Mask
filter, continued

200-spi image
133-lpi screen

Amount: 75 Radius: 2 Threshold: 3 *Amount: 125 Radius: 1 Threshold: 3*

Amount: 100 Radius: 2 Threshold: 3 *Amount: 150 Radius: 1 Threshold: 3*

Amount: 125 Radius: 2 Threshold: 3 *Amount: 175 Radius: 1 Threshold: 3*

Amount: 150 Radius: 2 Threshold: 3 *Amount: 200 Radius: 1 Threshold: 3*

FIGURE 9-9
Various settings
for Photoshop's
Unsharp Mask
filter, continued

*150-spi image
100-lpi screen*

Amount: 150 Radius: .7 Threshold: 3

Amount: 200 Radius: .4 Threshold: 3

Amount: 180 Radius: .7 Threshold: 3

Amount: 240 Radius: .4 Threshold: 3

Amount: 210 Radius: .7 Threshold: 3

Amount: 270 Radius: .4 Threshold: 3

Amount: 240 Radius: .7 Threshold: 3

Amount: 300 Radius: .4 Threshold: 3

FIGURE 9-9
Various settings
for Photoshop's
Unsharp Mask
filter, continued

150-spi image
75-lpi screen

Amount: 150 Radius: .7 Threshold: 3 *Amount: 210 Radius: .4 Threshold: 3*

Amount: 180 Radius: .7 Threshold: 3 *Amount: 240 Radius: .4 Threshold: 3*

Amount: 210 Radius: .7 Threshold: 3 *Amount: 270 Radius: .4 Threshold: 3*

Amount: 240 Radius: .7 Threshold: 3 *Amount: 300 Radius: .4 Threshold: 3*

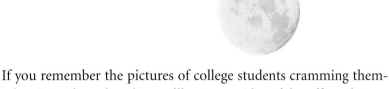

10 COMPRESSION

GETTING
SMALL

If you remember the pictures of college students cramming themselves into phone booths, you'll get some idea of the offices that we all share. We've managed to compress ourselves, a dozen other people, thousands of books, and what seems to be a million AOL membership floppies into the modern-day equivalent. So our desire for compression comes from rather obvious reasons.

In this chapter we provide an overview of the compression world: what it is, what it does, and generally how it does it. We also give you some guidelines for choosing between compression methods, depending on what you're doing and how you're doing it.

Compression takes the form of algorithms: descriptions of how to do a given mathematical or programming task, step-by-step. Compression algorithms describe how you can take raw data, like a TIFF image file, apply a series of mathematical operations on the data, and wind up with a smaller file than you began with.

The real trick, of course, is that later you want to take this compressed image and *decompress* it into what it was before. That's where the distinction between the two major kinds of image compression comes into play. When you're playing the game Twenty Questions, the first question you ask is, "Animal, vegetable, or mineral?" When you're playing the compression game, the first question you have to ask is, "Lossy or lossless?"

LOSSLESS

If you compress an image using *lossless* compression, after decompressing that file you have an identical image. No information is lost or changed in any way—guaranteed. If the algorithm can't guarantee it, it's not lossless. It's like a kitchen sponge: you can take the sponge and squeeze it down really small, and when you let go, it reverts to its original form. We could illustrate this by showing you two pictures—one before being saved in a lossless format, and one after—but since they'd look identical, it would be kind of silly.

Lossless compression is used in programs like WinZIP and StuffIt Deluxe for archiving programs and data, because you can't afford to mistake a single bit in a program or data file. It's also used for images for which you want to preserve everything about the image—which is often the case.

There are several kinds of lossless compression; each of them is used in one or more major image file formats, which we discussed back in Chapter 4, *File Formats.*

RUN LENGTH ENCODING

One of the simplest forms of lossless compression for images is Run Length Encoding (RLE), which is automatically used for the Macintosh PICT image format. RLE works by looking for the same value multiple times in a row. For example, let's say you have a black-and-white bitmapped image of a cow. A program that compresses image data with RLE sees that the first 245 sample points in the image are white, followed by 80 black points, followed by 16 white points, and so on. The program can then compress that data by just recording those values: "245 white, 80 black, 16 white," etc. (see Figure 10-1).

This compresses a simple image down to almost nothing, and a complex image by just a little; in fact, if an image is complex enough (or has noise in flat color areas), RLE compression can make the file *bigger*!

FIGURE 10-1
Run Length Encoding

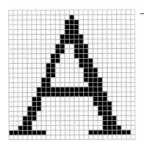

——————— 40 sample points of white
1 sample point of black
25 sample points of white
3 sample points of black
25 sample points of white
3 sample points of black
and so on...

LZW

LZW (Lempel-Ziv-Welch, though you really don't need to know that) compresses data by looking for patterns throughout a file. These patterns, called *phrases*, are identified and stored in a table. The table has short tokens or keys that correspond to these longer phrases. So if you had the word "ishkabibble" appearing 500 times in a text file and you apply LZW compression, "ishkabibble" would be replaced by a single number that might take only one or two bytes to represent. If you looked that number up in the encoding table, you'd find "ishkabibble." (See Figure 10-2 for an example with just nine substitutions.)

FIGURE 10-2
Partial LZW
compression
of text

Before phrase replacement
Of a certain knight that swore by his honour they were good pancakes, and swore by his honour the mustard was naught; now, I'll stand to it, the pancakes were naught and the mustard was good; and yet was not the knight forsworn.

After phrase replacement
Of a certain ❼ that ❽ by his ❺ they were ❸ ❹, ❷ ❽ by his ❺ ❶ ❻ was ❾; now, I'll stand to it, ❶ ❹ were ❾ ❷ ❶ ❻ was ❸; ❷ yet was not ❶ ❼ forsworn.

Phrase table	
the	❶
and	❷
good	❸
pancakes	❹
honour	❺
mustard	❻
knight	❼
swore	❽
naught	❾

Another example: If, in an image, you have pink, orange, and green pixels repeating 50 times, LZW notices this, gives that pattern a single number (let's say number 6) and then stores the data as the number 6, 50 times in a row.

The standard implementations of TIFF and GIF use LZW compression because it's an efficient way to represent patterns in color images even if there is some noise. Like RLE, it works best if you have areas of consistent, noise-free colors, but it's much better than RLE in compressing any arbitrary image data.

HUFFMAN AND CCITT ENCODING

We only mention Huffman and CCITT Encoding because you might see the terms as compression options in programs and should know why to choose them or not. Huffman Encoding was invented way back in 1952, and it's used as part of a number of other compression schemes, like LZW and deflate.

Huffman Encoding is a technique that takes a set of symbols, like the letters in a text file, and analyzes them to figure out the frequency of each symbol. It then uses the fewest possible bits to represent the most frequently occurring symbols. For instance, E is the most common letter in standard English text. In Huffman Encoding, you might be able to represent E in as few as two bits (1 followed by 0) instead of the eight bits needed to signal E in ASCII, which is used to store and transmit virtually all text on and between computers.

CCITT (the abbreviation for the International Telegraph and Telephone Consultative Committee) Encoding was developed for facsimile transmission and reception. There are several different standards, but you'll see the terms *Group 3* and *Group 4* most often. Huffman and CCITT Encoding aren't interchangeable terms; CCITT Encoding is a version of a narrow use of Huffman Encoding.

CCITT is used for compression of black-and-white bitmaps. If you own Acrobat, for instance, in the Distiller application you'll see CCITT options. In the Job Options menu's dialog box, there's a Compression tab from which you can choose CCITT Group 3 (identical to fax format), Group 4 (like fax format but without special control information, and the default option here), Run Length (same as RLE), and ZIP, a format that Adobe implemented using the deflate algorithm.

Neither Huffman nor CCITT are actual file formats; their algorithms are always used inside of other formats, like TIFF, EPS, or PDF.

DEFLATE

We try not to take you too far afield, but you will see references to *deflate* if you do any additional reading on this subject—or even just try to read Adobe's documentation for Distiller. After the flap about Unisys's ownership and licensing of the LZW patent—see "PNG" in Chapter 4, *File Formats*—a number of rather clever people helped design software that could be used without any patent claims. One algorithm is called *deflate*, and a common free implementation of deflate is the *zlib library*.

Deflate uses techniques similar to LZW to losslessly compress data, but the developers have made every effort to make sure the deflate algorithm isn't covered by the LZW patents. The ZIP format for Acrobat mentioned above uses the deflate method, as do PNG and some archival compression programs.

ARCHIVES

When you're moving files around or storing them for later use, it can be useful to group them together as a single entity. The easiest way to do this is with an archiving program that can take one or more files—or even an entire directory structure of files and folders—and put them together in a single archive file that's easy to transfer and store.

Even better, you can have the program that creates archives apply compression as it adds files, reducing space and making the resulting archive more efficient. StuffIt Deluxe and PkZIP are two well-known examples of archiving programs, although there are dozens.

What you get when you archive a file or set of files with these programs is another file that *includes* the compressed version of the original data, and, if you've added folders or directories, the location of files in the hierarchy. You can't do anything with that image until you use the archiving program to *extract* the file, creating new, uncompressed files on disk.

Some compression programs can read other compression programs' files (for instance, WinZIP and StuffIt can both extract from the Unix "gzip" format), but a program such as QuarkXPress or PageMaker can't read one of those archives. You have to extract the files from the archive first.

Archiving programs are great for all sorts of things: when a file can't fit onto a floppy disk, if you need to send the file via the Internet, or when you're storing large redundant data files on a disk (like images or plain text) and you won't be needing them very often.

For day-to-day use of image files, however, compressed file formats are where it's at, since they can be read and written by the programs you use to edit and place them.

There's no point in using an archive program to compress a bunch of GIF or PNG files, or TIFF files with LZW compression turned on; the compression programs can't do a better job than the graphic file formats' built-in routines. In fact, using compression on image files can often make their component of the archive take up more space than the original file.

Adaptive archiving programs skip compressing files that already incorporate compression; or, they can also test compression on a file and skip it if it can't be made more efficient.

Lossy

The second type of compression—*lossy*, a term going back to at least 1945, though it sounds like it was invented by software engineers—actually loses information in the process of squeezing the data. But it drops out data in a very intelligent manner. It's like tightly folding a cotton shirt into a suitcase. If you really cram it in, you might save some room in your suitcase, but when you unfold the shirt, it doesn't look as good as it did before you compressed it. (To extend the metaphor, if you squeeze the shirt in very tightly, it might have gone in a bright white, but it comes out of the suitcase a warm gray.)

Lossy algorithms start with notions encoded in them about what kinds of image information is most important. The most important information is retained even at the highest compression levels. The less important information can be dropped out depending on the quality level you choose. For instance, luminance information—or tonal values—is much more important than color information, because the eye is more sensitive to changes in tone. All lossy image compression stores more luminosity data than data about hue or saturation.

By losing less-important information, you can increase compression ratios enormously. Where an LZW-compressed TIFF might be 40 percent of original size, the same file saved with lossy compression could be *2 percent or less* of the original file size. Lossy compression methods typically give you a choice of how tight you want to pack the data. With low compression you get larger files and better quality. High compression yields lower quality and smaller files.

How much quality do you lose? It depends on the level of compression, the resolution of the image, and the content of the image. Lower quality means there are more artifacts in the image; *artifacts* are errors, such as grainy sample points, introduced by software.

Lossy compression is based on mathematical algorithms that are too complicated to include here (that's a nice way of saying we don't understand the math well enough ourselves).

JPEG

The most common lossy compression scheme is currently JPEG, which we discussed back in Chapter 4, *File Formats.* As we noted, although JPEG could be implemented inside of all kinds of image data formats, it's really used only with a very simple spec called JFIF that can do 8-bit grayscale and 24-bit RGB; Adobe uses a variant of JFIF for its JPEG format, which it's tweaked to handle 32-bit CMYK data as well. (See Figure 10-3 and Color Page D for examples.)

HOW IT WORKS. JPEG uses several tricks to maximize compression. It first converts image data to a LAB-like colorspace (see Chapter 8, *Color*). It then throws away half or three-quarters of the color information (depending on the implementation).

It next applies an algorithm (called DCT for Discrete Cosine Transform) that analyzes 8-by-8-pixel blocks in the file. For each block, it generates a series of numbers that represent features on a spectrum from coarse to fine. The first few numbers represent the

FIGURE 10-3
JPEG compression compared with the original image

Original image with detail marked

Blown up from the original image

Blown up from a JPEG version saved with highest compression

overall color of the block, while later numbers represent fine details. The spectrum of details is based on human perception, so the coarse details (or larger features) are most noticeable; the finest, least.

These DCT numbers don't correspond one-to-one with pixels, which is another reason JPEG is lossy; even when you save JPEG with the least compression, you still don't wind up with an exact representation of the original image.

In the next step, based on whatever setting you've chosen for your JPEG image, more or fewer of the numbers that represent finer details are dropped out. If you choose better compression, only coarse details are retained, making the resulting image look speckled; better quality, and you retain more fine detail, with just minor color shifts in certain areas.

In the last step, JPEG uses Huffman Encoding (see "Lossless," above, for a definition of this algorithm) to most efficiently store the resulting, pretty arbitrary data. It's important to recognize that at the end of the JPEG compression process, you're left with data that really has no correspondence with the original image. It has to be run back through the JPEG routine in the other direction to re-create your original data.

USING JPEG RIGHT. Here's a few tips on using JPEG the right way and for the right images:

▸ Images with hard, high-contrast, and angular areas are most likely to develop artifacts when you compress them using JPEG.

For example, a yellow square on a green background in a lower-resolution image would look pretty miserable after compression.

▶ Compressing and decompressing images repeatedly can make images worse than just doing it once. It's just like photocopying a photocopy. After the first few generations, your original image becomes unusable.

▶ If your image is somewhat grainy or impressionistic already, lossy compression probably won't hurt much at all, but JPEG won't do a great job of compressing it.

▶ The flip side is that photographs with large, smooth areas compress very well with JPEG. Images with lots of detail are better compressed as an LZW TIFF.

NEW MATH

Our crystal ball is in the shop; when we wrote the first edition of this book, fractal compression looked like it was going to take off. Four years later, we're still waiting for the rocket to launch. Both fractal and wavelet compression take advantage of relatively new methods of expressing complex patterns using mathematical formulas—just like JPEG uses its DCT algorithm. Fractal mathematics emerged in the late '70s, whereas wavelets are the hot new math to express curves and images in the '90s. Very few companies are incorporating these algorithms into their compression techniques, but we want you to be aware of them, just in case you bump into one down the road.

FRACTALS. In any real-world object or scene, such as a piece of wood or a landscape, there are many identical patterns that appear at different sizes and orientations. Think of a leaf on a tree: there might be thousands of leaves, many of which are very nearly identical in form, but not in size or location.

Fractal compression identifies these patterns—it's best at doing so in natural scenes like that—and builds up a representation of an image that uses formulas to represent these patterns wherever they occur and in whatever transformation (rotation, scale, skew, etc.). Doing the compression can take a hundred times longer than the decompression; the decompression just turns the patterns back into bitmaps.

Fractal compression shows itself off best when you need to compress the heck out of something—say, to a 40- or 100-to-1 ratio. You can also scale fractally compressed images to any size; you don't get more detail than the original resolution, but the enlargement doesn't start to look grainy or pixelated. We've heard this has been used for great effect on billboards. (See Color Page E.)

All currently employed fractal compression methods are patented, and Iterated Systems, the owner, has licensed its algorithms to just a few companies. Compare this with JPEG, which is used by hundreds of programs, and you'll understand one of the reasons why fractal compression hasn't taken off.

WAVELETS. Wavelets are a mathematical representation of the difference between two sets of data: an original set (like an image) and a set that's half the original's size (like a downsampled image).

Take an image file and downsample it to 71 percent to get half the pixels (downsampling to 50 percent would get you half the dimensions, but not half the area or overall pixels). If you blow it up to view at 140 percent and look at it side by side with the original, you'll see that two pixels in the original now represent one in the downsampled version.

Wavelet theory allows you to represent just the difference in data between those two resolutions. You can continue to downsample the data to some arbitrary point—though it could be down to just one value! Each of these differences can be stored more efficiently than the original data, because the differences are full of redundancy.

The lossy compression comes in at the point when you're deciding which and how many of these differences to store. The algorithm is proprietary—licensed from a Texas university to Compression Engines—but we can infer that it's doing something much like JPEG: using a compression scale to decide how much fine detail to retain (See Color Page E).

This kind of compression has two benefits: rapid viewing at many sizes without down- or upsampling, and substantial file-size reduction with less apparent loss than similar JPEG compression ratios.

OTHER RESOURCES

We spent a lot of time cramming information into the smallest place possible in our head in order to represent it compactly here on the page. One of the many sources we turned to for advice was the excellent and very heavy *Encyclopedia of Graphic File Formats* by James D. Murray and William vanRyper. This book is packed with information on how every file format works, and has an excellent and clear chapter on the most technical details of compression schemes. It also comes with the full text on a CD-ROM packed with other material.

You can visit our Web site at www.rwsh.com to find links to this title, on-line Frequently Asked Question lists (FAQs) about compression, and ideas on other books and resources.

SMALL IS BEAUTIFUL

Remember that the whole idea of compression is to make a file on your hard disk take up less space. Although there are many ways to do this, note that there's always the possibility of simply getting a larger hard drive. Compression always takes extra time somewhere (while compressing and decompressing), and that can be a hassle. Small is beautiful (hey, no comments about our height), but fast and efficient is next to godliness.

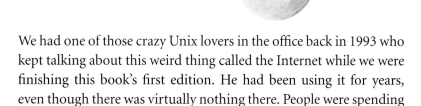

11 IMAGES FOR THE WEB

REAL WORLD WIDE WEB

We had one of those crazy Unix lovers in the office back in 1993 who kept talking about this weird thing called the Internet while we were finishing this book's first edition. He had been using it for years, even though there was virtually nothing there. People were spending a huge amount of effort to send text back and forth at low speeds.

That crazy guy was Glenn, of course. He wasn't successful in making anyone in the office excited about the 'Net until March 1994, when Steve saw a screen capture in *MacWeek* of a newly released and free program called Mosaic from the National Center for Supercomputing Applications (NCSA). Mosaic let you navigate the Internet by clicking on links that took you from one resource to another. But more importantly to Steve, it also incorporated graphics. Steve thought there just might be something to the Internet, after all.

What do the Web and the Internet have to do with scanning? As we say until you plug your ears, it's important where a scan will wind up while you're making it. The more you know about where and whether an image will be output and then ultimately viewed, the more work you can do at the time of the scan, and the more time you can save. This includes keeping a wider range of colors, which can also be more highly saturated; and making smaller scans, which speeds up the process and reduces storage requirements.

Often you'll hear the dread word *repurposing*, in which you're taking existing documents and reworking them for Acrobat PDF and

Web display. We like to talk about *prepurposing*—getting it right before you create the original document. For images that will be used in several different media—which could include Macromedia Director movies, color offset printing, and the Web—you might have to make a few scans of the same image to get the right results.

FILE FORMATS

Everything you want to know about how a graphic file format works can be found back in Chapter 4, *File Formats*. But we want to show you which files work on the Web and in what way browsers can handle them. Remember the bitmapped files table back in Chapter 4 (Table 4-1)? Table 11-1 compares the same formats for Web-specific issues. (Issues about formats' colorspaces are found in Chapter 4, and formats' compression in Chapter 10, *Compression*.)

STANDARDS. The current standard file formats for the Web are GIF and JPEG; these are well supported by almost every current browser releases. PNG has made some inroads, including support in both Microsoft Internet Explorer and Netscape Navigator's latest releases as we write this.

WINDOWS INTO BIG IMAGES. FlashPix and Photo CD (covered in depth in Chapter 4, *File Formats,* and Chapter 14, *Photo CD*) have limited application on the Web except as a way to let a visitor see pieces of larger images. Both formats store multiple resolutions of the same image. Browsers equipped with a plug-in for FlashPix or with Java turned on for Photo CD can display the image at one resolution, and allow the user to zoom in, zoom out, or pan across the file. This might be useful for real estate agents to show properties, museums to show off their collections, and other purposes where you want to provide high-resolution views without requiring the user to download a multimegabyte file.

COMPRESSION AND FILE SIZE. Although we devoted Chapter 10 to compression, you should also be thinking about the final file size

Format	Displays in browser	Inter- lacing	Transparency	Browser color models	Device-independent color support
TIFF	No				
EPS	No				
GIF	Yes	Yes	One color	8-bit indexed	No
JPEG	Yes	Yes[1]	No	grayscale or 24-bit	No
PNG	Yes[2]	Yes	One color or alpha channel	indexed, gray-scale, or 24-bit	Yes
FlashPix	Yes[3]	Yes	Alpha channel[4]	grayscale or 24-bit	Yes[4]
Photo CD	Yes[5]	Yes	No	24-bit	Yes[4]

[1] Multiple settings for interlacing. [2]Mac and Windows Netscape and Internet Explorer just added basic support at this writing. [3]Requires third-party plug-in for all browsers at this writing. [4]Part of image spec, but either not implemented for browsers, or unclear how it will be used in browsers. [5]Uses Java applet for display; built-in support in a few obscure browsers.

TABLE 11-1
Major bitmap formats as they work on the Web

of images you put on the Web. JPEG is often preferred to GIF because of its massive compression ratios: a full-screen image might turn into a several-hundred-kilobyte GIF but a 50 K JPEG. And though GIF can display the same way on many different machines, it's not the best way to represent photographic images. Flat colors compress well and do well in GIF; photographic images are better suited for JPEG even if there's some variation between how the image looks on different computers.

SCANNING AND CORRECTING

If you're planning on putting your scans directly on the Web, you have to think about computer monitors and how they display color and tone. Many computers lack video circuitry that will display enough different colors to let you use JPEGs with impunity. And no two monitors—especially one on a Mac and one on a Windows machine—will represent tones in the same way. We discussed the wherefore in Chapter 8, *Color*; the how-to-avoid is below.

BIT DEPTH

Bit depth, as we explained back in "Bit Depth and Dynamic Range" in Chapter 2, *Scanners*, is a way to measure how many different colors a sample or on-screen pixel can represent. Although most computers have a 16-million-color palette, an 8-bit video display can only show 256 of those colors at the same time. Although most new machines come with 16-bit video, there's no way to ensure that any given viewer will have the right machinery to see your images. (Real programming wonks could use JavaScript or other server-side tools to try to figure out the user's bit depth and feed out a GIF or JPEG as appropriate—but that's a little over the top.)

JPEG and PNG can both store images in 24 bits with colors coming from the entire palette of 16 million. Although it requires 24-bit video to best display a rich photograph, 16 bits (or thousands of colors) do a more than passable job using dithering. Dithering is also one of three techniques that copes with low bit depth; the other two require reducing all the colors used in a GIF (or indexed-color PNG) to a single common set.

NETSCAPE-SAFE PALETTE. For the Web, GIF files often use what's called the "Netscape-safe palette": a set of 216 colors that both Microsoft and Netscape's browsers can display without using a patchwork of other colors to simulate ones it can't display. (This patchwork is called *dithering*; see below.)

The safe palette limits itself to 216 colors, to leave 40 colors free on an 8-bit video display for the Macintosh or Windows (or even Unix) operating system to use for its own purposes.

SUPER PALETTES. The Netscape- or Web-safe palette is really just one of a large possible set of 216 colors that can safely be used across images on the same page without dithering. These palettes are called *super palettes*, and it's easy to create one from a set of images to maximize photographic quality. DeBabelizer offers the options of opening several images at once, determining an ideal palette of colors across these images, and saving this palette for future reference.

You can do this "manually" in Photoshop by selecting all of your images, pasting them into a single large canvas, and converting to Indexed Color mode. Choose Adaptive from the conversion's popup menu, and Photoshop will generate what it feels is an optimum set of colors. You can save that color map as a file and then load it for conversion for each of the images you're putting on the same page (or on a Web site).

We still recommend using only 216 colors; otherwise, you'll get dithering. The main reason to use a super palette is to represent natural images in a manner that's not as distorted as you'd get from the Netscape-safe palette.

DITHERING. The computer will substitute a patchwork of patterns of dots to simulate the color it can't produce. This doesn't help when editing images or checking details, for sure. But it's better than pure posterization, in which abrupt transitions appear instead of gradual tonal variation. Dithering is usually visible to the naked eye as a kind of speckling; it's a terrible thing in flat colors, where it stands out completely. It's better hidden and put to better use when it appears in photographs, giving the impression of a real tonal range. (See Color Page F–G.)

You can also get software packages and Photoshop plug-ins that do a nice job in presenting dithers made up of color palettes you select—like the Web-safe palette—in order to better control your final images.

SATURATION

You're probably used to de-emphasizing saturation—intense concentration of colors—when preparing images for prepress, because process color separation can't reproduce them well. The Web, being display-based, doesn't have this limitation. So go hog wild and saturate the heck out of images that need to be pumped up or that appear pumped up in the original.

GAMMA

Gamma measures how tonal values are distributed in an image or a video display. It's usually displayed as a graph, showing where values are compressed, expanded, or shifted. Macintoshes typically have a much lower gamma than Windows video, which means that an image that looks perfect on a Macintosh can be far too dark on a Windows machine. On the Web, this has been a significant problem, as the middle ground isn't great either. Typically, we try to aim for a 2.0, between the typical 1.8 level found on a Mac and 2.2 or higher found in Windows. The best way to adjust for gamma is to have standard Mac and Windows 16-bit or higher systems set up or available so you can do a few tests before committing.

PNG can store a gamma curve representing the display of the machine that created it, so that it theoretically could automatically display correctly on any computer. However, none of the browsers that support PNG have built this in, and a broader specification (called sRGB) is in the works to try to make this possible across lots of different software. (See Chapter 8, *Color*, for background on device-dependent color and how gamma enters into that.)

WEB SPECIALS

There are a few things you can do on the Web that you can't do in the prepress world. It's a cross between true multimedia, which encompasses animation, transparency, and fading effects, and flat media, which can use transparency and translucency to some great effect. Note that any technique can be overused, but transparency, interlacing, and animation can make Web pages seem a bit more interesting if done well.

TRANSPARENCY

An image that has transparency—whether a single color or an entire channel—allows other images or text behind it to show through wherever that color or tone appears. This is used to *knock out* shapes in prepress, and to better blend images and type on the Web.

The difference between doing composites in Photoshop that are intended for print and using an alpha channel in a Web-bound image is that you can combine and recombine different Web images on the fly with different backgrounds, or several times on the same page for varying effects.

GIF. GIF transparency is limited to knockout colors, not partially transparent mixes. Most programs that allow you to set transparency in a GIF let you select either a single or multiple colors. However, the colors you select don't mix with the underlying colors; a transparent GIF color sample just shows through whatever color underlies it in the browser window. It's either on or off, not a blend.

In Photoshop, you use the GIF89a Export plug-in to create transparent GIFs (see Figure 11-1). The export window shows your indexed color palette or color map, and you can just click on the

FIGURE 11-1
Photoshop's GIF89a Export plug-in used with RGB and indexed-color source files

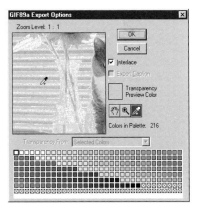

If you convert your file to indexed color (above) before using the GIF89a Export plug-in, you're presented with the full range of options for selecting transparency (right).

If you start with an RGB file, you select transparency before using the plug-in, and are presented with fewer choices (left).

colors in the image that you want to act as transparent. Any pixels that were transparent in your RGB file before you selected the export plug-in will have their transparency preserved. The preview shows you how a gray background will show through the image with those colors selected.

This can take a bit of back and forth to get perfect, because typically you have a color or a background image showing through the transparent images, not just a dark gray. Sometimes it's better to create "fake" transparency, where you create a GIF that uses the same color or colors as a background pattern or Web page color.

Some versions of browsers do a bad job of showing the same color the same way in a GIF and as a Web page background color, so it's important to test major browsers on both platforms before doing too much work. For example, Steve's conference business noticed a strange yellow tinge on some of their Web pages with the release of Netscape 4 for Macintosh. It turns out that Netscape changed (and broke) how it displayed standard indexed-color palettes just on the Mac. As of this writing, months after the initial release, Netscape's still broken, but Steve's site JavaScripter built a workaround to avoid the problem.

PNG. PNG supports a full alpha channel, allowing graduated transparency, so that some parts of an image might show 50 percent through, while others show 5 or 95 percent. Current major browser support for PNG doesn't implement the transparency features, but the potential is to make the Web seem even more photographic.

Because PNG supports a standard alpha channel, and because no browser currently displays it, we're not going to get into the intricacies of creating PNG transparency here. Any image-editing program that supports alpha channel transparency and can save a PNG file with the alpha channel—Photoshop can do both, of course—will allow you to create what you need. We recommend you consult *Real World Photoshop 4* by David and his colleague Bruce Fraser; they spend several pages on alpha channels, showing you the tools and how to use them.

INTERLACING

Interlaced images display gradually on a Web page by storing the image data out of sequence. Most image files store pixels in the same order they appear on screen: the file first stores the first line of pixels from left to right, then the next, and so on, until the end of the image. Interlacing—also called progressive rendering when you're talking about how it appears on screen—stores image data out of order. So instead of storing lines 1, 2, 3, 4, 5, 6, you might store the data in the order of lines 1, 4, 2, 5, 3, 6.

What's the advantage of doing this? Not any in terms of storage, but quite a bit from a user's perspective. Progressively rendered images start displaying the entire depth and width of the image in a Web browser before all the image data has transferred over the Internet or other network. This makes users feel like things are happening faster than they are. Realistically, it lets surfers click on buttons or images as soon as they get the gist, rather than having to wait for the full download to make their next action.

As you can tell, we're not entirely convinced that interlacing is useful, but it is widely used.

There are two kinds of interlacing: line at a time and two-dimensional. Line at a time works just as we describe above: lines of an image are loaded in alternation at some interval until the whole image appears. Two-dimensional interlacing loads just a few pixels from alternating lines in each pass, making the first passes appear very quickly indeed.

Here's how to set interlacing in GIF, JPEG, and PNG files.

GIF AND JPEG. GIF and JPEG use line-at-a-time interlacing, and these are both easily set. Photoshop lets you set interlacing at the time you save a file in GIF or JPEG format. When you select GIF or JPEG from the Format popup menu in the Save As dialog box and click Save, you're presented with dialogs that let you set interlacing options (see Figure 11-1, earlier). GIF interlacing is either off or on in Photoshop (see Figure 11-2), while JPEG can be set to 3, 5, or 6 lines of alternation for each pass; we don't notice much differ-

FIGURE 11-2
GIF interlacing over
four passes

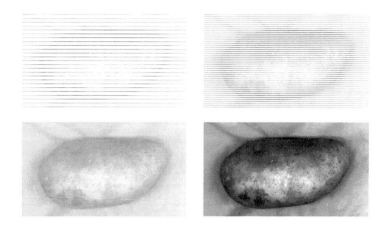

ence, really, although it can change how fast the first passes appear. Most other image-editing programs don't offer the full range of interlacing choices for JPEG, though newer versions keep catching up to Photoshop.

PNG. PNG interlacing is two-dimensional—a bit harder to picture. Single pixels are extracted both down and across the original image in a regular, progressive pattern. The PNG specs point out that the first pass of a PNG image can display in one-eighth the time of the first pass of a GIF image. There's less detail in each pass, but the effects are quite nice and it does appear to appear faster.

Photoshop's PNG options appear after you select PNG as the file format in the Save As dialog box and click Save. Progressive rendering is done through the Adam7 algorithm; it's not descriptive, just a funny name.

FIGURE 11-3
Ulead GIF Animator
preview window for
an animated GIF

ANIMATION

Animated GIFs made advertisers' hearts leap with glee, because it made the Web more like television. Animation works in a GIF file by having multiple images that represent sequential frames in the same file. Animated GIFs can be created through a lot of different shareware and commercial software, like Ulead GIF Animator; they let you sequence GIFs, control the timing between them, preview, and write the final file (see Figure 11-3). Because the full image, not just the differences between frames, is stored for each frame, it's important to choose easily compressible images—ones with few colors and no photographic detail or shading.

FTP HAZARDS

We don't intend to give you a lesson on using File Transfer Protocol (FTP); there are probably 500 books that can tell you about that. But we do want to make you aware of a few pitfalls in uploading and transferring images.

BINARY, ASCII, AND MACBINARY. Text files ignore the eighth bit of their bytes; this used to be an important distinction. Many systems formerly reserved the eighth bit of a byte to pass control signals on a network. And, way back when, many modems were limited to transmitting only seven bits of data. For the last several years, though, it hasn't been a problem to download or upload full 8-bit binary files.

Most FTP programs will give you the choice between binary and text. Sometimes binary is called raw data or 8-bit, and text is called ASCII or 7-bit. If you always set your default to binary, you'll never run into a problem. The binary format sends all eight bits even if the eighth bit isn't used. Sending in text mode means that you might be truncating a bit off a binary file by accident.

MacBinary is a special format created for Macintoshes to transfer the *resource fork* of certain Mac files. The resource fork contains all the icons, dialog boxes, system messages, and other organized data that a program needs to work in the Mac environment. However, MacBinary is only used for program data, not for documents; and it only works correctly between two Macintoshes.

If you need to upload a Mac program file, use StuffIt Deluxe or DropStuff from Aladdin Systems to turn the file into a binary archive; these ".sit" extension files can be transferred across all systems and are the standard.

If, for some reason, you need to transmit data in 7-bit ASCII format, you can encode your binary data in one of two 7-bit schemes: BinHex or uuencode. BinHex is a Mac-specific format that turns each 8-bit byte into a 2-byte, 7-bit hexadecimal (base 16) number. When you de-BinHex with StuffIt Expander or another program, the hexadecimal numbers are read and turned back into single binary bytes. Uuencode is more broadly used; it's an old Unix format that's been in use for decades.

FILE EXTENSIONS. As we noted in "File Types, Extensions, and Magic Numbers" back in Chapter 4, *File Formats,* different platforms identify files in different ways. The Web, fortunately, uses extensions—just like Windows—to identify the data in a file. If you name a file with ".gif" at the end, when that file is retrieved by a Web browser, the server will tell the browser that it's sending an image file in GIF format. We recommend using three-letter versions (like .jpg and .htm) if you're switching between platforms, rather than four-letter ones (.jpeg and .html).

CAPITAL VS. LOWERCASE AND SPECIAL CHARACTERS. Web images might be created on Macintosh, copied to a Windows NT machine on a floppy or via FTP for assembly in pages, and finally uploaded to a Unix Web server. Each machine has a little different understanding of what letters you can use in the file name.

The safest bet is to always use uppercase and to format names with the old-style DOS convention: eight letters, a period, and a three-letter standard extension, like .gif, .jpg, or .png. It's annoying, hard to use, and ugly—but works consistently. Also, avoid odd characters, like punctuation. Use numerals and letters, the period, underscore, and hyphen, and avoid everything else. Part of the reason is file transfer; part of it is how the Web deals with non-alphanumeric characters.

► *Macintosh.* Macs will let you use upper- and lowercase in a file name, and it will "remember" what you've typed. But it doesn't internally distinguish two names spelled identically with different capitalization. So "Frame.html" and "frame.html" are the same file to a Macintosh system.

▶ *Windows 95 and NT.* Long file names are great, but if you copy a file to a floppy disk, through older FTP software, or over many kinds of network servers or systems, the names will get rewritten from up to 256 upper- and lowercase characters to just the old DOS style. This often happens when copying from a Mac to a PC through a DOS-formatted floppy. There's no good way around this but to use our "safest bet" above.

▶ *Unix.* Unix is the most consistent and flexible, allowing virtually any character in any name, and never modifying a file name no matter how it's received or transmitted. You can name a file "!$*&#$*&(@#$&" and spend 20 minutes trying to rename it to something sensible.

BIG- AND LITTLE-ENDIAN. As we told you back in "TIFF" in Chapter 4, *File Formats*, there are different ways to store data on different processors—these methods are called "big-endian" and "little-endian." Some older Unix and PC hackers will tell you that it matters, but the truth is that virtually all of today's image-editing software doesn't care. It uses a little cleverness to make sure all the bytes come out in the right order. And the Web itself is byte-at-a-time, so there's no problem with different kinds of machines accepting image formats in the right order.

WELCOME TO THE WORLD

The Web is a remarkable medium, but trying to appeal to the least common denominator can be an ongoing and tiring effort. Choose your battles well, though: There's nothing like completing a project only to find that you have to redo every image on a site because of palette conflicts—or the CEO's old low-bit-depth video display. Our final piece of advice: Save your originals (in RGB mode, if possible); you'll be visiting them again to create new versions of the same images in the future.

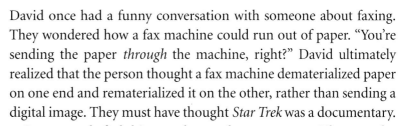

12 COLOR OUTPUT

MATCHING INPUT TO OUTPUT

David once had a funny conversation with someone about faxing. They wondered how a fax machine could run out of paper. "You're sending the paper *through* the machine, right?" David ultimately realized that the person thought a fax machine dematerialized paper on one end and rematerialized it on the other, rather than sending a digital image. They must have thought *Star Trek* was a documentary.

Some people feel this way about color output, too. They wonder how the color gets out of the monitor onto paper or film. The answer: Very carefully.

This book focuses on halftones and offset printing, but we want to include useful advice on preparation for color output, such as from film recorders, cheap color printers, and proofing devices. The choices are mostly about color and resolution.

Color output comes in two main forms: film recording, which is RGB output to photographic negatives or slide film; and CMY, CMYK, and other multicolor output to a variety of devices that transfer ink, dye, wax, or toner onto a paper or other substrate.

RGB output is the simpler of the two, because you can use your screen as a better guide to which colors will reproduce best. Output to paper or a substrate can be continuous-tone, halftone, or dithered color; but any of these methods combines some of the problems of offset printing with some of the advantages of matching the results better to your screen.

FILM RECORDING

Film recorders (also called slide recorders and film writers) create an image on very high-resolution, compact CRTs (cathode-ray tubes)—in other words, they make a picture on a tiny TV. But where a normal television can only display a few hundred pixels vertically and a computer monitor can do from, say, 400 to 1,000 pixels from top to bottom, film recorders use CRTs that can display up to 16,384 lines of pixels.

Typically, a film recorder has a set of three colored filters, and it does one pass each for red, green, and blue exposures; the CRT displays just grayscale, and the filters rotate into place for each different color exposure.

WHAT IT'S USED FOR

Film recording is used for a lot of different purposes, from creating slides for projection to writing large-format film—as big as 8 by 10 inches—that gets used to create billboard-sized prints. Optical duplication of film often loses color fidelity and introduces other problems like reduced sharpness; digital duplication is an alternative that's superior to the older techniques.

We know of one project that couldn't have been completed as well any other way. Nancy Skolos and Tom Wedell, Boston designers, used a Kodak Premier image-editing system to create an incredible series of digital composites for a book about guitars made by a California artisan. (The Premier system could scan and write out 8-by-10-inch film at a time when a Mac IIfx could barely rotate a 20 Mb image file.) The few dozen final pieces were output at 8 by 10 inches as transparencies, sent to Asia, and color-separated and printed at a high screen frequency.

Although the designers could have used digital files as the last step, the files would have been hundreds of megabytes each—an unmanageable size then and now—and wouldn't have preserved the range of tones they were able to get out of a deep bit-depth editing system. The high-end digital color separation used at the Asian printing plant also helped keep the photographic quality intact.

Film recording is used at the high end as part of multimillion-dollar film-editing systems that can read in an entire feature film, do correction and editing, and write the new version back out. When a movie is re-released as "digitally remastered," that's what they're doing—scanning hundreds of thousands of frames and later writing them all back out. The joy of digital remastering is that once you have it all in digital form, you can store it forever without film stock fading or getting scratches—or spontaneously combusting.

MATCHING COLOR

Because you're going from RGB to RGB, if you can get your monitor configured correctly, you have an excellent chance to see on screen a close approximation of what the slide or negative will look like. As we discussed in Chapter 8, *Color*, there are different gammas and temperatures you can set on a monitor to match different viewing and output conditions. Your service bureau or film recorder manual will have recommendations on setting up Photoshop and other programs, or how to load the correct color management profiles to achieve the best match. This means that you can predict results by looking at how much you like a scan or corrected image when you look at it on screen.

Most recorders support greater than 8-bit color, even though this is used to better create smooth gradients or render colors that are more difficult to express in RGB values than truly expanding tonal range. Some film recorder drivers and software can take PostScript or vector input and render it, and they can often take advantage of this bigger bit space to produce imperceptible steps in blends.

Film recorders use a color look-up table (LUT) to match colors specified in an RGB colorspace on the computer with the corresponding color necessary to match that color on film. These LUTs are highly film-specific and you can get different results depending on the film you choose; we explain more about film and color issues in Chapter 14, *Photo CD*.

FILM TYPE

Just as the difference between a flutist and a flautist is about money, so the difference between a slide recorder and a film recorder is typically about marketing language and price. Slide recorders take positive slide film, while units marketed as film recorders will often take both negative print film and positive slide film. Slide film usually requires some masking space for the slide mounts, reducing the overall imaging area; this varies by writer, and you should ask your service bureau about this limitation.

You would want to use slide film when creating presentations that will later be projected, or for creating positive images for color separation. As we note above, sometimes circumstances demand film instead of the digital file. This can often give you more control because you're providing an objective, "real-world" color scheme that the color separators can match by looking at the film you wrote out as their reference.

Film negatives (color reversal film) can be used to make photographic prints. The density of negative film is much lower—as much as $\frac{1}{30}$ of positive film—and can require a lot more tweaking to get what you want.

RESOLUTION

Every film recorder has a slightly different imaging area, but they're virtually always measured in units of 1,024 lines, or 1K; a recorder that can do 4,096 lines of resolutions is a 4K scanner, and so forth. In a film recorder, this measurement is always the longer side, or the width when outputting to 35 mm. So a 4K scanner might be able to image about 3K (3,072) pixels high.

This varies from scanner to scanner, so we've assembled a table showing several popular models from different manufacturers for reference (see Table 12-1). For 35 mm film, the aspect ratio—long to short side—is 3:2, while other formats are measured 4:3. In the table, we list the highest possible resolution in the second dimension, which is higher when a writer can expose larger-format films.

Different models can handle film ranging from 35 mm up to

8 by 10 inches. The highest-resolution devices are often used to write the same density of information to larger film. It's rare that you would need to write more than 4K resolution to 35 mm, but you might need 16K when recording on 8-by-10 film. If you output at 4K to 35mm, you're writing an effective 3,000 pixels per inch (ppi); 16K for 8 by 10 is only 1,650 ppi.

SIZING

Bitmaps are the business of film recorders, and for the simplest and easiest results, you need to create your artwork to the exact pixel dimensions that the device supports for a given resolution. You can rely on intermediate software to do some processing, but this means the software is either downsampling or interpolating to make a file smaller or bigger, and you might as well control the final result.

You can make a file exactly half the size of the resolution you want to write to in order to keep file size small, and high-end film recorders will do a good job of creating intermediate tones. This doesn't add detail, but it can make an image seem a little richer or deeper without increasing film size by a factor of four.

POSTSCRIPT OUTPUT

We remember with dismay the terrible convolutions we had to go through a few years ago to take output from a regular old DTP application like QuarkXPress or Adobe Illustrator and render the PostScript output into something the film recorder could handle. Even though PostScript was mature, the solutions for color output rendering weren't. This has all changed, though, and there are a dozen good, straightforward PostScript interpreters that either ship with film recorders or have specific settings for all models.

You still have to worry about color shifts, and solving the color fidelity problem differs from package to package and recorder to recorder. We recommend working with a service bureau to understand exactly what they want, and leaving yourself time and budget for a couple of tests before doing any large-scale projects.

PRINTING ON SUBSTRATES

The flip side of color output from film recording—where colors can be roughly matched to colors—is printing onto paper or special substrates, where all on-screen, emitted colors have to be converted to their reflective counterparts, and where you face many of the same issues as in printing offset process colors.

Color printing can simulate process color output and be used for proofing. If well calibrated and part of a color-managed system, it can save you money by allowing you to get a glimpse of what might be—and let you fix it before thousands of copies have rolled off a press (see Chapter 8, *Color*).

TABLE 12-1
Common film recorders and their maximum heights by pixel

Maximum pixels high by device	2K 2,048	3K[1] 3,072	4K 4,096	6K 6,144[1]	8K 8,192	16K 16,384
Agfa						
FotoColor and ProSlide 35	1,366		2,732			
PCR II Plus	1,536		3,072			
Matrix						
Alto	1,536		3,072		6,144	12,288
Lasergraphics						
Mark II	1,366		2,732			
Mark III			2,731		5,462	
Mark V			3,362		6,724	
Mark VI			3,362		6,724	13,448
Management Graphics Inc.						
Solitaire 16xps and Gemini	2,048		4,096		8,192	16,384
Sapphire Precision and Opal	1,366	2,048	2,732			
Sapphire Pro	1,366	2,048	2,732	4,096	5,464	
Opal Plus	1,536	2,304	3,072	4,608	6,144	
Opal 100		2,048	2,732			
Polaroid						
Digital Palette	1,365		2,730			

[1]3K and 6K are included by Management Graphics to match standard Photo CD resolution of Base*4 and Base*16; see Chapter 14, *Photo CD*, for more details on these sizes.

Making photograph-like output has been pushed heavily by manufacturers selling inexpensive ink-jet printers, from low-end devices like the Apple Color StyleWriter and dozens of similar devices to relatively cheap six-color printers, such as Hewlett-Packard's PhotoSmart device. The examples you see in ads and on television are often more compelling than your own output unless you carefully calibrate and test your printer.

Color printers divide into two major areas: continuous tone and patterned output. Currently, dye sublimation is the only reasonable example of continuous-tone color printing; for reasons of cost and longevity of the final printed piece, patterned output—dithered and halftone solutions—abound, including ink, toner, wax, and dye methods.

CONTINUOUS TONE

Although continuous-tone printers in the form of dye-sublimation output have relatively low resolutions (300 or 600 dpi) and a high per-piece price ($3 to $9 per sheet), they're the closest thing you can get out of a printer that looks like an actual photograph. No halftoning or dithering is involved because each printed dot can have a different tonal value.

Dye sublimation (or dye sub) uses a dye-covered ribbon, which tiny thermal pinpoints—like the individual jet heads on an ink-jet printer—heat to different temperatures to transfer varying amounts of dye onto an expensive coated substrate. The dye is sublimated onto the paper—it goes from solid dye to gas without hitting a liquid phase. The intense heat fixes the gas onto the substrate.

The costs of the dye ribbons and substrates are still high. The dye ribbons are one-time use, with a full sheet of dye for each color used for each print. (It's fascinating to look at a used-up ribbon; it's the negative of every image, color by color.)

Several dye-sub devices now can switch between wax or dye so you can get the best of both worlds—proofing cheaply on wax until you reach a final stage, when you switch to dye for the most accurate color. Wax ribbons are cheaper, but the colors aren't as pure and the output is patterned, not continuous tone; see "Patterned," below.

GAMUT AND PROFILES. Dye sub has a wider gamut than other color printing because it has purer colorants (the substances making up the colors) and it can print much higher saturations of color. High resolution isn't needed for the same reason; you don't need a density of dots to produce different colors the way you do with dithering (see "Patterned," below, for more on that).

You can use color-management profiles of dye-sub devices and produce proofs that have the restricted gamut of different offset printing methods. For instance, Imation's Rainbow proofer is a standard output profile in virtually every page-layout program and color management system.

DRAWBACKS. Dye sublimation has a few major downsides that make it appropriate for proofing, but not so great as a final output device. Dye-sub printing is highly susceptible to slight atmospheric changes in humidity and temperature, meaning that prints made at different times can have different colors fixed in them. In proofing environments, it's important to keep this in mind.

Although advances have been made, the substrates and dyes have a relative short life span, possibly less than a decade in perfect conditions. Lightfastness is a real problem; in under six months, an exposed print can be ruined. Different UV-protective coatings are available—and some are now part of the output pass—but these affect color fidelity.

PATTERNED

All dot-based output methods that use CMY and other colors have one thing in common: to make different colors, they use combinations of three to six single-color dots. They use collections of these dots to simulate the thousands of colors typically found in offset process-color printing. It's called *dithering* when it's done on the cheap or *stochastic* when it's done expensively. (For more on how this works, see Chapter 22, *Stochastic Screening*.)

This is a broad category of printer, and they range from 300 dpi to 1,800 dpi. The lower-resolution devices have to use patterned dithers to simulate halftoning. The higher-resolution devices can use a combination of techniques to produce halftone spots. (If this is a foreign language to you, the whole second part of the book is devoted to halftones and their alternatives, and you might want to jump ahead and come back to this part of the chapter later.)

Patterned-output devices include those that spray or burst ink onto a page, those that melt dyes and waxes, and those that use powdered or liquid toner. Each of these has different advantages of speed, cost, color fidelity, and reproduction. There are a few things you can do to ensure a reasonably accurate path from your computer to one of these printers, whether you're proofing for prepress or producing final pieces for distribution.

TYPES. Here's a brief rundown of the different kinds of patterned output available.

▶ *Ink jet and bubble jet.* Using replaceable ink cartridges or reservoirs, ink-jet and bubble-jet devices range from less than $200 to more than $50,000. The cheapest devices produce one or two pages per minute. The most expensive, like the Scitex Iris drum-based ink jets, can take dozens of minutes to produce a poster-sized art print. Even cheap jet printers can have 600- or 1,200-dpi resolution, while the top-of-the-line printers go up to effective resolutions of 1,800 dpi by using several sizes of printer dots. Some new, cheap devices (less than $500) use black and yellow plus a light and dark cyan and magenta for a total of six colors. The four cyan and magenta inks help create more realistic Caucasian flesh tones without having to increase resolution.

▶ *Phase change.* Printers that heat up solid ink just long enough to push a jot onto paper are called phase-change printers. The ink comes in sticks that get inserted into uniquely shaped holes to avoid the horrible accident of mixing colors. Tektronix pioneered this technology with its Phaser printer that does 300-dpi CMYK printing. Resolution is typically 300 or 600 dpi.

- ▸ *Toner.* The Canon Color Laser Copier (CLC) is the old-timer in the color photocopying crowd, going back to the late '80s. With a PostScript RIP—like the Electronics for Imaging (EFI) Fiery— and an Ethernet card, a color photocopier can be a network workhorse. The resolution on these copiers is often 400 dpi or lower.

- ▸ *Liquid toner/ink.* The Indigo Eprint is a beast on its own that uses a fast-drying, liquid toner (they call it ElectroInk) that allows it to act like a printing press but individually image each page like a laser printer. Resolution is up to 821 dpi, and they claim 200-lpi screens using their own halftoning technology. Its key advantage is that there's no make-ready like that needed for offset printing—you stick PostScript in one end and finished printed pieces come out the other. They're almost indistinguishable from commercial printing and getting better all the time. (If you rub a piece of Eprint output, it will feel just a little waxy, like an off-season cucumber at a grocery store.)

DITHERS. The best devices give you some choice on how the dithering or halftone creation is done. Some offer different draft modes or different types of output. Others come with, or can work with, a software PostScript interpreter. For instance, the Epson ink-jet printers, which can do from a few hundred to over a thousand dots per inch, work with a $90 product from Birmy that uses Adobe's Brilliant Screens stochastic software algorithms to create the dithering for the printer. (See also Chapter 22, *Stochastic Screening.*)

PAPER. A critical factor in getting good output from any of these devices is using the right substrate or paper. Many of them support dozens of papers, but require individual settings even when you're working on the image to get the right results. Color management can be a key aspect of getting this part of the workflow right.

COLOR. Each device has its own unique gamut and gamma, but many image-editing programs and color management systems have

custom, predefined curves already in the system. You'll need to tweak these to match individual devices, but you can, in many cases, get the same kind of accuracy in an on-screen preview to a color printer that you can when aiming for an offset press.

PROOFING. Any device costing more than $500 has targets, profiles, and other bits and pieces necessary to use it to proof output intended for offset color printing. Anything costing less than $500 typically is useful only for final pieces or photograph-like output for home use. The Hewlett-Packard PhotoSmart printer, for instance, is aimed squarely at the consumer market that wants to do scans, modify them a bit, and produce greeting cards or prints suitable for framing. (Just watch out for water- and lightfastness.)

The more expensive devices, even in the $750 to $1,000 range, will either come with profiles or supply software and calibration targets for building profiles. Many devices already have profiles as part of Kodak CMS or Apple's ColorSync software.

SPOT GAIN. We introduce this concept later in the book, in Chapter 19, *Setting Your Screens.* But let's just note here that the kinds of spot gain you see on printing presses aren't applicable to color printers. Spot gain occurs throughout the graphic arts production process, from creating negatives to ink spreading on paper on press.

With color printers, spot gain or printer dot spread is enormously reduced because the amounts of ink or toner are highly controlled. Paper is a major factor in how well toner or ink gets laid down, as you might guess. The smoother the paper or more highly coated, the less spatter, spread, or absorption, and the more accurately the printer reproduces an image.

An offset press might add 15 to 35 percent spot gain depending on the factors involved, while a color output device printing on smooth paper might add 5 to 15 percent. Of course, under worst-case circumstances, with an ink-jet printer and very porous, uncoated art paper, you could see the same spot gain as on a press.

PROOF POSITIVE

Our head swims when we think about the number of color output options we have these days. Our options used to be bounded by cost: we just couldn't afford to own or use devices like film recorders or dye-sub printers. With technology's relentless push, this equipment is now near our hands—which are never idle—and we spend more time figuring out how to get from screen to printer than what we're going to do with it once we succeed.

13 OCR

If a client, colleague, or boss has ever given you text that was once in a computer but now is just a pile of paper, you've probably sworn at the ceiling. Why retype something that was once digital? Shouldn't there be a way for a computer to recognize its own and turn it right back into text? Yes, there should be—and there is.

Optical character recognition (OCR) is the rubric for a variety of software techniques that analyze a scan of printed text and turn it into letters, words, and sentences. A computer has to work hard to do the analysis, and it's only in the last decade—as PCs have become really powerful—that OCR has become less hype and more truth as a real desktop solution.

In this chapter we take a quick romp through OCR, how it works, and what you can to do to improve your results.

HOW IT DO WHAT IT DO

Why is OCR so difficult? Can't the computer just see the words? The answer, in a word, is No. Human beings have specialized parts of the brain that identify textures, shape, color, and distance as separate characteristics; these systems help us to look at a tree and know it's a tree, or look at a page of type and read it. A computer, however, can't distinguish between a scan of a page of text and a scan of a photograph. It's all just a bunch of little dots, or samples, saved in the computer as zeros and ones.

However, specialized OCR programs can look through a scanned page and *recognize* characters on it, one letter at a time. There are two techniques for doing this: pattern matching and feature extraction. Then, in both techniques, a program can use context checking to ensure that it has chosen words or phrases that make sense.

PATTERN MATCHING

OCR programs that use *pattern matching* loosely compare each character to a file of stored bitmaps of standard typefaces and sizes. If it has a large library of stored characters, there's a reasonable chance that the program will choose a correct match. However, it might take a while to check each letter because it can never find an exact bitmap match; the software has to use techniques to find similar matches, often trying different versions of the same character.

Older OCR software couldn't automatically recognize different fonts, and had to be told whether it was reading Helvetica or Courier or Bodoni. Newer versions have the smarts to recognize several different fonts on the same page.

Not all matches are made in heaven, though, and you can *train* the OCR software to recognize letters and symbols that it couldn't identify using its built-in patterns. Some software lets you scan in a page of text and identify every character to define a new font. Others will do their best with their own know-how and then let you identify just the characters it can't figure out (see Figure 13-1).

FEATURE EXTRACTION

Another method for performing OCR is *feature extraction*. In this system, each character gets broken down into various features of the character: diagonal lines, horizontal lines, curves, and so on. The program then matches these features to its understanding of what characters look like. If it sees two vertical lines connected by a horizontal bar in the middle, it figures that it's probably looking at an H.

FIGURE 13-1
OmniPage Pro's
training window

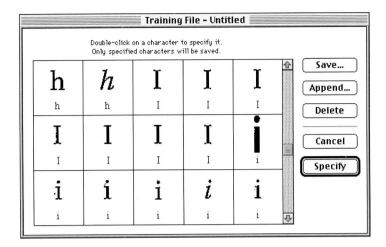

The nice thing about feature extraction is that it can recognize a number of different fonts because their basic makeup is so similar. That is, an "s" in one font is pretty similar to an "s" in another font. However, throw in a font with a really bizarre form, and the program chokes.

CONTEXT CHECKING

Most OCR programs try to do some context checking to double-check that their choices for combinations of letters—rather than just individual ones—are in the ballpark. For example, if a letter suddenly appears in the middle of a bunch of numbers, the program might reconsider its choice. Or, if the program thinks it's seeing a "ck" at the beginning of a word, it might be trained to know that it's more likely that the two letters are "ch."

Context checking can also include spelling and grammar checkers, which confirm that the words and phrases that have been recognized really make sense together. These checkers are usually language-specific, to take into account peculiarities in each tongue.

More sophisticated programs can tie in feature extraction and spelling checkers. If the OCR program identifies the word "loy," but it knows that "log" is a legitimate word and that both "g" and "y" look similar, it can drop in the right word without user intervention.

TIPS

OCR *is* rocket science, but getting the right scan and setting up the OCR software correctly is a walk in the park if you know the issues. Below, we've identified some of the most common problems and their solutions, to help you get the best results.

RESOLUTION. Virtually all OCR software expects to recognize standard type point sizes at 300 spi. Scanning at any other resolution makes the software work harder with worse results. Feature recognition software is more flexible, but it's still thinking about normal default type sizes, like 10, 12, 14, and 18 points.

The exception is for type below 10 points. You might consider scanning at 400 spi or even higher because the software is going to have to do a lot of work regardless; you might as well give it enough data to make better decisions.

Don't scan at a resolution that's higher than the optical resolution of your device.

LINE ART VERSUS GRAYSCALE. If the text you're scanning is in good shape, then the primary advantage to passing an OCR program a grayscale file instead of line art is that the OCR software can make the threshold decision itself. (Degraded text, such as a multiple-generation photocopy or low-resolution fax, can be handled better as grayscale images by some scanning software, such as OmniPage Professional.) Thresholding turns a grayscale image into line art by picking a gray value above which every tone goes to black and below which they all turn to white.

In some tests we did, the difference of a few percentage points in thresholding at scan time could cause documents to be unprocessable in the OCR software. However, using a grayscale file results in source art that's eight times as large—about 8 Mb for an 8.5-by-11-inch page at 300 dpi.

Clearly, if you're doing a lot of scanning, you have to test and find the optimum threshold percentage for the work you're doing; for small quantities, grayscale may be OK.

WINDOWING/ZONING. Picture a typical magazine page. There are perhaps a few columns of text, a photograph, maybe an illustration, and a heading. If you scan that page and process it with an OCR program, the program not only has to figure out where and what the text is, but it needs to figure out in what order the text flows, and so on. Some programs are very smart at this (see Figure 13-2) and some are...well, let's be polite and just say they *aren't* so smart.

FIGURE 13-2

Zone recognition

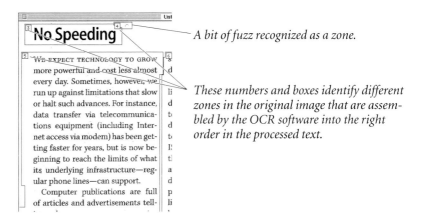

A bit of fuzz recognized as a zone.

These numbers and boxes identify different zones in the original image that are assembled by the OCR software into the right order in the processed text.

The key is to create zones or windows on the scanned page that the program can follow. One zone might be a graphic image that can be left alone, another zone might be the first column of text, then another column, and so on. Again, some programs can create these zones for you, and others let you do it yourself. Many programs can now not only identify graphics, but separate them out and save them as separate page elements automatically.

FORMATTING. If the text you're OCRing is formatted—such as with bold, italic, first-line indent, and so on—your OCR program may or may not be able to figure that out (see Figure 13-3). Therefore, you may either lose the formatting altogether or the program may not even be able to figure out what those letters are. An italic "a" is very different from a normal "a," and a "y" with an underscore looks pretty weird to an OCR program. If you have to do this sort of scanning, make sure your program can handle it well. Some programs allow you to turn off style recognition so it concentrates on just finding the right letters rather than the right fonts or styles.

No Speeding

WE EXPE**R**T TECHNOLOGY TO GROW
more powerful and cost less almost
every day. Sometimes, however, we
run up against limitations that slow

*Note just one small error
in this word (it should be
"expect") alongside almost
perfect recognition of
placement and style.*

STRAIGHTEN THAT SCAN. Many OCR programs have a lot of difficulty with text that has been scanned at an angle. In crooked scans, feature-extraction programs think that horizontal lines are diagonal lines, and pattern-matching programs just go nuts. Scanning the page straight is important to getting good results. However, there are tools you can purchase or make that help you keep the scanner and page parallel to one another. Some software packages will "autostraighten" the text—it recognizes that the type is tilted and puts it level. But image quality generally degrades with rotation, making character recognition more difficult, so it's better to do it right at scan time.

TRANSLUCENT PAPER. If you try to scan and OCR a page on semi-translucent paper, such as newsprint, you may have a helluva time. Characters from the back side show through and cause all sorts of havoc. One way you can sometimes get around this is by placing a piece of black paper behind the page when you scan it. Then, you can also bump up the scan's contrast somewhat to make the faint back-characters fade away (see "Linear Correction" in Chapter 7, *Tonal Correction*).

WORKFLOW

As with every scanning task, before settling on a product you should identify your workflow: where the scan's being done, how to correct the text, what formats it'll output to, and whether you need the look and feel of the original page.

not very lossy (see Chapter 10, *Compression*). Color fidelity is an issue when you're using resolutions above Base. Here's how Photo CD's compression scheme works.

We've talked repeatedly about how the human eye perceives variations in luminosity—differences from light to dark—more readily than differences in color. And just like the LAB colorspace that Photoshop supports, Photo CD's PhotoYCC colorspace uses luminosity as its main component, with two separate color channels (see Chapter 8, *Color*). Then, instead of remembering all three channels of the image at every resolution, Photo CD retains all the luminosity information and throws away almost 60 percent of the color information for the resolutions above Base.

That means that the resolutions above Base in each image pack contain progressively less color information. This sounds kind of dangerous, but the way Kodak does it is very clever. The biggest problem is that colors don't show as much variation and can seem flat in the highest-resolution images.

If you *really* care about color fidelity in an image, you should be careful about using the higher resolutions from Photo CD. We're not going to say don't use them, because we've seen some really spectacular images come out of the Photo CD system, but this drawback is something to be aware of.

ADJUSTING FOR OUTPUT

All the issues we've discussed throughout this part of the book, such as sharpening and tonal correction, apply to Photo CD images as well. A Photo CD image is similar to a raw, uncorrected scan you'd get off a good scanner. However, there are a few differences.

The Photo CD workstation handles the overall tonal balance for you if the SBA is turned on. Because Photo CD was originally geared for TV display, the image's saturation is boosted, and the tonal range is shifted to look good on a television screen. You may need to compensate by decreasing saturation a bit and adjusting the tonal range to compensate, or have the service bureau turn off or reduce the amount that the SBA is doing.

Photo CD images are not sharpened at all, so you'll need to take that step before placing images in your publications.

SINGLE AND MULTISESSION

Just because you can put more than 100 images on a disk doesn't mean you have to wait until you have that many images to make a Photo CD. If you put only a single roll of 36 exposures on a disk, you can go back and put more on later. That's because the PIW can write to the disk on more than one occasion or *session*.

Note that the overhead for each session's directories takes up space on the disk—about 13 to 15 Mb per session! Each session decreases your storage by about five images.

You need a multisession CD-ROM drive to read anything beyond the first session, but virtually every CD-ROM sold since 1993 supports multiple sessions. If you have older equipment and are really concerned about this, you should check whether your CD-ROM is an XA (eXtended Architecture) or a Photo CD-branded compatible drive. If it is either of those, no problems; if not, time to upgrade. You can also visit Kodak's Web site, where it occasionally updates a long list of which drive mechanisms support multisession Photo CDs.

ACCESSING IMAGES

As we said, Kodak licenses a tool kit for software developers to incorporate support for Photo CD within applications or utilities. Most major applications let you access Photo CD image packs right through the File menu's Open, Import, or Place item, but Kodak has its own Photoshop plug-in, which has a few more bells and whistles than the standard Open item. Also, with the right combination of Macintosh software, you can access Photo CD images from any program. (See Chapters 31 to 33 for application-specific support in programs like QuarkXPress and CorelPhoto-Paint.)

KODAK PHOTOSHOP ACQUIRE MODULE

Photoshop's built-in support lets you access the image from the Open dialog box, where you can then select resolution and color-management information (see Chapter 8, *Color*, for more on color management and Photo CD). However, Kodak also has a free acquire module that lets you select cropping, sharpening, and tonal balancing options (see Figure 14-1).

MAC OS

FIGURE 14-1
Kodak's Photoshop
Acquire module

If you've got a Macintosh with at least System 7.0, QuickTime 1.5, and the CD-ROM 4.0.1 drivers installed, all kinds of cool things

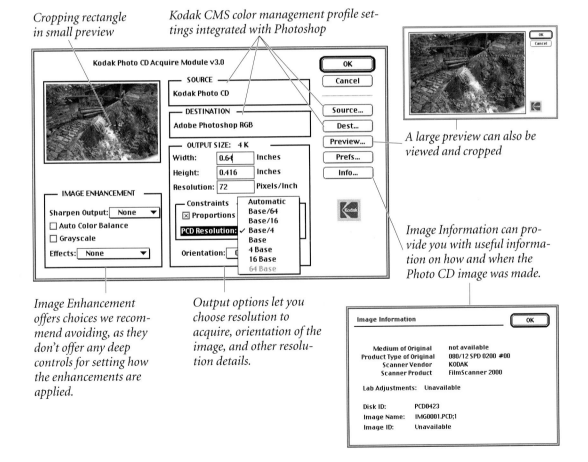

FIGURE 14-1
Kodak's Photoshop Acquire module

Cropping rectangle in small preview

Kodak CMS color management profile settings integrated with Photoshop

A large preview can also be viewed and cropped

Image Information can provide you with useful information on how and when the Photo CD image was made.

Image Enhancement offers choices we recommend avoiding, as they don't offer any deep controls for setting how the enhancements are applied.

Output options let you choose resolution to acquire, orientation of the image, and other resolution details.

happen. (All these version numbers are minimum configurations; if you're using later versions, like System 8.0 or QuickTime 2.5, it works even faster.)

THUMBNAILS. First, when you insert a Photo CD disk, you get a progress dialog that tells you the system is making Photo CD color icons. When it's done, you have a folder in the Photo CD's window on the desktop, called Photos. This folder, in turn, contains five (for Master) or six (for Pro) folders labeled with the picture resolutions described in Table 14-1. If you open one of those folders, you can see thumbnails of the images right in the Finder (see Figure 14-2).

FIGURE 14-2
Photo CD in the Macintosh Finder with QuickTime and the new CD-ROM software

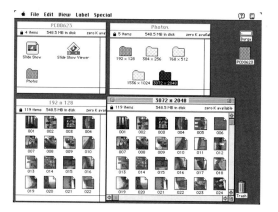

SLIDE SHOW. The next cool thing that you'll notice is the Slide Show file and application. Like the Photos folder, these don't really exist on the disk, but the Macintosh shows them to you just as though they did. If you double-click on the Slide Show icon, a window appears and lets you run through the images one at a time by clicking on buttons (see Figure 14-3). Slide Show works just like the standard QuickTime Movie Player, except it uses still images.

You can also automatically load the image you're looking at in Slide Show into a program using the View or View As items from the menus, or by double-clicking on the image.

APPLICATION SUPPORT. Perhaps the greatest feature of having the newer versions of system software and QuickTime is that they let

FIGURE 14-3
Slide Show

Basic Movie Player controls: play/pause, slide to specific image, fast rewind, and fast forward.

you open Photo CD files from within any application. Even if the program doesn't inherently support Photo CD itself, it can open the Photo CD images because the system fools the program into thinking that it's looking at PICT files. This trick also lets you drag any file from the Photos folder to another disk. The Finder acquires just that resolution and copies the file to your disk with a preview icon.

You can quickly make a desktop image in Mac OS 8 by dragging one of these PICTs to your hard drive, and opening the Desktop Pictures control panel. Select the Photo CD image that's been turned into a PICT and you get an instant desktop photo (see Figure 14-4.)

Once again, however, we typically like to open the image in Photoshop first and make our modifications. Then we save it as a TIFF image before we bring it into another program. But just to know that you *can* bring a picture in directly is a good thing, in our books.

PHOTO CD ACCESS PLUS

It's hard to imagine you'd be reading this book if you didn't have some image-editing program (like Photoshop), and most likely it's one that supports Photo CD directly. If you don't have one or, better yet, you want to be able to have people on a number of workstations processing images without the cost of an image-editing program for each machine, Photo CD Access Plus is an option.

FIGURE 14-4
Mac OS 8's Desktop
Pictures control panel

For less than $100, you can read any Photo CD image at any res-
olution; crop it, rotate it, downsample it, change its mode, or make
linear (or "bad") tonal adjustments on it; and then save it as TIFF,
PICT, BMP, EPS, or FlashPix (see Chapter 4, *File Formats*). This
isn't a lot of functionality, but you can batch process and export
images, and in a production environment—or for a kid's
machine—it might be a good tool.

WEB PLUG-IN

You can even view Photo CD images over the Web if you're using a
Java-enabled browser—or should we say, "browser that can use Java
and you've decided to turn Java on"? Kodak released a few free good-
ies for Web site developers that lets them put Photo CD images in
their image pack format right on a Web site. The Java applet that you
need in order to view these images is automatically downloaded by
your browser when you visit one of these sites. The controls show
you a small version of the Photo CD image, and let you pan, zoom,
rotate, and swoop over Manhattan. Well, not that last thing.

WHY USE IT?

So finally we get to the good stuff: How Photo CD can make your
life happier and your business more prosperous. Photo CD technology has a number of advantages over other forms of scanning,
including desktop scans or even drum scans. With Photo CD you

can get scans that approach the quality you get from drum scanners, but for only a couple of bucks an image. You also save money on storage.

COST AND QUALITY. Photo CD scans cost a *lot* less than any comparable scan. For a 35-mm negative, you could easily pay between $10 and $30 for a typical CCD scan, or $40 to $200 for a drum scan. On the other hand, one high-end, professional photofinisher we know of in Boston charges $5 per image for a calibrated and tweaked Photo CD scan. And you can get very good Photo CD scans for $1 to $2. Some photofinishers are now charging as little as 90 cents per image. (Pro Photo CD scans of larger formats can cost a bit more, in the $20 to $30 range.)

If the quality of a $2 scan is almost as good as a $100 scan, which would you prefer? As we noted earlier, you start to lose color fidelity in the higher-resolution images. But in many cases, the loss of color isn't noticeable on an offset press. And although early Photo CD scanners had a density of just 2.8D, the current generation are 3.3D—at or above the range you'll find in most film.

PERMANENCE. Kodak claims that its Photo CD–branded disc media will last 200 years without data degradation. This is a lot longer than you might expect your average floppy or even hard drive to survive. Of course, one hopes that CD-ROM technology is still usable in a decade, much less two centuries. The real advantage is that you can archive essentially "forever," and easily copy the image packs off onto the new permanent media—like writable DVD—whenever that appears on the scene.

SPEED OF ACCESS. One other great thing about Photo CD is that the technology stores a number of resolutions in one image pack. That means that you can open the image at just the resolution you need. If you only want a little preview or for-position-only image, you can import one at Base/16. That's much faster than opening the full-page high-resolution scan, and then downsampling to the size you need.

Also, because the images are stored together and can be quickly previewed, you save a lot of time in reviewing images for use. You can even use image database programs such as ImageAXS or Extensis Portfolio to keep track of multiple CDs.

NETWORK ACCESS. Because of the way Photo CD images are stored, you can access the pictures very quickly over a network. To see a thumbnail of a TIFF, for instance, your computer has to pull over the entire file. With Photo CD, it can pull over just a low-resolution image. Then, you can acquire the compressed, high-resolution image and let it decompress on your computer, saving even more time. Now, if you put six 100-disk jukeboxes (all SCSI-chained together) on your network, you could have more than a terabyte (a million million bytes) of images at your fingertips....

WHAT, ME WORRY?

If you're like us, when anyone talks for this long about how good something is, you get nervous. Well, it's true; Photo CD is not the answer to all of life's questions. It may not even be the answer to your image needs. But it might prove to have enough utility and quality to make it another weapon in your desktop publishing arsenal.

PART 2
HALFTONES

15 DOTS, SPOTS, AND HALFTONES

HOW HALFTONES WORK

When you look at a book of Georgia O'Keeffe prints, your first thought—unless you're us—isn't, "Look how well they reproduced those colors!" It's what we think about all the time, however: How colors and tones are represented on a printed page using halftones.

No printing press—or ink-jet or laser printer—can reproduce different tones; they can only print shapes in one solid color at a time. If you assemble equipment or toner cartridges together, presses and printers can lay down two, four, six, or more colors onto the same piece of paper—but still just one at a time. That is, they might be able to print cyan, yellow, magenta, and black, but they can't directly reproduce the different shades of gray or gradations in color that you see in a photograph. That's where halftones come in.

Halftones are used in virtually every piece of printed material, and when they're done well, you don't even notice them. When you're looking at the O'Keeffe book, you may see colors, but those hues and tones aren't what they appear to be.

So what are you looking at?

THE SPOT'S THE THING

Lithographers figured out in the late 19th century that they could create a tint of a colored ink by breaking the color down into a whole bunch of little spots. They could make gray, for instance, by printing small black spots really close to each other. Our brain tries to make order out of chaos by telling us we're seeing a tone instead of black spots.

This process of breaking a gray image up into black spots is called halftoning. Figure 15-1 shows an everyday halftone of a photograph, with a blown-up section showing the halftone spots.

FIGURE 15-1
A halftoned photograph

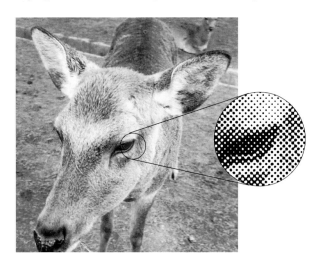

PHOTOGRAPHIC HALFTONES

Traditionally, halftones were photomechanical reproductions. Someone put a piece of photosensitive paper behind a finely etched *screen* (originally made of glass, and later of film)—and reflected light through the photograph, which exposed the film (see Figure 15-2). The result was a pattern of evenly spaced spots of different sizes. Because of *diffraction*—the spreading of light after passing through a narrow aperture—the spots in dark areas were big (even overlapping), and the dots in light areas were small.

TINTS AND TINT PERCENTAGES

Bear in mind that this kind of halftoning wasn't just for photographs. Flat tint areas were made using the same method

FIGURE 15-2
Photographic halftoning

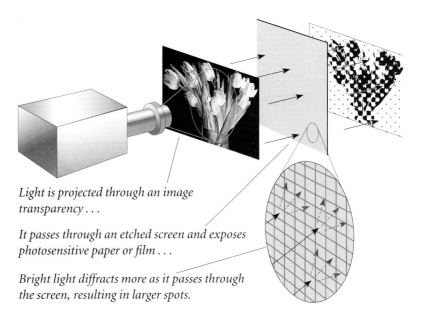

Light is projected through an image transparency . . .

It passes through an etched screen and exposes photosensitive paper or film . . .

Bright light diffracts more as it passes through the screen, resulting in larger spots.

described above, except that light was projected directly through a screen rather than passing through a photographic negative first.

Tints are referred to in percentages. A light gray tint, where the halftone spots are a tenth of their full size, is a 10-percent tint. A medium gray area might be a 50-percent tint, and in a dark gray area—let's say a 90-percent tint—the spots are 90 percent of full size. A 100-percent tint, of course, is black (see Figure 15-3).

DIGITAL HALFTONES

Photographic halftones in our part of the world are generally limited to older newspapers and magazines that haven't updated to digital techniques—but that's less and less common. Outside of North America, they're still used in quite a few places.

Computers coupled with laser printers and imagesetters are the main tools for creating halftones—though, of course, they don't use screens made of glass or plastic to make them. In order to understand how computers make halftones, we need to stop for a moment and look at how these devices make images in the first place.

FIGURE 15-3
Tint percentages

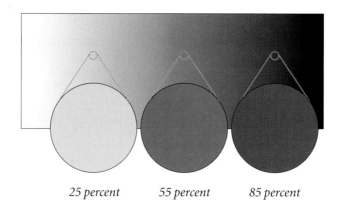

25 percent   *55 percent*   *85 percent*

DOTS

As we've talked about throughout the book so far, computers represent things in ones and zeroes: on or off. Fortunately, this corresponds to offset printing and laser output: You can either have black or not—there's no in-between. When a laser printer is creating an image, it simply turns the laser on and off—on where the paper should be white, and off where it should be black. The dots that the laser creates are so small and close together that there's no space between adjacent dots—a row of them looks exactly like a line. An imagesetter does the same thing with different effect: it uses light in the form of a laser turning on or off to expose a tiny dot on specially coated paper or film.

The dots that most desktop laser printers create are tiny. In fact, you can fit 600 of them next to each other in a single inch. That's why people call them 600-dpi (dots-per-inch) printers. Other printers (typically plain-paper output) and imagesetters (photosensitive paper and film) can create even smaller dots, as fine as 1,200, 2,400, or even several thousand dpi—dots that can be far too small for the unassisted human eye to see.

SPOTS

But how can you make halftone spots larger and smaller when a laser printer's dots are all the same size? The solution is pretty simple. The computer groups together a bunch of dots into a single halftone cell. This cell is a square grid of dots, each of which can be turned on or off. To create a dark area (a large spot), lots of the dots are turned on; to create a light area (a small spot), only a few dots are turned on (see Figure 15-4).

The important concept here is that the spacing of the halftone spots doesn't change. They're not closer together in dark areas. Only the number of dots turned on *within each cell* changes. The

FIGURE 15-4
A representation of digital halftone cells

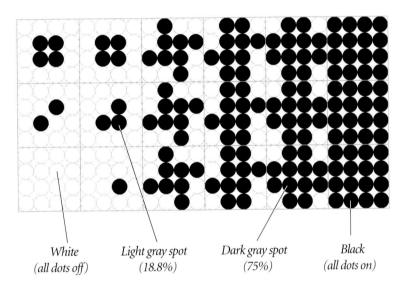

| White (all dots off) | Light gray spot (18.8%) | Dark gray spot (75%) | Black (all dots on) |

group of dots that are turned on is the halftone spot (see Figure 15-5). We'll talk more about these spots and their shapes in the next chapter. (There is a way of creating digital output without halftones that involves arrangements in space instead of changes in size; it's called *stochastic screening*; we devote Chapter 22 to this subject.)

HALFTONES, TINTS, AND SCREENS

There's one other piece of terminology that we want to clarify before we end this chapter: *screening*. We mentioned above that the etched

FIGURE 15-5
Halftone spots

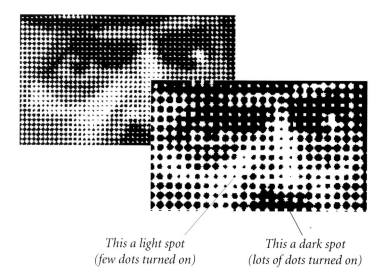

*This a light spot
(few dots turned on)*   *This a dark spot
(lots of dots turned on)*

piece of glass or film that's used to create photographic halftones is called a screen. The process of creating the halftone pattern is called screening. To confuse matters more, the pattern of dots that results from screening—the halftone pattern—is also called a screen.

The more you recognize halftones and how they're used and created, the more effective you can be in your own work. Next we look at some more details about halftoning: frequency, angle, and spot shape.

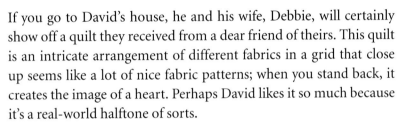

16 FREQUENCY, ANGLE, AND SPOT SHAPE

WHAT MAKES A HALFTONE

If you go to David's house, he and his wife, Debbie, will certainly show off a quilt they received from a dear friend of theirs. This quilt is an intricate arrangement of different fabrics in a grid that close up seems like a lot of nice fabric patterns; when you stand back, it creates the image of a heart. Perhaps David likes it so much because it's a real-world halftone of sorts.

As we noted in the last chapter, halftones are made up of bunches of spots, some larger and some smaller. These spots fool the eye into seeing grays and colors where only spots exist. Each spot is in a grid or *cell* made up of *printer dots*. These halftones cells are arranged in a pattern with three primary attributes: frequency, angle, and spot shape. Let's look at each of these in turn.

SCREEN FREQUENCY

Imagine eggs in an enormous egg carton. Each egg sits in its own place, with an equal distance to the eggs on the left and the right. If the egg carton were big enough, you wouldn't say it was a 6-egg carton or a 12-egg carton. Rather, you'd say there were 12 eggs per foot or 39 eggs per meter, or something like that. Each row is the same distance from the next row, so you can say that the "egg-per-foot" value (epf) is the number of rows of eggs per foot (see Figure 16-1).

FIGURE 16-1

Egg cells

Now let's look back at halftones: you've got a whole bunch of spots (eggs) that sit in rows of a big grid (egg carton). There are too many spots to count, so you simplify the problem by counting the number of spots—or rows of spots—per inch. This is called the frequency of the halftone, because it tells you how frequently spots occur within an inch.

The frequency is typically measured in lines per inch (lpi). Of course, in countries that use the metric system, it's measured in lines per centimeter (L/cm). Specifying screen frequency in lpi or L/cm confuses the issue slightly, because we're not really talking about lines here. We're actually talking about rows of spots. But if you keep that in mind, you won't go wrong.

People often talk about coarse and fine screens. The lower the screen frequency, the coarser the screen. That is, the cells are bigger and the image is rougher looking, and the dots are more visible and don't fool the eye as well. The higher the screen frequency, the finer the image, because the cells are really small (see Figure 16-2).

FIGURE 16-2

Screen frequency

20 lpi   75 lpi   130 lpi

Coarser screens are used in newspapers, because cheap newsprint can't reproduce a fine screen well; whereas exceedingly fine screens are found in books reproducing artwork printed on exquisite paper. (We talk about paper and screens in Chapter 18, *Reproducing Halftones*.)

SCREEN ANGLE

If we go back to our egg story, we see that the pattern of all those eggs not only has a frequency, but an angle, too. If you look at the eggs straight on, the rows of eggs are at an angle of zero degrees. If you turn the carton, though, the angle changes. Turn it to "1 o'clock" and the angle is at 30 degrees. Turn it to halfway between 1 and 2 o'clock, and the angle goes to 45 degrees (see Figure 16-3).

You can rotate a halftone screen almost as easily as turning an egg carton, and the angle to which you align the rows of spots is called the screen angle. A standard screen angle is 45 degrees because it's the most traditional and least noticeable—it does the best job of fooling our eye into seeing gray instead of a pattern of spots (see Figure 16-4). However, there's another good reason to change the angle of a screen: to improve color separations (see Chapter 25, *Rosettes and Moirés*).

SPOT SHAPE

The final element of halftone screens is the spot shape. Until now, we've been talking primarily about round spots. But remember that

FIGURE 16-3
Turning the
egg carton

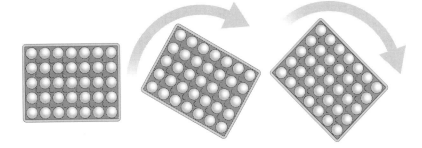

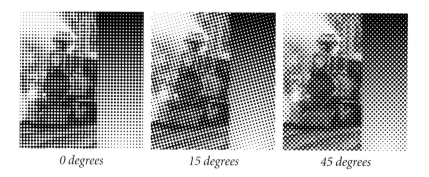

FIGURE 16-4
Halftone angles

0 degrees   *15 degrees*   *45 degrees*

these spots are made of tiny dots, and we can arrange the dots any way we want. So, our spots can be circles, squares, triangles, lines, or even little pictures of Barney the dinosaur (see Figure 16-5).

You almost never notice the shape of a halftone spot unless the screen frequency is really low—think Roy Lichtenstein paintings. (In a 10-lpi halftone, there are 10 halftone cells per inch, so you can see the shape pretty easily; in a 133-lpi screen, each cell is so tiny—$\frac{1}{133}$ inch—that you can barely see what it looks like.) However, the spot shape can make a difference in the appearance of your halftones. For example, a square spot often results in a sharper, higher-contrast look—especially in midtones—while an elliptical dot (actually a rounded-corner diamond) results in smooth transitions in graduated blends. Typically, though, you don't have to worry about spot shape unless you're trying to achieve a special effect.

EGGS-CELL-ENT

There's more you should know about spot shapes, but we put it off until Chapter 20, *The Glorious Spot*. However, we do think it's important to point out sooner rather than later that the egg-in-a-carton metaphor breaks down at this point. Do not (we repeat, do *not*) try to construct differently shaped eggs at home or in the office.

FIGURE 16-5
Spot shape

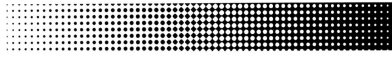

Round spot

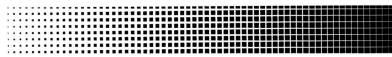

Line spot

Square spot

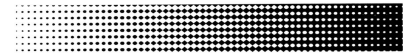

Elliptical spot

17 FREQUENCY VERSUS GRAY LEVELS

TRADE-OFFS IN DIGITAL HALFTONING

China's president visited the U.S. recently, and a picture of him ran on the cover of *The New York Times*. Glenn noticed something strange and pulled out his line-screen detector: The *Times* had accidentally run the photograph at such a high frequency that the image had a very high contrast and only a few tones in it.

In digital halftoning, there's an essential trade-off between screen frequency and gray levels: the more you have of one, the fewer of the other. In trying to achieve photographic effects, you can wind up with so few gray levels that the image looks somewhat like pop art.

Let's outline the problem first, and then take a little time to discuss why it's there and what you can do about it.

SCREEN FREQUENCY, GRAY LEVELS, AND OUTPUT RESOLUTION

Put succinctly, the halftone screen frequency has an inverse relationship to the number of gray levels possible at a given output resolution. Put more simply, the higher the screen frequency, the fewer levels of gray you can get at a given resolution. Reduce the screen frequency (or increase the output resolution), and you can get more levels of gray.

For example, on a typical 600-dpi desktop laser printer you can only get 33 different shades of gray (including black and white) in a 106-lpi halftone. If you make the halftone coarser—let's say 71 lpi, which is the lowest reasonable value for a good halftone on that printer—you can get 73 different shades of gray.

POSTERIZATION

When you don't have enough gray levels, what results is *posterization*—an obvious stair-stepping from one gray level to another, quite different, gray level—rather than a smooth transition. It's primarily a problem in graduated blends or halftones of photographs in which smooth transitions from white to black occur (see Figure 17-1). Posterization can also be an interesting special effect—but only when you want it. (In the example in the introduction, the *Times* certainly didn't want it.)

FIGURE 17-1
Posterization

SCARCITY OF DOTS

But why? Why should there be such a limitation on gray levels, when halftoning is so flexible? It's because the number of possible gray levels is determined by the number of dots in a halftone cell (see Figure 17-2). If a cell is made up of 25 dots, there are 26 possible gray levels (including white and black—all dots off and all dots on). If a cell is made up of 255 dots, there are 256 possible gray levels. The more dots per cell, the more possible gray levels.

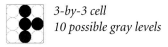

FIGURE 17-2
Dots per cell
and gray levels

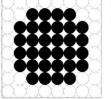

3-by-3 cell
10 possible gray levels

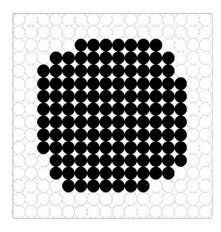

8-by-8 cell
65 possible gray levels

16-by-16 cell
257 possible gray levels

The goal, then, is to work with halftone cells that have lots of dots in them, so you have lots of available gray levels. Therein lies the essential problem of digital halftoning—there are only so many printer dots to work with. The finer the halftone screen, the fewer the number of dots there are in each halftone cell, and therefore the fewer levels of gray you have available (see Figure 17-3).

You can determine the number of dots in a single halftone cell with simple arithmetic. If you divide the resolution of the printer by the screen frequency, you get the number of dots on one side of the halftone cell. Square this number (multiply it by itself) to find the total number of dots in the cell.

For example, if you divide 300 dpi (the resolution of the printer) by 75 (the screen frequency of the halftone), you get 4. Then multiply that by itself (4 times 4) and you get 16. That's the number of

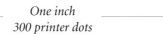

One inch
300 printer dots

4-by-4 cell
17 gray levels
75-line screen

6-by-6 cell
37 gray levels
50-line screen

10-by-10 cell
101 gray levels
30-line screen

FIGURE 17-3
Halftoning at
300 dots per inch

dots that can possibly be turned on or off in each halftone cell. That means that when five dots are turned on in that cell, you have a 31-percent gray dot; when six dots are turned on, you get a 38-percent gray dot; and so on. You can't cut a dot in half, so there's no way to get any levels of gray in between. (Some laser printers can print dots of different sizes; see "Variable Laser Dots," later in this chapter.)

To figure out the total number of levels of gray you can get, just add one to the number of dots in the halftone cell. In other words, if each level of gray is created by turning on an additional dot, you can get the same number of grays as there are dots in the cell, plus one. You have to add one if you want to include white as a level of gray (white is zero dots on). Figure 17-4 portrays the trade-off graphically. For those of you who like formulas spelled out, here it is:

Gray levels = (output resolution ÷ screen frequency)^2 + 1

For example: Let's say you're printing a halftone at 133 lpi on an imagesetter with a resolution of 2,400 dpi. Divide 2,400 by 133 and you get 18. Multiply 18 by 18 and you get 324 dots in the halftone cell. Add one for white, and you see that you can get 325 tones.

FIGURE 17-4
Gray levels versus
screen frequency

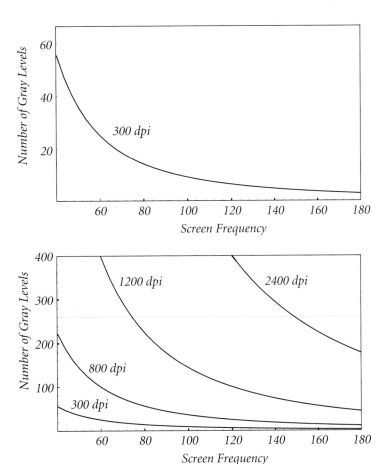

Or can you? As it turns out, PostScript Level 1 (the original) and Level 2 (the first big update) can really only render a maximum of 256 different halftone spot sizes in any given screen frequency. Anything over 256 levels of gray just renders as the next nearest tone.

PostScript 3, introduced in 1996, can conceivably create up to 4,096 spot sizes, according to our reading of the Adobe specifications. What all these extra spot sizes make possible is incredibly fine and smooth gradations, rather than necessarily producing better-looking photographs on press. (And PostScript 3 goes a step further—no pun—by dithering at the boundaries of tones in gradations; see Chapter 23, *Band Aid.*)

Also, there's a school of thought—propounded by Adobe Systems, the creator of PostScript, among others—that says the human eye can't perceive more than 256 levels of gray in a single visual field. (We live in Seattle, where the weather is gray, cloudy, foggy, and misty so often that we've developed the ability to discern *and name* more than 256 levels of gray.) What is certain is that job printing presses—those used for workaday brochures, posters, and books—can't reproduce more than 100 or so levels of gray.

Fine printers can often do much better because of the quality of materials, paper, and press conditions. If you're working on a project where subtlety at this degree of refinement counts, you'd better check with your service bureau as to what version of PostScript they're using.

THE RULE OF SIXTEEN

The practical limitation of 256 levels of gray means that you rarely need to do the calculations described above. Instead, you can simply focus on two questions: What is the highest (finest) screen frequency you can use, given the resolution of your printer? Or, what is the minimum-resolution printer you can use, given the screen frequency you're using?

The Rule of Sixteen gives you the answer to both these questions (it works because 16 is the square root of 256). You still have to do a little math, so don't put that calculator away too quickly. But this calculation is really easy. Here's the formula.

Maximum screen frequency = Output resolution ÷ 16
  or
Required output resolution = Screen frequency × 16

For example, if you want to print a halftone at 150 lpi, multiply that by 16 to find that you need a minimum of 2,400 dpi to get 256 levels of gray. Or, if you know you'll be printing on a 1,200-dpi printer, you can divide that by 16 to find that you shouldn't print a halftone at higher than 75 lpi.

VARIABLE LASER DOTS

Many laser printers on the market these days can create variable-sized laser dots, which to some extent bypasses the essential trade-off of digital halftoning, providing more gray levels at a given screen frequency and output resolution. Because the laser dots can vary in size, there is more control over halftone spot size, hence more potential gray levels. Apple's grayscale version of its Photo-Grade technology, for instance, provides 91 gray levels with a 106-lpi screen frequency at 300 dpi.

WHO NEEDS 256 GRAYS?

Many designers are now starting to realize that they really only need between 100 and 150 levels of gray in their scanned images (or even fewer). Graduated fills and some high-quality images almost always need 256 levels of gray (see Chapter 23, *Band Aid*), but if an image already has a lot of noise in it—or if you're printing on very absorbent paper—fewer gray levels might be fine for you.

By the way, if all your halftones are straight tints (no blends or photographs), then you probably don't have to worry about posterization and achieving a full 256 levels of gray. If you're producing a newsletter that has several 20-percent gray rectangles behind some type, you could easily print that at 120 lpi, even on a 1,200-dpi imagesetter. Sure, you can't get more than 101 shades of gray, but who cares? You've only got one shade of gray on your page!

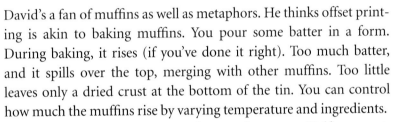

18 REPRODUCING HALFTONES

SPOT VARIATION AND THE PRINTING PROCESS

David's a fan of muffins as well as metaphors. He thinks offset printing is akin to baking muffins. You pour some batter in a form. During baking, it rises (if you've done it right). Too much batter, and it spills over the top, merging with other muffins. Too little leaves only a dried crust at the bottom of the tin. You can control how much the muffins rise by varying temperature and ingredients.

Halftones work the same way but aren't as tasty. Halftone spots get poured into halftone cells, just like batter into a muffin tin. Depending on the type and quality of the press, you have to choose paper, inks, and line screens carefully to avoid winding up with a not-so-delicious overflowed and burned batch.

SPOT VARIATION

After all your hard work making a perfect halftone, you still have to contend with a printing press. Those thousands of tiny halftone spots spread out or shrink, depending on their size, the pressure of the offset cylinders, and (primarily) the absorbency and smoothness or *calendarization* of the paper. Sometimes they spread or shrink just a little, but sometimes they spread out so much that your image will look like the blob that ate Cincinnati (see Figure 18-1). As dark tints fill in and become black, your nice photograph ends up like a shot of Night Life in Sioux City.

FIGURE 18-1
Simulated spot
variation on various
paper stocks

Without spot variation

*With spot variation. Note how shadows get darker
(to the point of going black) and highlights get
lighter (to the point of going white)*

The opposite problem also arises. The smallest spots tend to dis-appear. The tiny areas of ink don't adhere to the paper or they get filled in during the process of creating lithographic negatives or plates. This makes the subtlest tones in a snowbank blow out to white, or a 4-percent tint vanish entirely.

SPOT GAIN AND LOSS

The growth of halftone spots is traditionally called *dot gain*. This use of "dot" instead of "spot" is a holdover from conventional halftoning terminology, but we're going to call it *spot gain* to be consistent and avoid confusion. When small spots disappear, you say they're *blown out* (as in the phrase, "This picture of Yul Brunner's head is solid white; all the highlights are blown out!"). We refer to the two problems together as *spot variation.*

Spot gain is measured in percentages: people talk about 5- or 10-percent spot gain. Be aware, however, that 5-percent spot gain doesn't mean that 50-percent spots become 55-percent spots. Spot gain percentages refer to the increase in area covered by a spot. So with 10-percent spot gain, a 20-percent spot goes to 22 percent, and 50 percent spot goes to 55 percent.

It's also important to understand that because of this growth in area, spot variation is nonlinear. All the spots in an image don't just increase by 10 percent on press (which is the impression given by the term *dot gain*). Small spots might get smaller, midtone spots might grow by a few percent, and spots in shadow areas might grow by 20 percent. If your software has a dialog box that lets you correct for dot gain by typing in a single percentage value, you should eye it with some suspicion.

HIGH-FREQUENCY PROBLEMS

Spot variation is more of a problem with fine screen frequencies printed on presses or plates that are unable to handle small spot size, or on uncoated or textured paper. The spaces between spots are smaller at fine screen frequencies, so they clog up with ink quickly. In light areas, the spots are also small, so they're more likely to disappear entirely. If you work with a printer whose equipment and staff consistently reproduce screens of 175 lines per inch or higher, these problems are usually minimized or eliminated. For suggestions on setting screen frequency to control spot variation, see Chapter 19, *Setting Your Screens.*

REPRODUCING THIN LINES

The *blow-out* problem happens somewhat differently with rules or lines that approach the width of the smallest halftone spots, as in line art, boxes, and *callouts*—lines that point to elements in an illustration (We talked about scanning line art in Chapter 6, *Choosing Resolution.*)

The problem with lines is that it's immediately apparent to the eye when a line is a little broken up or it is missing pieces. Your optical processing center will pick up on that instantly when a few missing or lopsided spots are below the perceptual threshold.

With a scientific calculator, you can quickly calculate what the size of the smallest safely reproducible spot is and then figure out what is the associated thinnest line width you can use without fear of grottiness. Near the end of this chapter, we give you upper and lower spot-size percentages for different kinds of paper.

Let's say you were printing to coated paper at 133 lpi with the output coming from a 2,540-dpi imagesetter. Your minimum spot size should be 5 percent—below that, and the spot will disappear or break up. Now there are 133 cells per inch and a 5-percent spot takes up 5 percent of the overall area. So the formula to determine the width of the spot is:

$$\sqrt{(dpi/lpi)^2 \times percentage}$$

In English, you're dividing the printer resolution by the screen frequency to get the number of dots on each side of a halftone cell. You square that to get the area, multiply by 0.05 to get a 5-percent spot's area, and then take the square root of the remaining number to get the length of the sides of a 5-percent spot. In this case, that's $(2540/133)^2 \times 0.05 = 18$, the square root of which is about 4 dots on a side or $17/10{,}000$ inch.

The recommendation we make is to be about 2.5 times larger than that smallest spot's width to ensure a crisp line. That's about $35/10{,}000$ inch, or about 0.3 points in pica measurement. Not coincidentally, this is the usual recommended "hairline" width.

For comparison, if we were doing the same output to rough, uncoated paper, a 10-percent minimum spot is recommended. That gives you about a $23/10{,}000$-inch spot or a ½-point minimum rule.

WHAT CAUSES SPOT VARIATION?

Spot variation arises for a number of reasons throughout the process of turning digital information into real, physical spots on paper. Many factors can affect the reproduction of halftones; here's a list of a few of them:

- ▶ Laser-printer density setting

- ▶ Density of imagesetter or plate material

- ▶ Photographic reproduction

- ▶ Making—or printing—plates

- ▶ Excessive inking

- ▶ Transfer of image from plates onto blanket cylinders, and from blankets onto the paper itself (offset printing)

- ▶ Absorptive properties of paper, including texture

A little terminology is useful before we proceed. Imagesetter output is usually called *lithographic film* or *lithographic paper*. If you know your Latin, you know that has something to do with stones. It's called *lithographic* because it shares the same properties as offset lithography—it can only capture black and white, just as offset presses can only print a given ink color in a given location, or not. There's no tone in lithographic material, unlike photographic con-tone (continuous-tone) film and paper.

LASER DENSITY SETTING

If you're printing your final output from a laser printer, check to see if your laser printer has a density control. Just as with scanner or film density—see Chapter 2, *Scanners*—toner density affects how "black" the black is; too little density, and the darkest tones are mottled or washed out. Too much density is bad, too, as type and halftones are mottled or filled in. It's important to balance the two extremes, and often your print house can help you by measuring output tests on a densitometer (which we describe below).

DENSITY OF IMAGESETTER MATERIAL

Imagesetters expose photosensitive paper or film rather than applying toner to paper or transparencies. As a result, density is critically important to imagesetter output, just as it is to photographers developing their film. Let's look at some of the ways that density is affected in the imagesetting process.

DENSITY. When imagesetter film or RC (resin-coated) paper is photochemically developed, the areas of emulsion that were exposed get transformed into another chemical compound, while the unexposed emulsion simply washes off. Density is a measure of how much of that chemical compound is fixed on the substrate; essentially, it's the compound's ability to absorb light passing through (for film) or reflecting off (for paper)—its opacity. (We go into the input side of density in "Bit Depth and Dynamic Range" in Chapter 2, *Scanners.*)

You can measure this opacity with a densitometer; it can also measure halftone tint percentages. Any service bureau running film must have a densitometer or it can't calibrate its imagesetter.

Density is measured on a decimal logarithmic scale, like the Richter scale for earthquakes. A value of 4.0 means a 'quake (or density) 10 times greater than a value of 3.0. Lithographic film should have a density of roughly 3.5; lithographic paper should be around 1.7. Of course, these numbers vary according to material type, and they're almost never dead-on. In fact, in many cases density can usually be off by as much as a full point in either direction for lithographic film without causing problems. Consult your printers on ideal density for their systems, just as you would for ideal ink coverage or other printing variables.

If you take negative film—the standard for printers in the United States—that's not dense enough and contact it onto plate material, highlights can be too dark, and shadow areas can clog up (spots tend to be enlarged). If the film is *too* dense, the highlights blow out and images can appear too light overall. (The opposite is the case with positive film, generally required in Europe and Asia.)

IMAGESETTER DENSITY CONTROLS. Imagesetters have density controls similar to laser printers. Just as you can over- or underexpose film in a camera—causing images to be too light or too dark—you can over- or underexpose the film or paper in the imagesetter.

Service bureaus often bump up the intensity of their imagesetters for paper output so that solid black areas such as type or line art are good and black. However, this causes halftone spots to get "bumped up" as well, becoming too large and potentially clogging up dark areas. Most people don't output halftones to paper for reasons we describe below.

But the important rule here is to use a service bureau that calibrates its imagesetter. If you specify a 10-percent tint, you should get a 10-percent tint. A good test for a service bureau is to bring in a sample with tints, run it out, and watch them check the tints on their densitometer. Percentages should be off by no more than 2 percent, and should generally be as close as 1 percent.

CHEMICAL PROCESSING OF IMAGESETTER MATERIAL. Also like camera film, imagesetter output is developed using chemical baths. Material goes through a developer bath, a fixative bath (broken out in photography as a stop bath and then a "fix" bath), and a wash. The developer and fix are heated, while the wash is at room temperature and simply squeegees and flushes any remaining chemicals.

If the developer bath is below the correct temperature or depletes too quickly, the density of the output is affected, because too much emulsion is washed off. If the fix is weak or depleted, film can be fogged, or paper may fade or yellow within a few days or weeks.

You should use a service bureau with a "replenishing-bath" processor. This type of processor introduces new chemicals at a constant rate, and maintains them at an even temperature. The wash water should either be replenished through a feed from a water line or through a frequently changed tank. You can tell if wash water is stagnant, as your output will have traces of algae on it. True, *and* yucky.

CALIBRATION. It's up to the service bureau to calibrate the whole system, from imagesetter through processor. The service bureau can run tests from one of its computers to an imagesetter and through the processor, then, finally, check the results. With the correct software, a variety of tints and densities can be checked on the densitometer for the ideal value, and then any nonlinear values in tints can be corrected.

It's also possible to use color management system profiles when outputting on imagesetters as part of the closed loop. This way, a user needs only to calibrate their input and proofing loop, and the service bureau can use those profiles to get the right results. (See Chapter 8, *Color.*)

If your service bureau doesn't have a densitometer, or doesn't calibrate its equipment, it's impossible for you to trust the output. You could bring in a file on Monday and the same one on Tuesday, and have tint variations of 10 to 20 percent.

PHOTOGRAPHIC REPRODUCTION

Anytime you introduce a photographic or contact step to the process of going from halftones to press, you can introduce spot variation of a couple or more percentage points. It's not always possible to avoid—there may be film stripping involved, for instance, and the printer might require a single piece of composite film for platemaking—but you can avoid spot variation if you can avoid duplicating film or shooting negatives from RC paper.

If for some reason the printer can't use the imagesetter film directly, there are some things you can do to reduce spot variation during photographic reproduction.

OUTPUT TO FILM, NOT PAPER. Shooting film from paper originals results in much more spot variation than shooting film from film.

If you output film, the printer can make a *contact neg*—putting two pieces of film together and exposing one through the other. Contact negs generally result in 1- or at most 2-percent spot variation. If you supply RC paper, the printer has to actually take a picture of the paper, resulting in 2- to 4-percent spot variation.

Even if you're providing laser output, you can print on acetate (there are brands designed specifically for use with photocopiers and laser printers). This is especially helpful when you're using some of the high-resolution lasers and alternative halftoning methods, which are often more difficult to reproduce photographically (see Chapter 22, *Stochastic Screening*). If you *are* printing on paper from a laser printer, use a bright, hard, coated paper designed for laser printing of reproduction masters.

PROVIDE FILM TO SPECIFICATIONS. You can reduce the number of generations of photographic reproduction that your material needs to go through by providing film in the proper format. If you provide positive film and the printer needs negative, they may need to add a duplication step (producing an *interneg* or *internegative*). Ask the printer if he or she wants emulsion up or down, negative or positive, and ask if there are other ways to eliminate reproduction generations.

OVEREXPOSE WHEN SHOOTING FROM LASER OUTPUT. If you are delivering paper laser output to the printer, you might ask them to overexpose slightly when shooting film. Since they're creating negatives, white areas on your original (surrounding the halftone spots) become black on the film. Overexposing causes those areas to encroach slightly on the jaggedy-edged, toner-based spots, reducing the problem of spot gain (it can also improve the appearance of type and line graphics). Although this tends to wash out highlights more—because small spots are more likely to disappear—that's generally less of a problem with laser output than is dark areas clogging up.

MAKING OR PRINTING PLATES

Once the plate-ready film is done, the printer uses it to expose (or *burn*) plates. The process varies depending on the type of printing (offset, gravure, letterpress, etc.), but in most cases it's a contact photographic process, so it doesn't result in much spot variation.

Film is placed in a vacuum frame that is directly against paper or metal coated with photosensitive material, and exposed under intense ultraviolet light for short periods of time. Because the material is directly contacted, there's little room for spot variation through diffraction or other properties of light.

One of the biggest savings in time, materials, and effort is computer-to-plate (CTP) technology, in which there are no intermediate analog steps between the data and the plate that's used on press. A few years ago, we thought CTP might take a while to mature. However, here in 1998, we're seeing the results every day. In fact, this book was composed electronically with halftones in place and dumped directly to plates. (We called this direct to plate until we realized that those initials would be confused with desktop publishing; the graphic arts industry has been using CTP as the right term for a few years.)

The greatest advantage of reducing photographic and material steps is that the spot variation just from one process to the next is eliminated, and you can concentrate on the parameters of the press itself. It's a little scary for those of us used to seeing *bluelines* (blueprint-paper contact prints of negatives) so we can see tiny imperfections and fix errors.

For some jobs, CTP doesn't provide enough control before reaching the press-check stage; but for many, it's faster, cheaper, and easier.

INK ON PAPER

If too much or too little ink is used on the printing press, halftone spots tend to clog from spot gain, or blow out entirely. This can also happen if the ink/water balance is off. Similarly, any one of a number of problems with the printing press can throw off tonal values in the halftone. For example, *spot doubling* (which looks a lot like severe spot gain) often happens if the press blankets are too loose. *Spot slur* occurs if the paper stretches too much or *skids* slightly across the impression cylinder. If you don't understand these terms, don't worry; unless you're a printer, you shouldn't have to, because there's nothing you as a desktop publisher can do about them (except find a new printer).

There are also two factors in color printing that can dramatically increase spot gain: black replacement and rosette formation. Overprinting ink on ink can result in dramatic spot gain, and both of these techniques can reduce the amount of ink and the overlap.

BLACK REPLACEMENT. In four-color process printing, you can literally put down 400 percent ink—100 percent each of cyan, magenta, yellow, and black. However, ink is both sticky and moist, and putting that much ink on paper on a printing press is a bad idea (the paper could buckle, stick to the rollers, or cause all kinds of trouble). Therefore, most color separation software, including the routines in Photoshop, do *undercolor removal (UCR)* and *gray component replacement (GCR)* to remove various amounts of color and reduce the total ink percentage down to something reasonable (between 240 and 350 percent typically, depending on the press type, paper, and so on).

UCR replaces cyan, magenta, and yellow with black wherever they combine to form what should be black—in reality, those three colors have enough impurities to form muddy brown instead. GCR extends further into neutral areas where equal amounts of cyan, magenta, and yellow should combine to form grays; GCR replaces those with corresponding straight tints of black.

These techniques reduce the overall amount of ink on press. Printers may have a preference for one over the other; you may need to use GCR for a newsprint press that has a maximum of 240-percent ink coverage, for instance.

ROSETTE FORMATION. There are different ways to turn the different process color separations so that they don't form unintentional patterning. In Chapter 25, *Rosettes and Moirés*, we discuss what a *rosette* is—a pattern formed by the set of all the color separations— and how they work. For our purposes here, though, it's important to know that using an *open-centered rosette* reduces the number of places where larger halftone spots overlap, reducing the overall spot gain from printing ink on top of ink.

PAPER STOCK

The area in which you have to be most aware of spot variation is in the choice of paper stock. You'll always encounter noticeable spot gain on uncoated stock, because the ink is absorbed into the porous paper. An extreme case of this is on newsprint, where spots can easily gain 20 percent.

Coated stock reduces spot gain considerably, because the paper isn't as porous. Superslick paper, on the other hand, sometimes causes spot slur (which has an effect similar to spot gain) because it can slip slightly in the press. Once again, consult with your lithographer when choosing a paper stock.

We discuss paper stock in relation to screen frequency and spot gain in Chapter 19, *Setting Your Screens*. We also recommend reading anything and everything by Constance Sidles, currently the "On Paper" columnist for *Adobe Magazine*. Her tips and explanations of the problems and joys of printing on paper can help you get the most—financially, technically, and creatively—out of a part of the specification process that is often downplayed.

UPPER AND LOWER TINT LIMITS

There is one incredibly easy way to avoid spot variation in extreme highlights and shadows: eliminate them entirely. If no tint in your publication is too light or too dark, the problems of spot gain are somewhat reduced (but not eliminated; it's still a factor throughout the tonal range). We discussed how to manage this with scanned images using tonal compression in Chapter 7, *Tonal Correction*. In the meantime, Table 18-1 suggests tonal limits for tints and halftones on different paper stocks.

TABLE 18-1	Paper type	Minimum tint	Maximum tint	Minimum line width
	Coated	5%	95%	0.3 pt.
	Uncoated	10%	90%	0.5 pt.
	Newsprint	12%	88%	0.75 pt.

Upper and lower density limits

DTP VERSUS THE BLOB

You're probably getting the idea right about now that creating high-quality halftoned images is much harder than the salesperson at the computer store told you. Spot variation is a major issue in scanning and halftoning, though it's one rarely focused on. Fortunately, it's also one that's surmountable.

Although proper attention to paper stock, calibration, and the other elements we discussed in this chapter will put you well on your way to creating excellent-looking halftones, one factor is so important in the discussion of spot variation that we've given it its own chapter: screen frequency. That's where we go next.

19 SETTING YOUR SCREENS

FREQUENCY

AND

SPOT GAIN

As we've seen in the last two chapters, screen frequency is one of the most important factors you need to consider when working with halftones. We looked at the trade-offs between screen frequency and number of gray levels back in Chapter 17, *Frequency versus Gray Levels.* In Chapter 18, *Reproducing Halftones,* we discussed the factors that cause spot variation. Now we want to look at how screen frequency affects spot variation.

THE PROBLEM WITH HIGH FREQUENCIES

The key issue is that as the screen frequency of a halftone increases, it becomes more susceptible to spot variation and muddiness. There are two reasons for this frustrating little fact. First, because spot gain occurs at the edges of spots, when there are more spots per square inch, there's more spot gain happening (more spots mean more edges, which means more potential spot gain). Second, at higher frequencies the spots are so close together that any spot gain can fill in what tiny space there is between each spot.

But how do you know what screen frequency you can get away with? There's no hard-and-fast rule to this; rather, you need to take several factors into consideration.

FACTORS TO CONSIDER

Typically, unless you're trying to achieve some sort of special effect, you'll want to use the highest screen frequency you can. However, maximum screen frequency is dictated by many different factors. Generally, the rule is to ask your printer what the proper screen frequency should be; but of course that doesn't always work. We're often reminded of the time we brought some artwork to a quick-print shop where the kid behind the counter thought screens were used to keep flies out.

The primary factors you need to consider when setting your halftone screen frequency are output resolution, output method, and paper stock.

OUTPUT RESOLUTION

In Chapter 17, *Frequency versus Gray Levels*, we explained the relationship between gray levels, screen frequency, and output resolution. If you adhere to The Rule of Sixteen—screen frequency should not exceed output resolution divided by 16—you'll always get your full complement of 256 gray levels.

You can go higher than that if you don't need all those gray levels—if you're printing just solid tints and no blends, for instance. Or, if the imagesetter you're printing to does "supercell screening" where it can make irregular cells that can simulate a higher number of spot sizes. That's when you need to ask your service bureau or printer whether that can work.

Another option is to switch to a higher-resolution device; if you can't, you might output your scanned images and graduated fills— which require all 256 gray levels—at a lower screen frequency than your flat tints. That way you get a fine screen for type, lines, and

boxes, and 256 gray levels for photographs and graduated fills. See Chapter 27, *Controlling Halftone Screens*, and Part 3, *Applications,* to find out how.

OUTPUT METHOD

Output method refers to the sort of printer you're outputting your artwork on. If you're producing final artwork on any type of toner-based laser printer, don't expect to exceed 110 lpi, even if the printer prints at high resolutions. Even better, use 65 or 85 lpi. The ragged-edged spots that result from toner-based devices are more prone to dot gain. On the other hand, the maximum screen frequency on an imagesetter is limited only by its output resolution.

OUTPUT MEDIUM. Whether you use paper or film for your output makes a big difference in what screen frequency you use. If you're outputting to paper, you're limited to about a 110-line screen, because the photographic process of shooting lithographic negative film can't hold a screen much finer than that. If you want a higher screen frequency, you must output to film, which we recommend for almost every purpose anyway. (If you're doing line art and text, however, or halftones below 100 lpi, a 600-dpi-or-higher resolution paper laser printer can be just fine. And much cheaper.)

This is also a good tip for laser printer output: Print on a clear substrate instead of paper, and you can get away with a higher screen frequency because fewer visual steps are involved. Some laser printers have expensive substrates that can actually be exposed onto quick-printer plates without shooting negatives.

REPRODUCTION METHOD

The third factor in choosing a halftone screen frequency is the reproduction method that you're using. Different printing methods dictate different screen frequency settings. Here's a very quick overview of some methods.

OFFSET PRINTING. The limits on screen frequency particular to off-set printing are dictated by your printer's press and the skill of the presspeople, and the paper stock you're using. It can range from 75 lpi to as much as 300. Ask your printing rep for the proper frequency.

GRAVURE. This printing method can hold a fine screen very accurately. If you're using gravure, you're probably working with a top-notch printer, and don't need our advice to choose screen frequency. Ask your rep.

QUICK PRINTING WITH PAPER PLATES. You'll almost always want to use 120-lpi screens or lower.

PHOTOCOPYING. Screen frequencies up to 100 lpi are possible, and 85 lpi is pretty safe, though we've seen scans clog up at even this low frequency. Try 75 lpi with scanned images. Some insanely expensive and complex photocopying systems, like Xerox's DocuTech, can output directly from PostScript, allowing higher resolutions with perfect clarity.

PAPER STOCK

Perhaps the biggest consideration when choosing halftoning screen frequency is the paper stock you're using for printing. There are hundreds of different types of paper, each with its own amount of absorbency. However, the basic information to remember is that coated papers boast the least spot variation; uncoated papers suffer more because they're more absorbent; newsprint sucks up ink like the Sahara sucks rain water (printing newspapers has been compared to putting kerosene on toilet paper at 200 miles per hour). Table 19-1 suggests screen frequencies for various stocks and printing methods. For in-depth information on paper, consult International Paper Company's *Pocket Pal*.

	Final reproduction method	Paper stock	Screen frequency
TABLE 19-1 Choosing screen frequency	**Photocopier**	Uncoated	50–60
		Laser paper*	50–90
		Coated	75–110
	Quick printer with paper plates	Uncoated	50–75
		Matte bond	50–90
		Coated	75–110
	Offset printing	Coated	120–150+
		Uncoated	85–133
		Newsprint	60–85
	High-quality offset/gravure	Coated	150–300

*Laser paper has a smooth, matte finish, the better to hold toner.

MAXIMIZING YOUR FREQUENCIES

The name of the game is getting the best-looking images on your pages, right? But as clearly as the game has its rules and regulations, it also has an individual personality. We can't truly sit here and tell you that you can do this or you can't do that. Last time we did that, we said there was no way to produce and print a good-looking 400-lpi image from the desktop. We were wrong. When enough thought and care go into planning and executing your work, it's amazing what you can do.

20 THE GLORIOUS SPOT

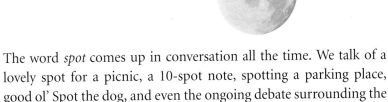

SPOT SHAPES FOR QUALITY AND SPECIAL EFFECTS

The word *spot* comes up in conversation all the time. We talk of a lovely spot for a picnic, a 10-spot note, spotting a parking place, good ol' Spot the dog, and even the ongoing debate surrounding the Grafenberg spot. But we notice that even in heated discussions on halftoning, people rarely talk about the details of the halftone spot.

We understand. In the majority of printing situations, spot shape is admittedly a minor quality factor. Halftones generally go through so many processes on the way to print—camera work, plate burning, offset blankets, paper—that carefully created elliptical spots (or whatever) might just as well be simple round blobs.

There are situations, however, where choosing a spot shape can make a real quality difference. If you're producing cosmetics catalogs, or need to solve tonal shift problems printing on newsprint at coarse screen frequencies (to use two examples), controlling the halftone spot can definitely improve the quality of your job.

ON THE SPOT

As we mentioned back in Chapter 16, *Frequency, Angle, and Spot Shape,* you can create halftone spots in a number of different shapes. Why would you want to alter the halftone spot shape? First, you might want to create special-effect screens for design reasons.

We discuss some of these effects at the end of the chapter. It's more likely, however, that you will choose spot shapes to minimize spot variation in the reproduction process, and avoid a phenomenon called optical jump.

OPTICAL JUMP

Remember those muffins back in Chapter 18, *Reproducing Halftones,* and how they can overflow to form an inchoate lump? There's a point in the tint spectrum from white to black at which halftone spots (and muffins) start to blend together into a single mass and no longer look like individual entities.

With halftones, that merging can result in an apparent jump in gray level. Figure 20-1, for instance, shows a smooth blend from black to white. At about the 75-percent point, however, where the halftone spots meet and begin to merge, there's an apparent jump in the smoothness of the blend.

FIGURE 20-1
Optical jump

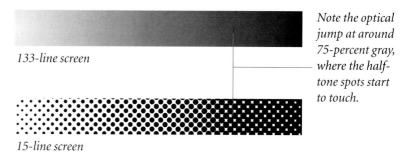

133-line screen

15-line screen

Note the optical jump at around 75-percent gray, where the halftone spots start to touch.

You can reduce optical jump by choosing your spot shape—especially important when you're working with graduated fills (or blends, or fountains, or whatever you want to call them) and with photographs that include smooth transitions in the midtones (as in Caucasian faces).

SPOT VARIATION

You might also want to consider spot shape because different spots fare differently in the tortuous path through the reproduction process. As we've noted before, spots tend to vary in size as they move through the process. Most spots get bigger (spot gain), though some very small spots (5 or 10 percent and below) tend to disappear entirely. The shape of the spot can affect the variation because some spots retain their shapes well in highlight areas, some in the midtones, and some in shadow areas.

Spot Shapes

We discuss how to alter spot shapes in Chapters 28 and 29, and in Part 3, *Applications*. For now, let's take a look at various spot shapes and their relative merits.

ROUND SPOTS

The simplest halftone spot is round (see Figure 20-2). The spot starts small, and then gets progressively bigger until it fills the half-tone cell. The round spot fares well in light tints and highlight areas; 5- and 10-percent tints with round spots are less likely to wash out and vanish. The round spot is especially prone to optical jump, however, and to serious spot gain in dark tints and shadow areas.

FIGURE 20-2
Round spot

110 lpi

20 lpi

The first problem with the round spot is that all four sides of a round spot touch its neighboring spots all at once—at a given tint level. So at about 75 percent, where all four sides meet, there's a marked optical jump.

The second problem occurs in the dark tint areas (over 80 percent or so). The round spot that held the ink in place so well in highlight areas is now touching other spots. The technical term for the white shape between the spots (the area not covered by ink) is "that strange square pointy thing that looks like a diamond in a deck of cards." The fine, pointy areas in this shape have a tendency to fill in with ink, obliterating the subtle differences in dark tones and clogging up everything to black.

Other than the original PostScript version 23 Apple LaserWriters, there are almost no printers that use this simple round spot. However, if you don't use a PostScript output device and are relying on your scanning, image-processing, or page-layout software to do the halftoning (see Chapter 21, *Who Does the Halftone?*), there's a reasonable chance that you'll get these simple spots. You can check by printing a graduated tint from black to white with a coarse screen frequency, and examining it carefully.

THE NEW POSTSCRIPT SPOT

Starting long ago with PostScript version 38, PostScript devices started using a variation on the round spot as their default. It actually changes shape as it gets bigger, so we call it a transforming spot (we discuss another transforming spot—the transforming elliptical spot—later in this chapter). In *PostScript Screening: Adobe Accurate Screens*, author Peter Fink calls this spot a Euclidean spot.

This new PostScript spot actually changes shape as it gets bigger. It starts out round, then at around 50-percent gray it changes shape, first becoming square, and then inverting so that instead of a big black round spot, it appears as a small white spot on a black background (see Figure 20-3). This is similar to the effect you'd get if you were creating halftones traditionally (photographically).

This spot is less prone to spot gain than a normal round spot, because the round white spot in dark areas doesn't fill in with ink as

FIGURE 20-3
The New
PostScript spot

110 lpi

20 lpi

easily as the strange square pointy thing. However, in many cases, it makes the optical jump problem even worse because there's a definite visual effect made by the checkerboard at around the 50-percent mark. This effect is especially noticeable in small graduated blends because the gray levels are densely packed in a small space.

OVAL SPOTS

In another attempt to solve the problems of round spots, some programs produce an oval spot (see Figure 20-4). This shape reduces the optical jump somewhat, because there are two meeting points—first where the ends meet and next where the sides meet. So instead of a single, large optical jump at 70 percent, you get two lesser optical jumps, at about 50 and 80 percent (the percentages where the ends and sides touch vary depending on how elongated the oval is).

While the oval spot has some advantages (like the round spot, it holds up well in highlight areas), it's really just a poor imitation of the true elliptical spot, which we discuss next. It's the shape you get

FIGURE 20-4
Oval spot

110 lpi

20 lpi

when you choose the Elliptical Spot in QuarkXPress. Other programs may also use an oval spot when what you really want is elliptical. Again, you can tell what you're getting by printing out a sample at a low screen frequency (coarse enough to see the spots easily).

ELLIPTICAL SPOT

Lithographers and screen printers have used an elliptical or "chain" spot (Figure 20-5) for years because it effectively battles both optical jump and spot variation. First of all, note that the elliptical spot is not really an ellipse. It's more of a rounded-corner diamond—slightly squashed, or elongated, so it's a bit bigger in one direction than in the other. The shape addresses the problem of optical jump very nicely because—like the oval dot—there are two meeting points: at the ends, and on the sides. So you end up with two smaller optical shifts—at about 50 and 80 percent—instead of one big one at 70 percent. Also, since the pointy ends of the diamonds merge slowly, the optical jump is less marked.

FIGURE 20-5
Elliptical spot

110 lpi

20 lpi

The elliptical spot holds up pretty well in dark areas, because the area that remains white is shaped like a diamond, as well. That shape doesn't fill in as easily as the strange square pointy thing that results with round and oval dots. It still doesn't hold up quite as well as a round or oval white area, however.

Note that this elliptical spot is not very elongated—it's actually close to a rounded-corner square—because if it was very elongated, you'd end up with something that looked like a line screen (or a chainlink screen, or what some lithographers call a corduroy screen) in tints between about 35 and 65 percent (read: really ugly).

TRANSFORMING ELLIPTICAL SPOT

The best halftone spots we've seen are the transforming elliptical spots that Photoshop creates when you select the Elliptical Spot option (see Figure 20-6). The transforming elliptical spot starts out as an oval, changes into an elliptical spot at around 45 percent, then inverts, appearing as an oval white spot on a black background.

FIGURE 20-6
Transforming
elliptical spot

110 lpi

20 lpi

Transforming elliptical spots have all the advantages of elliptical spots in that they avoid optical jumps in the midtones, but they have the advantages of oval spots in highlight and shadow areas. Light areas don't wash out, and dark areas don't clog up. The only tiny improvement we'd hope for is that there be one more transformation—from oval to round at about 15 and 85 percent, since round spots are even better than oval for holding the ink in light areas, and holding out the ink in dark areas. Well, maybe someday.

SQUARE SPOT

Square spots (see Figure 20-7) are often used in high-quality color catalog work, because they give the impression of sharpness—especially in the midtones that are so important to cosmetic photography and the like—without having to use a whole lot of sharpening on an image (see Chapter 9, *A Sharper Image,* for more on sharpening and its problems). They give this impression partially because

FIGURE 20-7
Square spot

110 lpi

20 lpi

the corners of the dots suggest sharpness to our visual system, but also because they result in an optical jump in the midtones. That optical jump gives the midtones contrast—notably in human faces—and makes them look "sharp."

Square spots have also been used traditionally in photoengraving for letterpress printing. Many programs offer the option of using a square spot. Though it's mainly useful for the somewhat specialized worlds of catalog and letterpress printing, it's also useful for creating special-effect screens, which is what we cover next.

SPECIAL-EFFECT SPOTS

Up to this point, this chapter has concentrated on spots for run-of-the-mill halftoning situations—for reproducing photographs and tints using relatively high screen frequencies (50 lpi and higher). However, when you get into low screen frequencies where you can actually see the spot shape, it's another world. In this world, spots can be fun, fun, fun. You can use them to produce trendy and hip designs, and to give photographs an eye-catching, stylized look.

You can use any of the spot shapes discussed above at low screen frequencies, of course, but there are some spot shapes that are really useful only in coarse screens. Let's look at a few of these popular special-effect spot shapes.

LINE SCREENS. A line screen, in which the halftone appears to be made of straight lines, is a commonly used special halftone effect. There's really nothing special about it: it's also just a pattern of spots. It's just that each spot is shaped like a little line. The little line spots blend with each other to form long lines through the image (see Figure 20-8).

OTHER SPECIAL-EFFECT SCREENS. There are a number of other special-effect spots you can create in PostScript—triangles, donuts, diamonds, pinwheels, and so on. Figure 20-9 shows a few of these. We explain how to create them in Chapter 29, *Spot Functions*. Again, remember that there's no reason to use these at high screen frequencies. In fact, there's rarely any reason to use them at all. But it's nice to know they exist, just in case.

Also, note that some PostScript imagesetters, especially those that are called "PostScript compatible" (that is, they aren't licensed from Adobe, but imitate Adobe's PostScript) can choke on these patterns or give you bizarre results you didn't expect.

SPOTS

Altering a halftone spot shape won't help much with getting rid of a moiré problem (see Chapter 25, *Rosettes and Moirés*) or improving the appearance of a lousy scan. In fact, it probably isn't even something that most people will see. Like good typography, the spots should rarely stand out and announce their presence. But if you're interested in high-quality work or in creating special effects in your halftone images, spot shape can help.

FIGURE 20-8
Line screen

110 lpi

20 lpi

FIGURE 20-9
Special-effect
spots at 20 lpi

Triangles

Propellers

FIGURE 20-9
Special-effect
spots at 20 lpi,
continued

Doughnuts

Strange circles

21 WHO DOES THE HALFTONE?

PRINTERS AND SOFTWARE

Steve doesn't spend much time pounding nails these days, but that wasn't always the case. One of his lesser claims to fame is that he spent one summer building a Ponderosa Steak House.

One thing he learned that summer was that the order in which you do things makes a big difference. In some situations it's better to build a whole wall lying flat, then tip it up into place. Other times, you need to build the wall vertically, assembling it where it stands. The order in which you build has a big effect on what you can build, how easy it is to build, and when you can build other things. And it's all dependent on the tools and materials you're working with.

The same is true with halftoning. Most often, you can rely on a PostScript printer to do the halftoning for you, when you print the job (see Figure 21-1). But in some situations, you might rely on your software to do the halftoning. And sometimes a printer comes with a special software package designed to improve dithered output.

HALFTONING IN POSTSCRIPT

You almost never have to think about when the halftoning happens, or who does it, because PostScript manages it all for you. You simply build publications, specify tints, and place scanned images, then

253

FIGURE 21-1
Comparisons
of halftoning in
software, and at
output time

Scanner	Software	Printer

Grayscale scan, non-PostScript printer. The software creates the halftoned bitmap from the scanner's grayscale image. You get a result much like the one above, but you can scale it and print to a higher-resolution output device, because halftoning doesn't happen until print time. Tonal correction is also possible because of the grayscale data.

Grayscale scan, PostScript printer. The software passes the grayscale data through to the printer, without halftoning. The PostScript interpreter handles the screening.

print. Your software tells the PostScript output device what gray levels it wants (along with what screen settings—frequency, angle, and spot shape), and the PostScript interpreter turns those grays into halftones using the specified screen settings.

HALFTONING IN SOFTWARE

There are times, however, when it's advantageous or necessary for your software to do the halftoning before you get to the printer. There are three primary reasons you might call on your software to do the halftoning:

► You're neither printing to a PostScript printer nor using a PostScript rendering package.

► You want to use a halftoned image for some effect, and you can't achieve the effect with PostScript's halftoning machinery.

► You're using a stochastic-screening package like Icefields—technically, not a halftone pattern—that creates the pattern on the computer. (We discuss this in the next chapter, *Stochastic Screening*.)

HALFTONING ON NON-POSTSCRIPT DEVICES

Non-PostScript printers, like the Apple StyleWriter series or Canon bubble jets, don't know *bubkes* about halftoning. They certainly don't know how to build those beautiful little halftone spots. In most cases, all they understand is, "Turn a dot on, turn a dot off." So in order to create halftones on these devices, your software has to tell them explicitly which dots to turn on.

If you're printing from PageMaker to a run-of-the-mill bubble jet, for instance, PageMaker can't ask the printer to "make that box 90-percent gray." Instead, PageMaker has to create a big, 600-dpi or even 1,200-dpi black-and-white bitmap (halftoning it in the process), and send that halftoned image to the printer. The same is true with a simple tinted box. It has to convert the box to a big 300-dpi halftoned bitmap (*rasterizing* it, or converting it to a raster—a.k.a. bitmapped—image) and send the whole bitmap to the printer. If you're sending a color image, it has to do this from *four to seven times*—one for each color the printer outputs.

Often it's not actually your application program that handles the halftoning in this situation. In many cases, the printer driver does the halftoning at the request of the application program. So you tell CorelDraw that you want a 90-percent tint. It sends that request to the Hewlett-Packard PhotoSmart printer driver; the driver creates the halftoned bitmap and sends it to the printer.

The main limitation of halftoning in software is control over screen settings. Few applications (or drivers) provide the control over frequency, angle, and spot function that PostScript does.

HALFTONES AS PATTERNS

Another scenario: You want to create a halftone-like pattern for the background of some groovy ad. So you fire up Photoshop, CorelPhoto-Paint, or the like, create a gray box, then convert to black-and-white ("bitmap") mode. One of the options for the conversion is Halftone, which lets you choose the frequency, angle, and spot shape of the resulting image. The program converts the image to a black-and-white halftoned bitmap at the resolution you specify (see Figure 21-2).

FIGURE 21-2
Converting to a bitmapped halftone in Photoshop

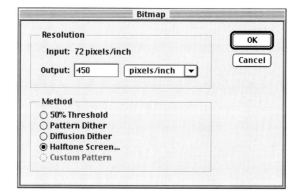

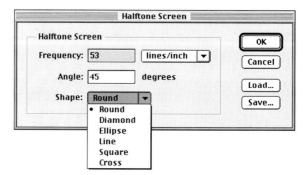

Photoshop even has a Color Halftone filter, which creates images that look like overlaid process color screens (see Figure 21-3). You'll see dozens of examples of this halftoning-in-software technique throughout the book, since we used it extensively to create the illustrations.

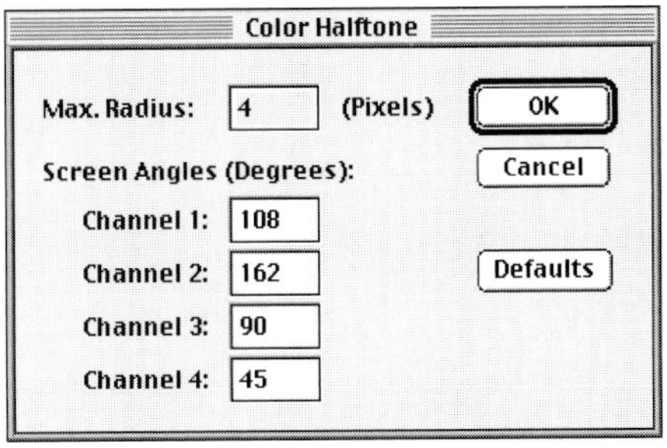

FIGURE 21-3

Photoshop's Color
Halftone dialog box

Color Halftone		
Max. Radius: 4 (Pixels)		OK
Screen Angles (Degrees):		Cancel
Channel 1: 108		
Channel 2: 162		Defaults
Channel 3: 90		
Channel 4: 45		

STREAMLINING THE PROCESS

It's true, you might not need to know the detailed mechanics of who does the halftoning, when, and how. But the time will come (probably tomorrow) when you will. By understanding when and where halftoning happens, you can really control the process, and get the kind of results you want without swallowing your hard disks, clogging up your laser printers, and short-circuiting your imagesetter.

22 STOCHASTIC SCREENING

HALFTONING
ALTERNATIVES

The way we're talking, you'd think that there's only one method for making tonal values with one color of ink: halftones with a frequency, angle, and spot shape, in which spots are big in dark areas and small in light areas. Well, in this chapter, we say that's just not so. A halftone is a black-and-white simulation of gray using different-sized spots. But who says you have to make grays that way?

It was a while ago that a new technology took amusement parks by storm: you could go into a booth and have your face printed on a T-shirt, calendar, or poster. Did they use ink-jets or dye-sub printers? Did they use lasers? No! Your face came out printed with teletype characters: the letters of the alphabet, numbers, and symbols. The closer the characters were, the darker the image; the farther apart the characters, the lighter the image. The gray values, although a little rough, certainly worked.

In this chapter we look at *stochastic screening*, which is a method of creating tonal values through random distributions of specks of the same size. The more specks in the same vicinity, the darker the gray. The difference between dithering and stochastic screening is marketing hype, but we'll examine that terminology split, as well as a little-used halftoning alternative.

Terminology is a confusing thing, and although stochastic screens are a different technique from halftoning, most books and software call the stochastic pattern a dot or spot. For clarity's sake, we call a stochastic pattern element a *speck*, because it's so small.

WHY A SPECK?

Stochastic screening suddenly rose to prominence because of several simultaneous developments in printing and graphics arts preparation: computer-to-plate (CTP) output, CMYK-plus-other-color printing, better graphic arts materials, and ever more processing power in computers and imagesetter PostScript interpreters. This combination both made stochastic screening possible, and helped motivate its advance.

COMPUTER-TO-PLATE (CTP). Computer-to-plate (CTP) output removes all the intermediate photographic and contact steps that can introduce errors, spot gain, and density problems (see Chapter 18, *Reproducing Halftones*). Without these steps, it's easier to reliably image stochastic patterns.

CMYK+ COLOR. To get better, more saturated, more accurate printing of color images, several systems came out that use CMYK plus two or more other inks, including High-Fidelity (Hi-Fi), Pantone Hexachrome, CMYK+RGB, and others. The problems with printing four inks using halftones are severe enough—see Chapter 25, *Rosettes and Moirés*. Stochastic screening removes the moiré hurdle by not having a grid or angles that interfere for patterning (see "Stochastic Advantages," later in this chapter).

BETTER GRAPHIC ARTS MATERIALS. The actual plate material or lithographic film that's exposed, output, or contacted has a resolution of its own that's a chemical limitation. In the '90s, these materials improved, allowing reproduction of higher halftone screens and tiny stochastic specks with more reliability and consistency.

PROCESSING POWER. It takes a lot of horsepower to process images into stochastic patterns—much more than halftoning. The ever-doubling performance of computer chips lets even entry-level imagesetters and personal computers run software that can create high-resolution (1,200-dpi or higher) stochastic output without real delays versus conventional halftoning.

WHAT'S IN A SPECK?

Stochastic means "involving a random variable." Stochastic screening is so named because it uses a randomly distributed, same-size speck in varying concentrations to create tonal values. There's no grid or varying speck size. When you see many specks together they look like a darker value than when we see just a few. Regular halftone screening, in contrast, uses a grid with a spot that can be different sizes, but always in the same pattern and location. Collections of larger spots seem like darker tones than collections of smaller spots (see Figure 22-1).

FIGURE 22-1
Round halftones (left) and stochastic screening (right)

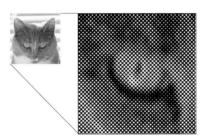
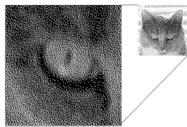

RADIO, RADIO

Halftone screens are amplitude modulated (AM) while stochastic screens are frequency modulated (FM). It's just like AM and FM radio. With AM radio, the signal is a waveform that has cycles of identical duration that are equal distances apart; the height of the waves encodes the sound. FM radio varies the space between cycles to achieve the same effect.

AM and FM radio and screening have another thing in common. AM radio can use relatively low frequencies, in the 500- to 1,200-kilohertz (thousands of cycles per second) range, because the amplitude is what's conveying the information. AM halftones can be created at relatively low frequencies as well, like 133 lpi in a grid using just 1,270-dpi printers.

FM radio requires a much higher frequency, from about 88 to 108 megahertz (*millions* of cycles per second) because the information is being conveyed down near the resolution of the radio signal itself—the shifts from frequency to frequency requires a finer resolution to achieve. Stochastic screening likewise requires much higher resolutions to express itself—at least 1,200 dpi versus just 133 or 150 lpi.

There are other names for FM screening, like dithering; and others for AM halftones, like regular-pattern halftones. We'll talk about both of these near the end of the chapter.

SPECK SIZE

Specks have to be tiny to represent tonal values without being recognizable by the human eye. Agfa's CristalRaster stochastic imagesetting software, for instance, creates specks between 14 and 31 microns—millionths of a meter, written as μm. (In English measurements, those are from $^6/_{10,000}$ to $^{12}/_{10,000}$ inch.) Expressed another way, these individual specks are about the size of a 1- to 3-percent halftone spot at 150 lpi-—or one printer dot at 1,200 dpi to one printer dot at 3,360 dpi.

DISTRIBUTION

Although we say that a stochastic pattern is random, in fact it's not exactly so, depending on the software behind it. Some developers say that true randomness is too much like noise, so there is some less-than-probabilistic correction in how the distributions are done. Some systems generate areas of the image like halftones, using a cell structure and repeating patterns for the same gray values, limiting the perceived gray values. Most of the hardware-based solutions, like Agfa CristalRaster, Linotype-Hell Diamond Screening, and Harlequin SuperFine screens, and the application Icefields from Isis Imaging, use a true FM conversion that's as random as random gets.

RANDOM DIFFICULTIES

We don't want you to think that printing stochastic screens is all wine and roses; there still are problems in knowing what you'll get in some areas of the printing process.

PROOFING. Both film-based and digital proofing devices have a hard time showing what a stochastic image will look like when printed. This partly due to the resolution of film-based proofers, where you expose negative film to sheets of process- and other-colored dyes, like the MatchPrint system. The dye can't reliably hold a speck. Digital proofers have a similar resolution problem; these proofers typically output at 300 to 600 dpi, while the stochastic speck might be the size of single printer dot at 1,200 or even 3,360 dpi. This problem is, of course, being worked on, but proofing systems are wrapped around halftoning, and have to be rethought and retooled to deliver a real preview of stochastic-screened images.

SPECK GAIN. Because you can't reduce speck size to compensate for spot gain or variation like you can with a halftone spot, it takes more effort to ensure the right tonal spread. It's impossible to preview a stochastic image on screen after it's been converted (and often you'll be doing the conversion in an imagesetter RIP, anyway). Isis Imaging's Icefields software package actually has a "dot gain" setting so you can attempt to soft-proof on screen, and other stochastic software attempts to compensate for press conditions when generating the images.

SPECKLING IN FLAT COLORS AND HIGHLIGHTS. The easiest way to identify a printed image that's been screened using stochastic algorithms is that the speck distribution, although close to random, looks like speckling in regions of flat colors and in highlights where the specks are more widely dispersed. The larger the speck size, the more obvious the speckling. But the trade-off compared to regular halftones is detail versus speckling. Often, the detail is more important (see below).

DUST. Yeah, it's nutty, but dust can be in the 15- to 30-micron range and appear in final printed pieces when you print on a press that can hold out the speck. This argues for reduced-dust, controlled environments for film- and platemaking. This might force you to use a printer for CTP or film output, or to find a service bureau that can produce output in those clean conditions—and pack and ship the film in an almost hermetic container.

STOCHASTIC ADVANTAGES

Now that we've brought stochastic screening back to earth, we'll erect a small pedestal to describe its virtues. The stochastic speck lacks so many of the halftone spot's characteristics that it bests the spot when halftone's features aren't benefits. The speck has no angle, frequency, or shape. There's no place at which you point and say that tones make a tonal jump or where straight lines get fuzzy. And because you're working at the effective resolution of the output device—1,200 dpi or higher—you can actually work with lower sample resolutions in your images without loss of quality.

HEY, HEY, NO MOIRÉ

We're getting a little ahead of ourselves in talking about moirés, or patterns that appear when halftone screens are overlaid at certain angles—we illustrate that concept in Chapter 25, *Rosettes and Moirés*. But because there aren't any angles with stochastic screening, you can't get patterns that arise from the way in which colors combine. In fact, it makes it possible to print with more colors than just CMYK (see "Why a Speck?" above) without fear of patterning.

There's also a subset of unintentional patterning called *content moirés*, which occur when a grid appears in an image—like the knit in a sweater—that matches the frequency of a halftone screen. These content moirés are insidious because they sometimes don't show up in proofs, and many techniques have been developed to work around them. Often this involves outputting at higher and higher screen frequencies—which often isn't possible for catalog work in which clothing typically appears. Stochastic specks solve this problem perfectly while retaining the detail of the original pattern in the content itself.

Because there aren't overlapping spots, you lose rosettes as well—there's no easy way for the eye to discern slight misregistration. Press registration has a wider latitude with stochastic screening because it's harder to see when it's off. (This doesn't mean the colors can slide over the page, but it does lessen an expensive and difficult problem.)

SHARPENING FACES

The original, unsharpened image

Taking the unsharpened image at left and applying the Unsharp Mask filter with Threshold set to 0 results in a grainy facial texture (lower left).

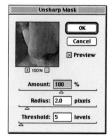

Setting Threshold to 5 results in a less pixelization in the face, although the background stays a little fuzzier (lower right).

The image sharpened with Threshold at 0

The image sharpened with Threshold at 5

SHARPENING WITH LAB LIGHTNESS

The original image (left) has highly saturated colors that sharpening in RGB mode would overaccentuate. So we converted the image to LAB mode.

After converting to LAB, the uncorrected Lightness channel.

After unsharp masking on the Lightness channel.

The final sharpened image preserves the saturation but appears substantially crisper.

SHARPENING SELECTIVELY

The original image (left) has a strong figure in the center of the picture, while the background is a little out of the depth of field and blurred. The face to the right of the central figure could distract from the overall composition if it were as sharp as the foreground figure.

Sharpening the whole image (lower left) makes the out-of-focus background noisy and too crisp. It also brings into sharper focus the face to the right of the central figure. Sharpening just the central figure's face (lower right) helps keep attention in the right spot and reduces noise. The face is sharpened with Threshold set to 3.

LOSSY COMPRESSION

Original image: 3.8Mb uncompressed and 2.2Mb LZW compression

 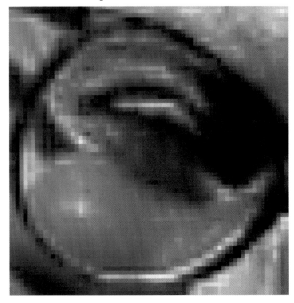

JPEG out of Photoshop with maximum compression and baseline optimization: 80K

 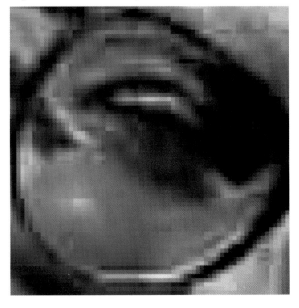

Wavelet compression at highest possible setting: 10K

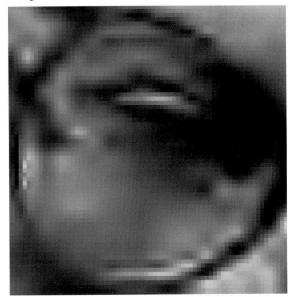

Fractal compression: 440K. It's designed to allow better enlargements with interpolated details.

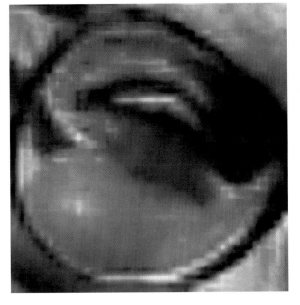

INDEXED COLOR PALETTES

24 BITS

Photographic

Flat colors

216 COLORS

216 colors, adaptive to the photograph

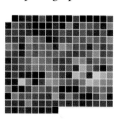

Most Web graphics experts recommend using a common set of 216 colors for all images on a page to avoid dithering. At left, you can see the effects of using an adpative 216 color palette that creates a custom set of colors for the photographic image; at right, the standard Web-safe palette which comprises colors shared between Windows, Unix, and Mac.

Web-safe palette 216 colors

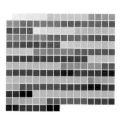

256 COLORS

128 COLORS

64 COLORS

32 COLORS

Photograph using photo's palette

Flat-color using photo's palette

Flat-color using its own adaptive palette

ROSETTES

A rosette is a circle of dots formed in separations by the arrangement of each color plate at a different angle. You can create open-center rosettes (at right and lower right) or close-centered (lower left). The difference between open- and closed-center rosettes is the left-to-right offset of the black plate which aligns the grid to determine whether a black spot appears in the center.

MOIRÉ

The bottom image shows a moiré pattern resulting from non-standard screen angles.

STOCHASTIC SCREENING

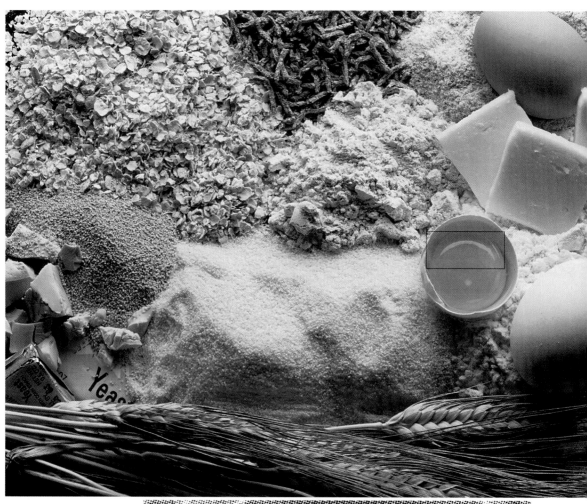

A conventionally screened image above, with a detail from the magenta plate called out. Halftone spots create the tonal values.

The same image printed in four colors as a stochastic pattern using Isis Imaging Corp.'s Icefields 3.0 software. The detail at right shows the same magenta plate detail made up of tiny concentrations of dots.

SUPER PALETTES

DeBabelizer provides options for creating a super indexed color palette (dialog box at right) from a set of images such as those below right. You can simulate this in Photoshop (below left) by pasting all the images into a single window and selecting the Adaptive option when converting to Indexed color.

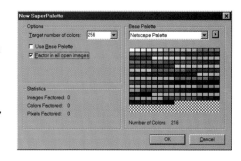

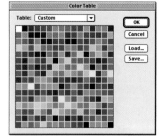

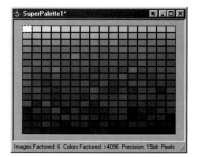

Blends

QuarkXPress linear blend from 100% red (magenta+yellow) to 100% green (cyan+yellow)

Photoshop linear blend

Photoshop linear blend with Gaussian noise added

Illustrator blend using 256 objects

FreeHand linear blend

FreeHand logarithmic blend

For comparison, FreeHand black and white blends as linear (above) and logarithmic (below)

COLOR MODELS

RGB

The standard RGB model can be conceived as a cube within which all combinations of red, green, and blue mix. (The views as the colors meet to form all white and all black are shown at left.) It's not a particularly intuitive way to think about color, but it is the way in which computers—and TVs—represent it.

LAB

The LAB model split lightness into one channel (L) and uses one channel each with a spectrum from red to green (A) and yellow to blue (B).

HSB

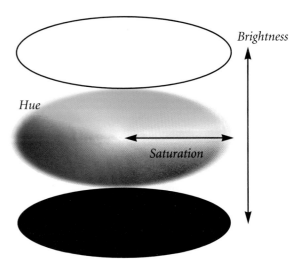

The HSB (Hue Saturation Brightness) model puts hue on a color wheel where the spectrum runs around the perimeter. Moving in towards the center of the circle decreases saturation, while moving up and down changes the brightness

SCANNER TARGETS

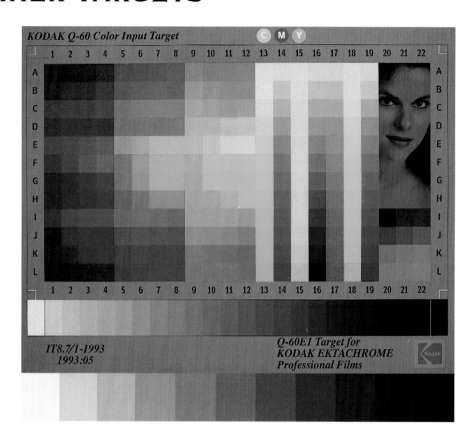

The IT8.7 target above, known as a Q60 target as well, is almost universal in its application as a method of calibrating scanners and presses. Scanning the target and running software that analyzes each of the hundreds of color squares can allow color management software to compensate for scanner color shifts. Printing this on an offset press or proofing device and then using a densitometer to measure critical colors allows you to create custom profiles that will help bring color output into some relationship with reality.

The Kodak step table at left contains 37 steps of density from 0.1 to 3.7, and is a useful way to find out the kind of shadow detail your scanner can capture.

P

RGB & CMYK Plates

Black

Magenta

Red

Yellow

Green

Cyan

Blue

DETAIL DEFINITION

Is it God or the Devil in the details? Neither—it's specks. You'll often note that images with fine detail, like a person's hair, grass, texture of clothing, or other natural objects, require high-frequency halftone screens to even approach a photographic feel. Stochastic screening doesn't suffer from this problem, because the detail can be resolved down to the speck or printer resolution. Halftoning, on the other hand, is limited to either the resolution of the cell (like 150 to the inch), or maybe the resolution of a quarter of the cell. But it's hard for halftones to resolve detail any further than that.

TONAL SHIFT AND COLOR FIDELITY

Halftone spots reach a point in their tonal scale when they become large enough to start touching their neighbors. You can monkey with spot shape—elliptical instead of round, supercells instead of a regular grid—but you're still left with a point at which tonal values jump as the ink fills in and the interstices are suddenly white holes in a black grid.

Stochastic screening doesn't suffer from this problem, because there is no discrete tonal point at which specks start to touch. The distribution of specks allows better color fidelity and a smoother tonal range because of this.

The quarter-tone and three-quarter-tone values tend to have the most spot gain, but the gain is diffused out, avoiding real jumps. The gamma curves that are device-, paper-, and even press-dependent for creating stochastic-screened images can take the pain out of this as well. And you can create your own custom curves for specific projects to hone in more exactly.

LOWER RESOLUTIONS

Because the frequency of stochastic screening is so much higher, relatively speaking, than regular halftone screening, you can use lower-resolution images (fewer samples per inch) and lower-resolution output (fewer printer dots per inch). We're not entirely convinced that a 150-spi image output with stochastic screening at 1,200 dpi outperforms a 225-spi image output at 150 lpi using halftone spots. But see Color Pages J–K for a side-by-side comparison of a conventional halftone and a stochastic version of the same image.

Of course, there's one tricky variable in this. If you would normally use a 150-lpi screen and 1.5:1 spi:lpi ratio, what ratio do you use for stochastic screens? We tend toward using a lower ratio to whatever lpi we would have used in the same circumstances. So if we would have used a 150-lpi screen, we'll use a 175- or 200-spi image.

REGULAR PATTERNS AND DITHERING

As we noted earlier in the chapter, there are other AM and FM screening terms besides the ones we've discussed so far, so we take a slight detour before finishing this chapter up.

REGULAR-PATTERN HALFTONES

Regular-pattern halftones are similar to the halftones you know so much about now, except that tonal values aren't represented by spots that grow from the middle out. The printer dots get turned on in the halftone cell in any order the software or you define (if you can program in PostScript). If you look at Figure 22-2, you'll see how tonal values increase.

We know how to create these regular-pattern halftones, but we've never particularly found a use for this except for experimenting with PostScript. Regular-pattern halftoning is actually suspiciously similar to some of the cell-based stochastic methods that use repeating, not really random repeating patterns.

DITHERING

Dithering has been talked about in various chapters in this book already, and you may wonder what makes it different from stochastic screening? One word: Marketing. Dithering is a catchall term

FIGURE 22-2
Regular-pattern
halftones

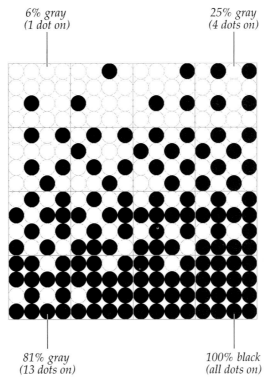

6% gray
(1 dot on)

25% gray
(4 dots on)

81% gray
(13 dots on)

100% black
(all dots on)

that used to distinguish low- and high-resolution FM screening. But FM screening, stochastic screening, and dithering are all really synonyms. We haven't seen a case in which we called one of them either of the other two terms and were contradicted.

GIVE SPECKS A CHANCE

Stochastic screening was originally seen as a technique for only the highest-end output. But if you can afford to use a waterless press that runs plates at 200 or even 300 lpi, you already have many options that are unavailable for job work, catalogs, or web-fed color.

But we think the talk of stochastic screening being too hard to generate and print are dying down as more designers and printers are exposed to it and have to figure out the often-small adjustments in proofing, printing—and thinking. It should be possible to use stochastic screening on the kind of jobs that form the bulk of a printers' workload. The best application we've seen in this area is for catalogs, where the fine detail that stochastic screening makes possible also increases the "touch" value of the pictures in the catalog—turning more browsers into buyers.

COLLISIONS AHEAD

We now leave the safe world of stochastic specks, where angle, frequency, and moiré simply don't exist, to go back into our workaday land of color shift, registration problems, and the collisions of grids. In the next chapter, *Band Aid*, we address how a journey of a thousand miles is stopped at the 255th step.

23 BAND AID

FOUNTAINS, BLENDS, AND VIGNETTES

"Why can't I get a smooth graduated blend? Why are there all these bands in my fountain? How can I get rid of this shade-stepping?" These questions get asked every day, every place where people do desktop publishing. The problem is easy to see (see Figure 23-1), especially in graduated fills that extend over a large area. And it's usually almost as easy to fix.

Before we go any farther, for the sake of everyone's sanity, let's agree that the terms *fountain, blend, degradé, vignette,* and *gradient* (or *graduated*) *fill* all refer to the same thing. Some people fight over what they consider to be the best term, but finally it seems to come down to religious preference. Whatever you want to call it, this kind of fill is very popular among desktop publishers, especially among those doing illustrations.

FIGURE 23-1
Banding in gradient fills

We start out this chapter by looking at how banding occurs, then talk about how blends are made and how you can create them so as to avoid banding.

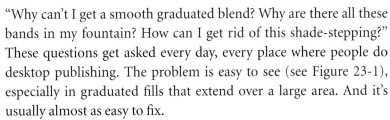

Running from 30-percent to 50-percent gray over 34 picas, this blend displays noticeable banding.

269

SHADE-STEPPING

Banding typically appears in blends because of digital halftoning's inherent limit in reproducing gray levels. As we discussed back in Chapter 17, *Frequency versus Gray Levels,* there are only so many levels of gray that you can achieve at a given screen frequency and output resolution. For example, if you're printing at 133 lpi on a 1,270-dpi imagesetter, you cannot achieve more than 92 levels of gray. So, when you're printing a nice, smooth blend that contains all 256 levels of gray, you're still only getting 92 of those grays. If the blend extends over a large enough area, each step is large enough that you can see it clearly. It looks like 92 bands of gray.

What can you do about this? You've got two choices: lower the screen frequency of your halftones, or print on an imagesetter with a higher resolution (or both). Either way, you raise the number of potential gray levels, and reduce banding.

Let's look at the example above again. If we change the screen frequency from 133 to 80, we can achieve 252 levels of gray at 1,270 dpi—reducing banding considerably, but producing coarse, highly visible dots.

A better solution is to print the higher screen frequency on a 2,540-dpi imagesetter, where we'd theoretically be able to print 366 levels of gray. But PostScript imposes a top limit.

PostScript Level 1 and Level 2 can only create 255 different halftone spot sizes; this is a real limit when doing gradations. PostScript 3, the latest version, can apparently create up to 4,096 spots sizes for PostScript vignettes, making it possible to achieve the 326 levels in the above example. If you went up to, say, 3,360 dpi, you could have 640 levels—a smooth blend, indeed.

TO MAKE A BLEND

How you create a blend can have a big impact on whether you get banding, and how much. There are (at least) three different ways to create blends in desktop publishing.

▶ Use the blend option in the Fill dialog box of an object-oriented drawing or page-layout program.

▶ Use the blend (or similar) command in a drawing program to create a number of intermediate objects between two objects.

▶ Use the blend (or similar) command in a paint or image manipulation program.

BLENDING IN FILL DIALOG BOXES

Some programs, such as Macromedia FreeHand, do all the work for you; you just say, "Fill this box with a graduated blend from black to white" and it does it. Figure 23-2 shows FreeHand's Graduated fill option. Other programs, such as QuarkXPress, Adobe Illustrator, and CorelDraw, use similar techniques. These programs send PostScript instructions to the printer on creating the fill—the on-screen display is just a preview.

FIGURE 23-2
The Graduated fill option in FreeHand's Fill and Line dialog box

If you use a graduated fill from a program's fill dialog box, the program should calculate the proper number of steps needed to print the blend without banding (see the next section). Some programs, such as Macromedia FreeHand, let you choose between a linear and a logarithmic fill. Because of the way that the eye perceives light—see our density discussions way back in Chapter 2, *Scanners*—logarithmic fills often appear to have a smoother transition from black to white.

BLENDING BY CREATING ADDITIONAL OBJECTS

Some programs also give you tools for creating gradients a different way: by blending two objects. You select the two objects containing the beginning and ending tints, tell the program how many steps you want in between, and it creates that many new objects between the two end points (see Figure 23-3).

But how many steps should you use between the objects? The following formula makes it easy.

Number of steps = (output resolution ÷ screen frequency)² × percent change in color

FIGURE 23-3
Creating a blend
between two objects

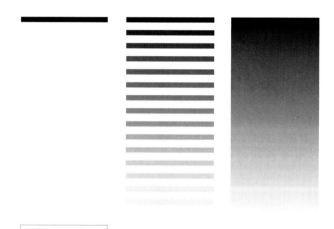

We know this might be a daunting equation at first, but let's look at why it's really pretty easy. The first part of the equation is the same as the one we looked at back in Chapter 17, *Frequency versus Gray Levels*. By dividing the output resolution by the screen frequency and then squaring that number, you find the number of gray levels that you can possibly print. Because PostScript Level 1 and Level 2 can print no more than 256 levels of gray, any value above 256 should just be rounded down to 256. Next, by multiplying that value by the percent change in your blend, you find the number of gray levels that are possible in your particular blend.

For example, if you have a blend that transitions from 10-percent to 90-percent gray, and you're printing it on a PostScript Level 2 2,540-dpi imagesetter at 150 lpi, you know that your blend has a maximum of 204 gray levels possible (80 percent of 256 levels, or 256 multiplied by 0.8). Because this is the maximum number of grays you could possibly achieve in this situation, there's really no need to use more steps than that in the blend (each step has its own gray level).

If the resulting number of steps causes gaps between objects, add more steps or make the objects wider. Otherwise, your blend will look like garbage. This formula simply ensures that you have *at least* enough steps to take advantage of 256 possible gray levels.

HOW BIG THE STEPS ARE

There are two factors to consider when figuring out whether your blend will contain shade-stepping. First, if your blend doesn't contain about 256 levels of gray, there is an increased likelihood that you'll see banding. Note that this banding is much less visible at coarser screen frequencies. However, often a bigger problem is how big each step is. Imagine 256 steps of gray from black to white over a 1-inch space. Each step is going to be really tiny, because each step is only $1/256$ inch.

Okay, now stretch your imaginary blend out to 20 inches. Now each step has to be much bigger to fill the gap. You can figure out how big one step is by dividing the total length of the blend by the number of gray levels possible for that blend (which we just figured out in the previous section). For example, if you know that you only have 204 levels of gray possible for a blend over 10 inches, then you know that each step will be .05 inch (10 inches ÷ 204 steps).

If the step is big enough, then it becomes obvious next to its neighbor steps. Typically, values between .01 inch and .03 inch (.25 to .75 millimeters, or 1 to 2 points) are small enough to blend together well. In the example above, the .05-inch step may be too large for a smooth blend, especially since you are not achieving a full 256 levels of gray.

COLOR BLENDS

Remember that when you separate process colors, each plate becomes in essence a black-and-white image. That means that shade-stepping can and does occur on each plate separately. Therefore, when you're figuring out how likely it is that you'll get banding, you need to look at each color plate. Typically, banding is worst in the color with the smallest percent change. For example, if you're blending a color made of 70-percent cyan and 40-percent magenta to white, then the magenta plate is more likely to band than the cyan because it's only using 40 percent of the available grays (see the equation earlier in this chapter).

On the other hand, if banding occurs on the yellow plate, chances are that it won't appear as prominently as it would on the cyan plate. Also, color blends are sometimes less likely to band because each color can mask the aberrations of the other. That is, the sum of the colors is smoother than each of the parts.

BLENDS IN BITMAPPED IMAGES

Programs that work with bitmapped images, such as Adobe Photoshop or CorelPhoto-Paint, create blends in a different way—on your computer, not in the PostScript processor. The interface is similar: you tell the program that you want a blend from this color to that color, and it does it for you (see Figure 23-4). However, because the program works with bitmapped images rather than objects (see Chapter 3, *Scanned Images*), the blend is described as a giant grid of dots, each of which can have a different gray level.

FIGURE 23-4
Using Photoshop's
Blend Tool

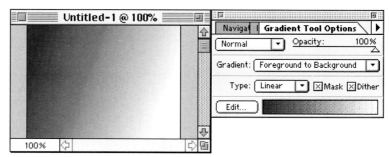

With bitmapped blends, the smoothness of the gradation is mostly dependent on the resolution and number of gray (or color) levels in the bitmap. If you're working with an 8-bit (256-gray) file or 24-bit (16-million-color) file, and your image resolution is at least equal to halftone frequency, you should be fine.

There is a real advantage to creating blends in a bitmapped program as opposed to an object-oriented program: the ability to add "noise" that disguises banding. If you include in each gray level some pixels that are of a slightly different gray level, your eye merges all those pixels together, resulting in an apparently smoother blend (see Figure 23-5 and Color Page M).

FIGURE 23-5
Adding noise
to a blend

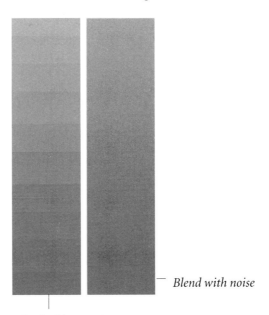

Blend with noise

Blend without noise

Some output devices (such as those using PostScript 3) can add noise to their gradient blends at printing time. If you're not using a device like this, you have to add it in Photoshop. The best way to do this is to select the gradient area and use the Add Noise filter. In typical images, where the image resolution is about 1.5 or 2 times the halftone frequency, we suggest using a noise level of about 4 or 5. If the ratio is less, you might have to reduce the amount of noise.

BANDING AND REPRODUCTION

Believe it or not, banding is one area where your final printed output may look better than what you see on screen. We've seen many situations in which banding is obvious and annoying in Chromalins or MatchPrints, but completely invisible in the final printed output. The vagaries of printing mechanics—notably the spot variation we discussed in Chapter 18, *Reproducing Halftones*—actually tend to mask the banding, blurring the bands together so they're much less noticeable.

So, when there's a lot of spot variation—on uncoated stock and newsprint, with colored papers, and on web presses—this "band-blurring" is more pronounced. It's not a sure thing, however; sometimes you'll still get the banding effect even in these circumstances.

GETTING GREAT BLENDS

When it comes right down to it, you probably shouldn't try to create blends larger than about 6 inches using an object-oriented illustration program like Illustrator, FreeHand, or CorelDraw—at least not in high-quality printing situations. If you expect more band-blurring in the print job, you can go up to 9 or 10 inches. On the other hand, smaller blends work fine with these programs. If you need blends larger than that, create them in a bitmap-editing program, adding a little noise to smooth out the banding.

24 WHEN GRIDS COLLIDE

AVOIDING PATTERNS AND MOIRÉS

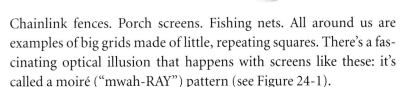

Chainlink fences. Porch screens. Fishing nets. All around us are examples of big grids made of little, repeating squares. There's a fascinating optical illusion that happens with screens like these: it's called a moiré ("mwah-RAY") pattern (see Figure 24-1).

Moiré patterns are caused by our eyes' perception of straight lines and repeating patterns. Anytime you overlay a bunch of straight lines or grids on top of each other, you have the opportunity for moiré patterns. One grid, all by its lonesome, never has a problem with these patterns. It's when you have two or more overlaid on each other that the wires in your perceptual system get crossed, and these little gremlins start to appear.

One way to think about moiré patterns is by thinking of a pool of water. If you drop one stone in the water, you get a radiating circle of concentric waves. If you drop *two* stones in the water, however, you get a complex pattern of high points where two waves meet and low points where two troughs meet. Moiré patterns are based on the same kind of *standing-wave* or *interference* pattern.

With scanning and halftoning, we're often faced with the kind of multiple overlaid grids that tend to result in moiré patterns. What are the halftones, after all? Big grids of spots. What is scanning? It's turning a real-world picture into a grid of sample points. What is laser printing and imagesetting? It's laying down a grid of black dots. Everywhere we turn in the scanning and halftoning world, we

277

FIGURE 24-1
Moiré patterns

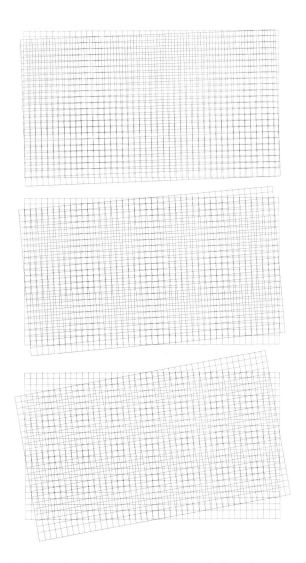

find ourselves looking at grids. And, therefore, we all too often find ourselves looking at moiré patterns.

There are four main situations in which you might run into the problem of conflicting patterns:

▸ Printing color separations, which in most cases involves overlaying two or more halftone screens

▸ Scanning and printing previously halftoned images

▶ Printing halftones of grayscale and color images that include regular patterns

▶ Printing black-and-white images that include repeating patterns

COLOR SEPARATIONS

By far the most common cause of moiré patterns is improper screening in color separations. If the angles and frequencies of the overlaid screens aren't just right, moiré patterns result (see Figure 24-2 and Color Page I).

FIGURE 24-2
Moiré patterning in process separation

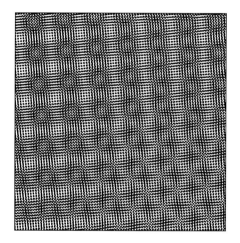

We discuss moirés in color separations in Chapter 25, *Rosettes and Moirés*, and Chapter 26, *Angle Strategies*.

HALFTONING HALFTONES

If you see a photograph in print, it's most likely been halftoned. That's not the only way to print it, but it's the most common (see Chapter 22, *Stochastic Screening*). But scanners can't tell if an image is already halftoned; they just scan it in, sample by sample, as though it were a normal photograph. The halftone spots on the printed page aren't turned back into gray levels—they're scanned as collections of black samples.

There are two opportunities for interference patterns here: between the original screen and the scanner sample grid, and between the original screen (which is picked up by the scan) and the output screen. Fortunately, there are a few things you can do to reduce the patterns in the scanned image.

FIXING THE PATTERNING

You can sometimes reduce the patterning in these cases by adjusting the image scaling and output screen frequency, using trial-and-error until you get it to work. The idea is to have an integral relationship between the original's screen frequency and the output frequency (1:1, 2:1, etc.). If the screen angles don't match, however, that's another potential source of patterning. Unfortunately, that's a pretty darn hard thing to adjust for. A better solution (though still not perfect) is to eradicate the original halftone pattern before you print, using Photoshop, CorelPhoto-Paint, or some other program.

PHOTOSHOP. When our friend Jeff McCord agreed to produce a program for the Seattle International Film Festival a few years ago, he didn't realize that the artwork he needed to scan included many images that were pulled from previously printed material, even clippings on newsprint. If he learned anything from the job, it was how to scan, clean up, and print previously halftoned photographs using Photoshop.

His favorite method for grayscale images is to apply the Despeckle filter in Photoshop before anything else. Then you can adjust levels and apply unsharp masking (see Chapter 7, *Tonal Correction*, Chapter 8, *Color*, and Chapter 9, *A Sharper Image*). The Despeckle filter is excellent for removing the weird traces of patterns in the scanned images. On the other hand, you have to be very careful with the Unsharp Mask filter (and other sharpening techniques) because they can re-accentuate the halftone pattern in the scan.

For scans of color halftones, Jeff likes to use Photoshop's Median filter with a specification of no more than 2 or 3 pixels. This filter has much the same effect in evening out the moiré patterning, but he finds it works better on color images.

Other people prefer other methods. Using blurring filters, followed by sharpening, often works well to remove some patterning. However, you lose detail, which you can't get back by sharpening. Similarly, downsampling the image (reducing its resolution) to as low as 25 percent of original size and then upsampling it (interpolating samples) back up to the original size has much the same effect, and similar problems.

Note that people are often concerned with patterning they see on the screen with scans of previously halftoned images. However, the thing to remember is that the patterns you see at a 2:1 screen ratio may go away when you look at the image at 1:1. This is simply a conflict between the original screen and the monitor's pixel grid. The 1:1 screen ratio is the one you should pay attention to most.

SCANNING SOFTWARE. Most scanning packages now include a *descreening* option that tries to take advantage of higher-bit depths, and other combinations of factors, to do a better job at the time of scanning than a software package could do later. Linotype-Hell's LinoColor software, for instance, lets you select the nearest screen frequency—which you can determine from a nifty halftone frequency finder that Linotype-Hell includes with the software—and it tries to do the rest (see Figure 24-3).

FIGURE 24-3
Image before (left)
and after LinoColor
descreening

CONTENT MOIRÉS

A less common problem, but one that we think you should at least be aware of, arises when you're scanning images that themselves include repeating patterns—the tight weave in a close-up of a silk tie, or the mesh screen on the front of an electric heater, for instance. These patterns can interfere with the grid of the printed halftone screen, resulting in *content moirés*. Fortunately, content moirés don't happen often, and they're often not important if the object only has a small role in the picture.

You can correct for content moirés by adjusting the image size or the output screen frequency, once again seeking to establish an integral relationship between the image pattern and the output screen frequency. Unfortunately, with content moirés it's a trial-and-error process. Stochastic screening is another way to reduce content moirés by eliminating spots altogether (see Chapter 22, *Stochastic Screening*).

Content moirés can also be a problem when printing grayscale or color screen shots from Windows or the Mac, which include repeating patterns in their scroll bars and other interface elements. Best bet: Adjust the interface colors to get rid of patterns before you grab the screen shots.

BLACK-AND-WHITE BITMAPS WITH REPEATING PATTERNS

Any black-and-white (or bilevel) bitmap that includes a repeating pattern can cause patterning, because the pattern conflicts with the grid of laser printer or imagesetter dots. Bilevel screen shots from Windows and the Mac are especially subject to this problem, due to the repeating patterns in their interfaces (see Figure 24-4).

The worst offenders, however, are images that are halftoned at scan time (see Chapter 21, *Who Does the Halftone?*). These scans—which are just big grids of black-and-white dots grouped

FIGURE 24-4
Patterning in
a black-and-white
screen capture

FIGURE 24-4
Patterning in
a black-and-white
screen capture

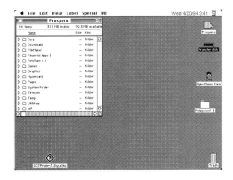

into a regular pattern of halftone cells—result in a special kind of patterning. We call this—for want of a better name—*plaid patterning* (see Figure 24-5).

Whether it's screen shots or scanned halftones, the solution for patterning in bilevel bitmaps is to scale the image so image resolution has an integral relationship to output resolution. That is, if you're printing on a 300-dpi printer, your images (at their final size, *after* they're placed on a page and scaled) should have a resolution of 100 dpi, 150 dpi, or whatever. There should be a 1:1, 2:1, or similarly integral relationship between image samples and printer dots.

This requirement imposes limitations on the scaling percentages you can use for these types of images. The best advice is to decide in advance exactly what size you need an image to be on a page, then scale and crop images as you scan them, rather than scaling them in your page-layout software. However, if you've already got the scans and need to make them fit your spread, you can calculate the acceptable scaling percentages using the following formula:

FIGURE 24-5
Plaid patterning in
a black-and-white
halftone

Scaling percentage = original image resolution ÷ output resolution × any integer

Output resolution in this formula is for your *final output device,* not for your proofing device (if they're different, that is). You may still get plaid patterns on your proof output, but you won't when you imageset the file.

By substituting different integers in this formula, you can build yourself a little table of acceptable scaling percentages for a job. Since different programs have different levels of percentage scaling accuracy, it's a good idea to test some images at different scaling percentages on your final output device.

If you're working with PageMaker, you can use its magic stretch feature (see Figure 24-6). If you set your target printer resolution in the Preferences dialog box, you have two methods of scaling images automatically—and proportionately to acceptable percentages, avoiding plaid patterns. When you use magic stretch, images jump to acceptable sizes as you drag. You can either hold down Command-Shift (Mac) or Control-Shift (Windows) while dragging with the mouse; or you can check the Printer Resolution Scaling button in the Control palette to use the nudge buttons.

FIGURE 24-6
Setting magic stretch options in PageMaker

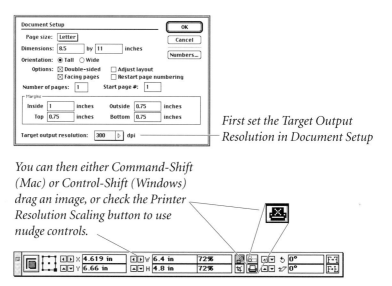

First set the Target Output Resolution in Document Setup

You can then either Command-Shift (Mac) or Control-Shift (Windows) drag an image, or check the Printer Resolution Scaling button to use nudge controls.

LOVE THOSE PATTERNS

We've spent this whole chapter telling you how to avoid patterns that result from overlaid grids. But there's another option: You could simply grow to love them, as David has. Of course, there's still the problem of getting your customers or clients to love them as well.

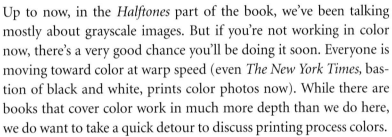

25 ROSETTES AND MOIRÉS

BEAUTY AND THE BEAST

Up to now, in the *Halftones* part of the book, we've been talking mostly about grayscale images. But if you're not working in color now, there's a very good chance you'll be doing it soon. Everyone is moving toward color at warp speed (even *The New York Times,* bastion of black and white, prints color photos now). While there are books that cover color work in much more depth than we do here, we do want to take a quick detour to discuss printing process colors.

In this chapter, we talk about how halftone screens interact when you make color separations and overlay them on press. These overlaid screens are what provide the flexibility of color printing, but they can also pose real moiré problems. Moirés are mainly a problem with process color work, in which four (or even more) screens might be overlaid, but they are also a consideration with spot-color work (especially with duotones and tritones), where two or three screens might collide.

MINIMAL MOIRÉS

As we said in the previous chapter, *When Grids Collide,* when you overlap two or more grids, you'll likely create a moiré pattern. The pattern is the result of our eyes' and brain's tendency to see lines and patterns even when we don't want them to. However, there are some angle combinations that minimize the optical illusion.

The larger the difference in angle between two overlaid grids, the smaller the resulting pattern, and the less apparent it is (see Figure 25-1). So if one grid is at 0 degrees and another is at 5 degrees, there is a very apparent pattern. If you rotate the second grid to 45 degrees, the pattern shrinks to the point that—at a sufficient viewing distance—it seems to disappear.

Note that a 90-degree grid is essentially the same as one at 0 degrees, just as a 135-degree grid is the same as a 45-degree one (though with asymmetrical spot shapes, the orientation of the spots varies around the full 360-degree arc—not a major factor in moiré patterning). So the largest angle difference possible between two overlaid screens is 45 degrees. If you're creating duotones for a two-color job, the angles of the two color screens should be offset by 45 degrees (put the dominant color at 45, because it's least apparent; the secondary color—often black—should be at 0).

Continuing with this logic, the largest angle offset we could hope for between three screens is 30 degrees ($90 \div 3$). Angle offsets smaller than this produce moirés that are too large, hence too apparent.

But, hey: There are four process colors, not three. If you want the angle offsets to be at least 30 degrees, what do you do? Through years of trial and tribulation, the printing industry has standardized on a combination of four halftone angles: three at 30-degree offsets, and one 15 degrees off. Cyan is at 15 degrees, black at 45, magenta at 75, and yellow at 0.

Because yellow is the lightest and least noticeable color, it can safely be set to 0 degrees, even though 0 degrees is a highly noticeable angle, and it's only 15 degrees from its nearest neighbor. Note that cyan is sometimes set at 105 degrees; however, with symmetrical spots it's really the same thing as 15 degrees (and even with asymmetrical spots, it doesn't make much difference).

When you overlay the four process colors using these angles, the resulting moiré patterns are as small as they can be. If these angles are off even slightly, however, you can run into big-time patterning problems. We discuss the problem of getting accurate frequencies and angles in the next chapter, *Angle Strategies.*

FIGURE 25-1
Moiré patterns with
different angle offsets

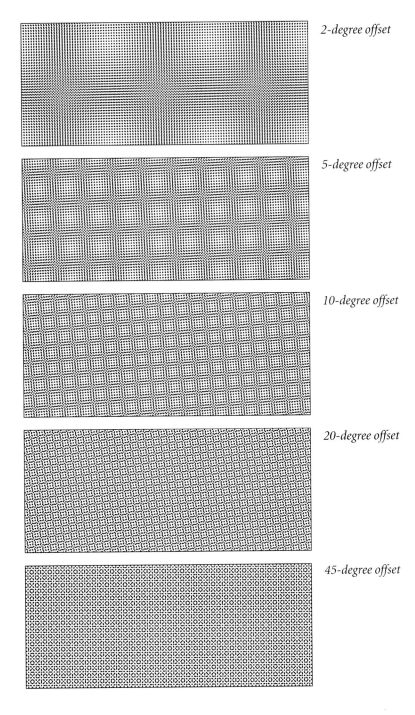

2-degree offset

5-degree offset

10-degree offset

20-degree offset

45-degree offset

THE ROSETTE

It's a popular misconception that when you overlay four halftone screens at the angles we just described, you don't get any patterning. You do, in fact, produce a pattern. It's just that the pattern is small and relatively innocuous, to the point where people don't call it a moiré; it's called a *rosette* (see Figure 25-2).

Whenever you're printing halftones, you have a pattern of cells—the squares in the grid in which a halftone spot is formed. Since halftone spots are formed from the center of the cell and grow to the outsides, when you overlay a number of cells at different angles, the rosette form is shaped. Because of the rotation, it looks roughly circular. (You can only see rosettes clearly when the spots haven't grown too large.)

FIGURE 25-2
An open-centered
rosette

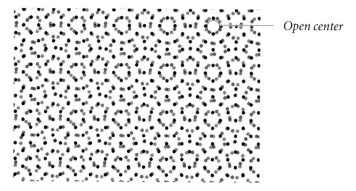

Open center

At low screen frequencies, the rosette pattern is quite evident, as any pattern would be. But at higher screen frequencies, the thousands of rosettes blend together to create a smooth "surface" for the image. At a sufficient viewing distance, the patterns blend together to give an impression of photographic detail.

There are two sorts of rosettes you can make in a four-color image: open-centered and close-centered (Figure 25-2 shows an open-centered rosette).

OPEN-CENTERED. Open-centered rosettes don't have a spot in the center of the rosette; this center is created by sliding the overlaid rotated screens to one direction or another to control where the rosette is formed. The open-centered pattern is sometimes called *robust* because it resists color shifts in the image even when slight misregistration occurs. On the other hand, images with open-centered rosettes display a more visible pattern, and tend to be somewhat lighter than similar images produced with closed-center rosettes at lower screen frequencies. This makes sense because so much white paper shows through and there's less spot gain due to ink overlap.

Because of the more pronounced pattern in open-centered rosettes, they are most appropriate for use at higher screen frequencies where the patterns are small and hard to see—150 lpi and above. Agfa's Balanced Screening produces open-centered rosettes (but it can be coerced into producing closed-center rosettes by setting the imagesetter to positive and the imaging application to negative).

CLOSED-CENTERED. A closed-center rosette pattern lets much less paper show through, so you have a better chance of color brilliance, and the rosette pattern is less apparent, so it's more usable at lower screen frequencies. However, registration is more critical; minor misregistration can cause significant color shifts. It also grows spot sizes, by spreading ink more. Linotype-Hell's High-Quality Screening (HQS) produces closed-centered rosettes. Note that a closed-centered rosette becomes an open-centered rosette in the highlights of an image.

MOIRÉ REDUCERS

Moiré patterns can easily appear in your four-color images due to even minor flaws in either halftone angle or frequency. We talk about how to reduce those patterns in the next chapter, *Angle Strategies*, but we'd like to throw out just a couple of ideas here that don't relate directly to accurate frequencies and angles.

IMAGESETTER SOFTWARE. Every imagesetter company has a different approach to it, but they all have built-in solutions to moirés. Linotype-Hell has High-Quality Screening (HQS) and Agfa uses

Balanced Screens; even Adobe built a system called Accurate Screens that's part of several other imagesetters. All of these systems use either one or more of the solutions we describe in the next chapter, such as irrational screening or supercell screening, or their own proprietary combination. Usually, you shouldn't have to even ask; any major imagesetter manufactured in the last five or so years will have a perfectly reasonable solution built right in.

STOCHASTIC SCREENING. In Chapter 22, *Stochastic Screening*, we mentioned that stochastic, or frequency-modulated, screening is a viable alternative to traditional halftone screening. One of the great benefits of stochastic screening is the impossibility of moiré patterning: there are no angles or frequencies to speak of, so no patterning can occur.

GO FORTH AND MOIRÉ NO MORE

There's really no reason you should ever see a moiré today in process color work when you're creating output from a modern RIP and imagesetter. But you may have to watch who you work with.

Glenn sent a job to a service bureau that output it on its Linotype-Hell Linotronic 330 that he knew used HQS to avoid moiré. He got the job back and the proof was riddled with patterns. He went back and forth with the shop and couldn't get a decent result. He took the very same PostScript dump to another bureau with the same equipment—and it came out perfectly.

The moral of the story: Part of the equation for dealing with any printing or output problem is knowing that the imaging center you work with knows how to run its own equipment to meet your needs.

In the next chapter, we offer some strategies for reconciling software settings with equipment requirements.

26 ANGLE STRATEGIES

GETTING
IRRATIONAL

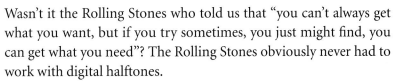

Wasn't it the Rolling Stones who told us that "you can't always get what you want, but if you try sometimes, you just might find, you can get what you need"? The Rolling Stones obviously never had to work with digital halftones.

The curious paradox with digital imaging is that although it allows incredible precision—a precision well beyond what the eye can see—the precision results in significant limitations in the real world. The first limitation we looked at was back in Chapter 17, *Frequency versus Gray Levels*: the higher your halftone screen frequency, the fewer gray levels you can achieve at a given resolution.

In this chapter, we look at some other limitations: attainable angles and screen frequencies. The fact is, not only do you often *not* get what you want, but you sometimes can't even get what you need. For example, if you ask for a 60-lpi, 45-degree screen on most 300-dpi laser printers, you'll actually get a 53-lpi screen. If you ask for the same screen but with a 44-degree angle, you'll get the 60-line screen, but the angle snaps to 37 degrees.

We explain why, why it matters, and what you can do about it in the course of this chapter.

WHO CARES ABOUT ATTAINABLE VALUES?

Before we jump into looking at what halftone angles and frequencies you can and can't achieve and why, let's think about why anyone would possibly care. The main reason is color separation.

In Chapter 24, *When Grids Collide*, we explored how moirés can creep into your grayscale scanning and output, and ruin your life. Grids over grids, we learned, can cause horrendous patterns in your artwork. And in Chapter 25, *Rosettes and Moirés*, we talked about the problems of moirés that can happen when you offset print the four process colors.

This chapter addresses how PostScript and imagesetter software gets rid of color moirés by an interesting combination of angle, frequency, and halftone cell creation. When it comes to avoiding patterns, the most important attributes of a halftone are its angle and frequency. Keep those to their proper values, and moirés can often be avoided. But let them wander off to other values, and your image looks as bad as a teenager's facial complexion just before a big date.

Typically, if your angles are within .001 degree and your frequency is within .01 lpi of the optimal values discussed in the last chapter, you'll not have patterning problems. As we'll see, this is often impossible. It depends on your equipment.

Requesting Angles and Frequencies

In earlier chapters, we've shown how you can specify a halftone screen in all sorts of ways: a given angle, a particular screen frequency, often even a special spot shape. However, due to the limitations of the digital world, you don't always get what you ask for.

Remember that the halftone spots are built inside halftone cells, which are made up of device dots. In typical digital screening, each of these cells looks exactly the same. They're like complex patterned tiles, and they have to fit together seamlessly. But there are only certain frequency/angle combinations at a given resolution for which this seamless tiling is possible.

CHANGING THE ANGLE AND FREQUENCY

In order to rotate a halftone screen, you have to rotate the cell. Similarly, if you want to lower or raise the screen frequency, you have to make the halftone cells larger or smaller (see Figure 26-1). The limitations occur because the halftone cell must fall on exact printer dot boundaries (see Figure 26-2), and the cells have to tile.

Because cells have to tile, there are only so many combinations of frequencies and angles available at a given resolution. If the frequency/angle combination that you request isn't available, the default action is for PostScript to use its best guess at the nearest approximation (see Table 26-1).

INCREASING PRINTER RESOLUTION

Although $1/300$ inch seems pretty small, when you're trying to build halftone screens with dots of that size, it's like building an oak dining room table with only two-by-fours. If you make the dots smaller, for instance, by using a high-resolution imagesetter, you not only get better-looking halftone spots, but you increase the number of available frequency/angle combinations. When working at a finer resolution, you can rotate or adjust the size of the halftone cell, and have more possibilities of whole dots to snap to (see Figure 26-3).

If you had an infinite number of dots, you could have any combination of frequency and angle you wanted. However, despite David's experience with the transcendental in his book *The Joy of Pi*, none of us has had much experience with the infinite.

RATIONAL VERSUS IRRATIONAL SCREENING

All the halftone screening that we've talked about in this book so far is called *rational tangent screening*. We also want to talk about *irrational* tangent screening. Both of these terms have been thrown around in the press a lot, so we'd better clarify them.

These names derive from the sort of "snapping to the nearest dot" that we've been talking about here. When you can describe an

FIGURE 26-1
Halftone cells

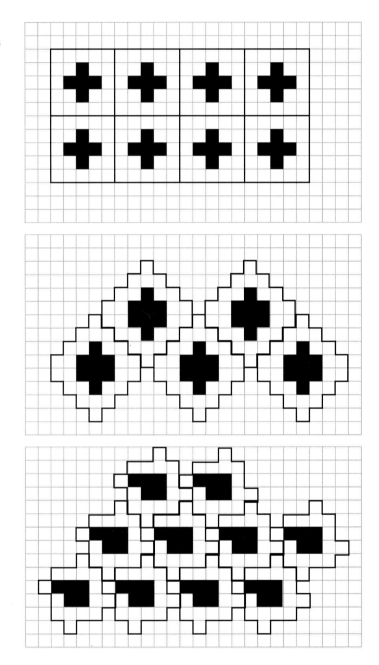

TABLE 26-1
Requested versus
actual frequency and
angle at 300 dpi

	Requested Frequency			
	50 lpi		*60 lpi*	
Requested Angle	*Actual Angle*	*Actual Frequency*	*Actual Angle*	*Actual Frequency*
0	0	50.0	0	60.0
1	0	50.0	0	60.0
2	0	50.0	0	60.0
3	0	50.0	0	60.0
4	0	50.0	0	60.0
5	9	49.3	0	60.0
6	9	49.3	11	58.8
7	9	49.3	11	58.8
8	9	49.3	11	58.8
9	9	49.3	11	58.8
10	9	49.3	11	58.8
11	9	49.3	11	58.8
12	9	49.3	11	58.8
13	9	49.3	11	58.8
14	9	49.3	11	58.8
15	18	47.4	11	58.8
16	18	47.4	11	58.8
17	18	47.4	11	58.8
18	18	47.4	22	55.7
19	18	47.4	22	55.7
20	18	47.4	22	55.7
21	18	47.4	22	55.7
22	18	47.4	22	55.7
23	18	47.4	22	55.7
24	22	55.7	22	55.7
25	31	51.4	22	55.7
26	31	51.4	27	67.1
27	31	51.4	27	67.1
28	31	51.4	27	67.1
29	31	51.4	27	67.1
30	31	51.4	37	60.0
31	31	51.4	37	60.0
32	31	51.4	37	60.0
33	31	51.4	37	60.0
34	31	51.4	37	60.0
35	31	51.4	37	60.0
36	37	60.0	37	60.0
37	37	60.0	37	60.0
38	37	60.0	37	60.0
39	37	60.0	37	60.0
40	37	60.0	37	60.0
41	37	60.0	37	60.0
42	45	53.0	37	60.0
43	45	53.0	37	60.0
44	45	53.0	37	60.0
45	45	53.0	45	53.0

FIGURE 26-2
Cells and dot
boundaries

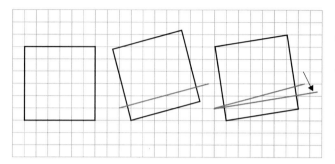

*With fewer
printer dots,
there are
fewer possi-
ble angles.
The spots
snap to the
nearest
printer dot.*

FIGURE 26-3
Finer-resolution dots

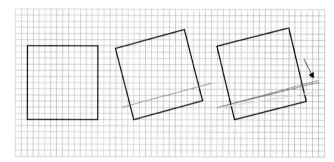

*With a finer
resolution,
there are
more dots to
snap to, so
more angles
are possible.*

angle by saying "move over eight dots and up three dots," you're describing a rational tangent angle. In fact, any angle that you can get by using whole integers is rational. The digital halftoning that we've been describing works this way.

However, as we've seen in this chapter, many angles can't be generated this way, at least not at a particular screen frequency and output resolution. For example, with rational screening there is no way to get a true 15-degree halftone screen from an imagesetter. You can get close, but you can't achieve exactly 15 degrees because there are no integer values of dots that result in that angle.

Irrational tangent screening was developed and implemented on various RIP/imagesetter combinations to deal with this problem. In irrational screening, each halftone cell is not exactly the same size; some have more printer dots in them, some have fewer (see Figure 26-4). By fudging the process like this, you can achieve a halftone grid that is extremely close to the requested frequency and angle.

The problem with irrational screening is that it's incredibly processor-intensive (read: slow to print). Unlike rational screening,

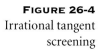

FIGURE 26-4
Irrational tangent
screening

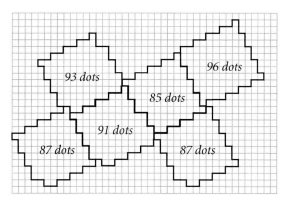

in which each of the 256 possible spots is built and cached for fast access, with irrational screening, each and every spot must be calculated on the fly, as the image is being generated.

SUPERCELL SCREENING

If you take rational and irrational screening technologies and mix them together, you get an interesting hybrid called supercell screening. A *supercell* is a collection of smaller halftone cells, each of which may be made up of a different number of printer dots. So, while each of these small halftone cells may have different printer dots (much like irrational screening), the whole supercell collection is repeated and tiled throughout the halftone (more like typical, rational screening; see Figure 26-5).

The supercell can produce a more accurate screen/angle combination because it's much bigger than its constituent halftone cells, so there are more potential corner points to snap to. This sort of screening can be a great help in reducing or eradicating patterning; however, there's often a performance hit. It's faster than irrational screening, but not as fast as standard rational screening.

WHEN YOU NEED AN ANGLE

It probably seems, after reading this chapter, that the situation is almost hopeless. But that's not so. There are more and more ways to get great, moiré-free color images. The supercell method is one of

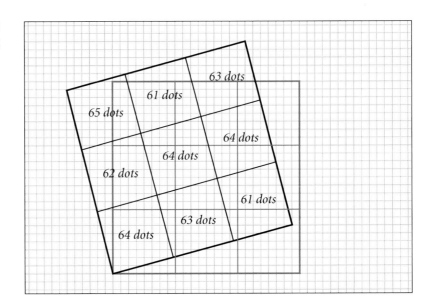

them. Another one may be by simply working with the screen/angle combinations that your imagesetter manufacturer recommends.

Many lithographers are so caught up in the old way of doing things that if you show them a set of digitally created screens at weird (to them, at least) angles and frequencies, they'll say it won't work. But sometimes you know more than they do about what you can get, and about what you need.

27 CONTROLLING HALFTONE SCREENS

WHAT OVERRIDES WHAT

Whether or not you're a control freak, you're going to end up wanting to control your halftone screens at various stages of your work. You might want the picture of Aunt Jean to be a 45-degree, 40-lpi image, that photo of Uncle Izzy to be much coarser, and all the other tints on your page to have 133-lpi screens. So how do you go about controlling those screens, making sure the right screen comes out at the right time?

The answer is (you saw this coming, right?): It depends. Screening controls work differently with different combinations of hardware and software. There is a basic hierarchy we can set down, though, of which screening controls override which others—in other words, which controls predominate.

Figure 27-1 shows, in brief, the order in which screening controls override each other. Let's look at each item in order.

DEVICE'S DEFAULT SETTINGS. Every PostScript output device has a built-in default screen setting. That means that if you print a plain ol' job with no halftone screen settings in it, you get that device's defaults for the whole job. On imagesetters and other devices with hard disks, those defaults can be changed. (Be careful of the settings discussed below—especially driver settings for Windows users; you may be unintentionally getting halftone screens that you don't want because of the application or driver controls).

FIGURE 27-1
What screen settings
override what

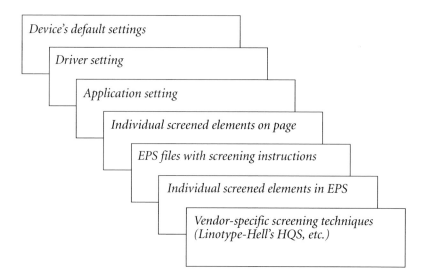

Device's default settings

Driver setting

Application setting

Individual screened elements on page

EPS files with screening instructions

Individual screened elements in EPS

Vendor-specific screening techniques
(Linotype-Hell's HQS, etc.)

DRIVER SETTING. Printer drivers are the software modules in the background that "drive" printers; PostScript drivers actually write much or all of the PostScript code that gets sent to the printer. Halftone settings are pretty minimal in print drivers, although the Windows 95 PostScript driver allows you to choose between printer defaults and choosing your own screen frequency and angle.

APPLICATION SETTING. Many applications provide control over halftone screens for your print jobs. In QuarkXPress, this control is in the Print dialog box's Output tab. In PageMaker, it's in the Print dialog box's Color setting. In Photoshop, you get to it via the Screens button in the Page Setup dialog box. It could be in a variety of places depending on the application; the important thing to understand is that any screen information you set here overrides the driver and device default settings for the whole document. (We cover this thoroughly in Part 3, *Applications.*)

INDIVIDUAL SCREENED ELEMENTS WITHIN PUBLICATIONS. In some applications—FreeHand and CorelDraw are examples—you can select individual objects (text or graphics) and set a screen for those objects. In others (such as PageMaker and QuarkXPress), you can apply screens to individual bitmapped images. These are called object-level settings, and they override the application-level settings, which apply to the rest of the job.

EPS FILES THAT INCLUDE SCREENING INSTRUCTIONS. Almost every program lets you save pages as EPS files (even if the program won't, PostScript printer drivers will). These files are often saved with halftone screening information included. When you place this file in another program, those internal screening instructions override any screening controls set by the program you're printing from. The custom screening affects only the EPS that contains the instructions. The application, driver, or device defaults apply to the rest of the job.

INDIVIDUAL SCREENED ELEMENTS WITHIN EPS FILES. An EPS file that contains screening instructions can also include individual elements within the file that have *their own* screening instructions. For example, an EPS from Macromedia FreeHand might have a gray box that has an object-level halftone screen applied to it. The EPS file's settings apply to the whole graphic, but are overridden for individual objects within the EPS that have their own settings.

VENDOR-SPECIFIC SCREENING TECHNIQUES. If you're printing to an imagesetter that uses a specialized screening technique such as Linotype-Hell's HQS, you may not get the screen settings you expect. These techniques use screening "filters" that catch all screening instructions, and replace the frequency/angle combinations with the closest settings that are available in their optimized sets. These screening technologies can override all the screening you specify, whether it's in an object, an application, or a driver. Sometimes specifying an odd screen can cause problems, too. Linotype-Hell uses 102 and 108 lpi to turn on different levels of stochastic screening in the imagesetter's RIP! It's unlikely you'd choose these frequencies, but take care, nonetheless.

WHO'S ON FIRST?

Trying to figure out what's controlling the screens in your print jobs can seem confusing. In most cases, however, you simply specify some halftone screen settings in the Print dialog box, and that setting applies to the whole job. Case closed. But, if you're not getting the screens you want, or if you want different screen settings for different parts of a job, this hierarchy of what overrides what should be a good road map for finding your way to the output you want.

28 POSTSCRIPT HALFTONING

SETSCREEN, SETGRAY, IMAGE, IMAGEMASK, AND SETTRANSFER

Our officemate Ole Kvern dreams in lines, shapes, and fills. Ole is one of the few individuals on this planet who can walk up to his machine, crack his knuckles, and start programming in PostScript. Sure, PostScript is called a "page-description language"—a structured method of defining the exact appearance of objects on a page—but that's usually just a figure of speech. Of course, Ole has a Mac, a PC, and a NeXT workstation all within inches of each other, and to see his fingers fly...well, you'd think they'd be teaching it alongside French to elementary schoolchildren.

If you've ever read any of Ole's columns in *Adobe Magazine*, read his book *Real World FreeHand*, or taken a stab at deciphering PostScript yourself, this chapter and the next may make some semblance of sense to you. On the other hand, if you've taken the more familiar path (believe us, you're not alone, and with good reason), you probably don't know anything about PostScript—or want to—and you can just skip this chapter and the next, and go straight to Part 3, *Applications*.

On the third hand, if you're a developer or a real wirehead, for goodness' sake, put down this book and rush out and buy Adobe's *PostScript Language Reference Manual, Second Edition,* and then download the addenda for Level 2 and PostScript 3 from the developer's section of the Web site.

BUILT-IN GOODNESS

It is to their credit that John Warnock and Chuck Geschke, when developing PostScript almost 15 years ago, saw fit to include a powerful but simple halftone generator in the PostScript engine. Printing grays to non-PostScript printers requires the software on the computer to generate the appropriate halftone screens at the resolution of the printer. For the application to print to a PostScript printer, however, it only needs to send the screen angle, frequency, spot shape, and gray level—hardly a daunting task.

The functions we describe below came out of PostScript Level 1, which was a bit simpler than the Level 2 and PostScript 3 revisions (yes, they removed "Level" from its name for version 3). PostScript 3, released in late 1996, especially raises the bar, as it's almost a complete publishing environment. You can even do things as weird as tell a PostScript 3 printer to retrieve a page off the Web and print it.

However, Adobe likes backward compatibility, and everything we tell you about here will work with every printer from early LaserWriters to the latest 9,600-dpi drum imagesetters.

We're not going to turn you into PostScript programmers in this chapter. We do, however, explain the basic PostScript operators for scanning and halftoning, so you can recognize them and understand their operation when you're perusing PostScript code. Maybe you're just curious. Maybe, someday, this will save your butt at three in the morning.

PostScript Operators

There are five PostScript operators of primary importance for scanning and halftones: *setscreen*, *setgray*, *image*, *imagemask*, and *settransfer*. We like to think of the commands below as simple ingredients to make complex recipes versus the gourmet meal that the later versions of PostScript offer.

Here's a brief rundown of the five operators.

SETSCREEN. This is the basic PostScript halftoning operator. You use it to specify frequency, angle, and spot shape.

SETGRAY. This operator simply specifies a gray level, from 0 to 100 percent.

IMAGE. This operator is used to image all bitmaps.

IMAGEMASK. Only 1-bit images can be used with this operator.

SETTRANSFER. This operator adjusts a PostScript device's gray-response, so you can control what actually gets printed when a given gray level is requested.

SETSCREEN

The key to assigning halftone screens, angles, and spot shapes in PostScript is the *setscreen* operator. This operator takes three arguments: the frequency, the angle, and the spot function. While the first two are obvious, the third is a little more complex, so we've written a whole chapter on it (see the next chapter, *Spot Functions*). A very simple example, which sets a 75-lpi, 45-degree line screen, reads *75 45 {pop} setscreen*. Here's a more real-world example of *setscreen* in action.

```
currentscreen          % put existing screen arguments on stack
/spot exch def         % save existing spot function in "spot"
pop pop                % throw away frequency and angle
133 45 spot setscreen  % put frequency, angle, and spot function
                            on stack, call setscreen
```

The *currentscreen* operator loads the device's existing screen arguments onto the stack in the same order as *setscreen* requires. In the above code, "spot" becomes a variable defined as the spot function of the existing screen, preserving it for use in our new screen. The frequency and angle settings are thrown away (popped). Finally, new frequency and angle settings are placed on the stack, followed by the spot function. The *setscreen* operator uses those three arguments, resulting in a 133-lpi, 45-degree screen with the previously existing spot function.

SETGRAY

There are simpler operators than *setgray* in the PostScript lexicon, but not many. To define a gray level for an object in PostScript, you use *setgray* with a value between zero and one (zero is black; one is white). Here's an example that draws a 100-point square, and fills it with a 40-percent tint.

```
100 100 moveto
0 100 rlineto
100 0 rlineto
0 -100 rlineto
closepath
.6 setgray
fill
showpage
```

The *.6 setgray* line sets the gray level, and the *fill* operator fills the current object with that gray. The percentage is reversed from how we normally talk about gray, so a 40-percent tint is specified .6 (60-percent white).

IMAGE

The *image* operator, which is used to image most bitmaps, is somewhat more complex than most PostScript operators. Rather than providing a uniform gray fill, *image* goes through each sample point in a string of data, setting the gray level for each sample.

The *image* operator takes five arguments: the width and height of the bitmap, the number of bits per sample point, the image matrix (the relationship between the image's coordinate system and PostScript's), and the data acquisition procedure (the method for reading the ensuing image data). What you get is an image in a one-unit square at the coordinates 0,0 (a unit is one point large until you scale it up). Here's *image* in action:

```
/width 20 def            % Number of sample points horizontal
/height 19 def           % Number of sample points vertical
/BitsPerSample 8 def     % Bits per sample point
/TheMatrix [width 0 0 height neg 0 height] def
                         % Image matrix
/picstr 20 string def    % Convert width to string and save in picstr
/DataRead {currentfile picstr readhexstring pop} def
                         % Data reading procedure
100 100 translate        % move to right place on page
200 190 scale            % scale the image up from a one-unit square
width height BitsPerSample TheMatrix /DataRead load image
DFDDDDE0E1DEE1E8E0D0D0DAE4E1DBDCDAD3D4D9DDDCDBDDDCD9C08B5C313056
96BBDFE0DEDBE0D3D5D7D6D4D8C94911190D0D10213C93DCDDDCE1CED0D4D4D6
C3643A576F687167716C439DDDD5D7D0D3D6D2D8B131617A91AEB7A590855342
CDD5D7D9D9D6D4D7C24A61738EA4A5A18A7E5F3AA6D8D7D7D8D7D0D5B35C3A33
346A8F5E404645479AD3D3CFCAD3CFD0AF772217241C281D230F245BA2C9D2C9
C2C4C9C8BA96575766658D69735D4D65BDCCD2CBCDD0D2C9C2BA5C6467658E68
777A68A5D0CCD1CACBC8C2A97A543854603D3B50686960B8D1CECCC6D0C38E4C
16041E3B665A63637B5F2F3096C9C9C6CCC19C672B0C3739367481804F453B38
87BDC6C3C9C9BB9151293C9B552A3340678A4B75AEC0C1BBD1CFCEBB916746B9
CB684D96CD9073A6BDC1C2BDD3D6D4D2C6AC8CBFA353A9DDC59AADC2C9C5C3C2
D4D3D4D6D7CFBBC4938ED0D4BDB7C9CCCCC7C1BDD5D1CFD3D7DAC9C7B0BFD0D2
C8C9D0D1CDC6C2BFD8D5D3CAC4C1BFC0B1B7C0BFC0C3C5D3CEC5C1C1
showpage
```

Note that if the image is saved in binary rather than hexadecimal format, you need to use *readstring* rather than *readhexstring*.

IMAGEMASK

While it's similar to *image, imagemask* serves a somewhat different purpose, and it only works with black-and-white (1-bit) bitmaps. The *imagemask* operator uses a 1-bit image to set up a mask through which "paint" can be applied to the page. It takes the same width, height, image matrix, and data acquisition parameters as *image.* But instead of the bits-per-sample value (the image is expected to be one bit deep), it takes a true/false boolean argument that tells it which areas to paint. True paints the black areas of the bitmap; false paints the white areas. (PostScript 3 supports more complex masking, which can involve alpha channel transparency; it requires different operators than *imagemask*. We describe alpha channels in "Transparency" in Chapter 11, *Images for the Web*.)

SETTRANSFER

The *setgray* and *image* operators tell the PostScript device what gray level to spit out. But what if the actual, printed gray level isn't what you want? What if you (or your software) ask for a 15-percent gray, and you get 20 percent instead? It's a common scenario: The output from laser printers and imagesetters varies based on many factors.

Given that variation, there's obviously a need for some overriding operator that controls how a device images grays, without the need to go through a whole PostScript program changing all the *setgray* and *image* values. That metaoperator is *settransfer*. Its job is to map the grays requested to a set of grays that PostScript uses for imaging.

The *settransfer* operator takes a gray level and converts it into another gray level, depending on the algorithm you give it. For instance, *settransfer* can be used for simple things like producing negatives through the command *{1 exch sub} settransfer*. Or it can be used for strange things, such as in this procedure written by Bill Woodruff, to convert all the values between .25 and .75 to .5, while passing all the others through unaltered: *{dup .25 ge 1 index .75 le and {pop .5} if} settransfer*.

The most interesting uses of *settransfer* come when you start correcting the gray curve for the output device you're using. The following bit of code, for instance, adapted from Pat Wood's work in *The PostScript Language Journal*, maps the grays to provide a more even density transition on the original Apple LaserWriter at its default frequency. The same method can be used for posterization (stairstepping the gray values for special effects) or for linearizing an imagesetter so a request for 10-percent gray yields a 10-percent tint.

```
/transarray [
0 0 0 0 0 0 0 0 1 1 1 2 2 3 3 3
4 4 5 5 5 6 6 6 7 7 8 8 8 9 9 10
```

```
10 10 11 11 12 12 12 13 13 14 14 14 15 15 15 16
16 17 17 17 18 18 20 20 20 22 22 24 24 24 26 26
26 28 28 31 31 31 34 34 37 37 37 40 40 42 42 42
44 44 46 46 46 48 48 48 49 49 51 51 51 52 52 54
54 54 55 55 57 57 57 59 59 60 60 60 62 62 62 63
63 65 65 65 66 66 68 68 68 69 69 71 71 71 72 72
72 72 72 73 73 73 74 74 75 75 75 76 76 77 77 77
78 78 78 78 78 79 79 79 80 80 81 81 81 82 82 83
83 83 83 83 84 84 84 85 85 85 85 85 86 86 86 87
87 87 87 87 88 88 88 88 88 89 89 89 89 89 90 90
90 90 90 91 91 91 91 91 92 92 92 92 92 93 93 93
93 93 94 94 94 94 94 94 95 95 95 95 95 96 96 96
96 96 97 97 97 97 97 97 97 97 97 97 98 98 98 98
98 98 98 98 98 98 99 99 99 99 100 100 100 100 100
] def
{255 mul cvi       %multiply gray times 256 and make integer
transarray exch get        % look up gray value in array
100 div   % return gray setting in 0 to 1 range
} settransfer
```

The array consists of 256 values, one for each of 256 gray values. You could just as easily use 50, 100, or 200 values. The important thing is the grayscale mapping. Let's say the requested gray level is .5. The transfer function multiplies it by 255 and converts it to an integer, yielding 127. It looks up the 127th value in the array (72), and divides it by 100, resulting in .72 setgray (a 28-percent tint) when you request .5.

This array is designed to work on LaserWriters and other Canon "print black" CX engine printers at their default frequency (nominally 60 lpi, actually 53). If you change the frequency, you will need to change the array as well, since spot variation is more pronounced at higher frequencies (see Chapter 19, *Setting Your Screens*). Figure 28-1 shows two graduated fills from white to black. In the first, *settransfer* is unaltered. The second shows the results with the transfer array above.

Typically, this sort of calibration is extremely time-consuming and tedious; fortunately, in this case other people have done most of

FIGURE 28-1

settransfer and grays with unaltered output on top and linearized output on the bottom

the hard work for you. Service bureau's imagesetter linearization programs use a densitometer to measure strips of output as they print. They can then create custom transfer functions for particular types of paper stock (newsprint, coated, etc.), or even paper that you might be using regularly. They typically have an array into which you can type densitometer readings from sample output. The main limitation is that you have to be able to offset print your tests to make it work. (There is some hope about building this into an entire color-managed approach, which we describe in Chapter 8, *Color.*)

So you don't really need to know how to program transfer functions, but it can be useful to know what these programs are doing behind the scenes—especially when some program insists on overriding the transfer functions you've set up with one of those calibration programs.

THE WEIRD WORLD OF POSTSCRIPT

PostScript's halftoning engine is extremely powerful, providing you with all the tools you need to create great screens. If you're not already overloaded, then hold tight: the next chapter explores this world a little further with an in-depth look at spot functions.

29 SPOT FUNCTIONS

INSIDE THE HALFTONE CELL

Now it's time to don your helmet, grab hold of your pickax, and play the part of a spelunker—one of those wild-eyed explorers who seem to thrive on the atmosphere of deep, dark, dank caves. But we won't be looking at stalagmites and stalactites today. Rather, we're going deep into the heart of the halftone spot. What makes up these tiny critters? What mysterious algorithm decides a spot's shape?

In Chapter 20, *The Glorious Spot*, we described a variety of spots for different purposes; in the previous chapter, *PostScript Halftoning*, we quickly passed over the concept of spot functions, saying that they were just part of the *setscreen* operator's variables. In this chapter we see exactly what makes a spot function tick.

Note that we're talking about normal ol' rational tangent screening here. Many developers have created alternate screening methods (see Chapter 22, *Stochastic Screening*), but those are proprietary methods that we won't discuss in detail here.

THE DOT GRID

As soon as you call *setscreen*, PostScript begins to create a perfect halftone cell, something that can be repeated (tiled) over a large area—the whole page, if necessary. The cell's shape and size depend on the printer's resolution, the screen angle, and the screen frequency (see Figure 29-1).

FIGURE 29-1
Various halftone cells

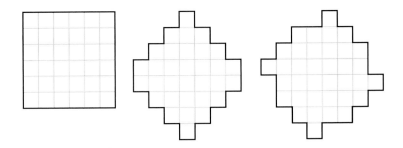

Once the cell shape is determined, the PostScript interpreter can build a halftone spot inside it. To do this, it needs to look at each printer dot that falls inside the cell. Each dot has a particular coordinate value from (-1,-1) to (1,1). The value (0,0) is right in the center (see Figure 29-2).

THE FUNCTION

The spot shape is generated by a tendency for dots to turn on. The interpreter assigns a "tendency value" to each dot in the halftone cell. This value corresponds loosely to gray levels that the halftone cell will be asked to simulate. Tendency values are always between -1 and 1.

For example, at a 25-percent gray level, all the dots in the cell that have a value of -1 to -.5 would turn on. To create a 50-percent tint, all the dots with values up to and including 0 would turn on. (The tendency values resulting from a spot function don't actually have to span the whole range from -1 to 1. They could go from -.4 to .6, for instance; the important part is the *relative* ranking of dots within the cell.)

Spot functions work by taking two arguments—the x and y coordinates of the dot in the cell—and handing back a tendency value for each dot. So the dots are ranked, in the order in which they're to be turned on. When the interpreter receives a gray value, it turns on the first five dots, the first 50 dots, or whatever is necessary to achieve that tint percentage. To make this clearer, let's look at a simple example—a spot function that creates line screens.

FIGURE 29-2

Dot coordinates
in a cell

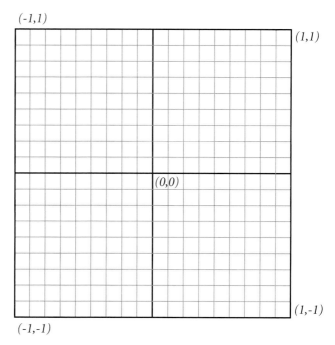

LINE SPOT

Perhaps the simplest spot function is *{pop}*, which creates a line screen. The PostScript interpreter puts the x and y coordinates of each dot on the stack (so y is on top, with x next). The line spot function simply throws away the top (y) value (the *pop* operator removes the top item from the stack).

The result? Each printer dot is assigned a tendency equal to its x value. So all the dots on the left side have low values, and therefore turn on first. All the dots on the right side have higher values, and turn on later—only with darker grays. Figure 29-3 shows a representation of this cell, detailing each dot's coordinates, tendency value, and ranking. The dots always turn on in the order that they're ranked; each dot of a higher ranking is turned on only after all lower-ranking dots have been turned on.

FIGURE 29-3
Line spot

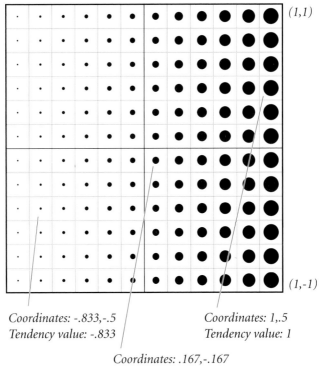

(1,1)

(1,-1)

Coordinates: -.833,-.5
Tendency value: -.833

Coordinates: 1,.5
Tendency value: 1

Coordinates: .167,-.167
Tendency value: .167

ROUND SPOT

The next spot we'll look at is the normal round spot: *{dup mul exch dup mul add 1 exch sub}*. This is the PostScript equivalent to "$1 - (x^2 + y^2)$." The result is a round spot that increases in size until it fills the entire cell. Figure 29-4 shows a representation of this cell.

The more common alternate to the standard round spot is *{abs exch abs 2 copy add 1 gt {1 sub dup mul exch 1 sub dup mul add 1 sub} {dup mul exch dup mul add 1 exch sub} ifelse}*. This spot function is conditional: up to a certain point in the cell (corresponding to an approximately 50-percent spot), the normal round spot is used. Beyond that, an inverted spot is used. That is, the spot starts to be built from the corners into the center rather than from the center out.

FIGURE 29-4
Round spot

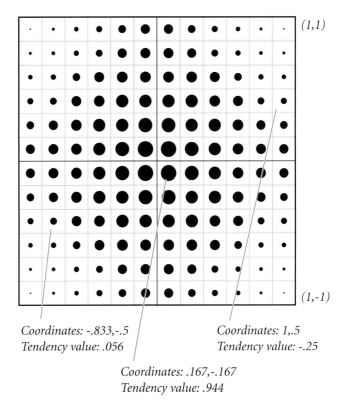

Coordinates: -.833,-.5
Tendency value: .056

Coordinates: 1,.5
Tendency value: -.25

Coordinates: .167,-.167
Tendency value: .944

MORE SPOTS

As long as you can come up with a PostScript function for it, you can create spots of almost any shape. Here are some of our favorites (see Figure 29-5). If you're hacking PostScript code, you can type them into a *setscreen* argument. Or, if you use a program that supports custom screens (as Photoshop does via the Screens button in the Page Setup dialog box), you can type them into a dialog box. With Photoshop, don't type the procedure name (the slash and the word)—just the curly brackets (a.k.a. *braces*) and what's inside them (you can also include the "bind" at the end; it can make the code run faster).

FIGURE 29-5
Some favorite
spot functions

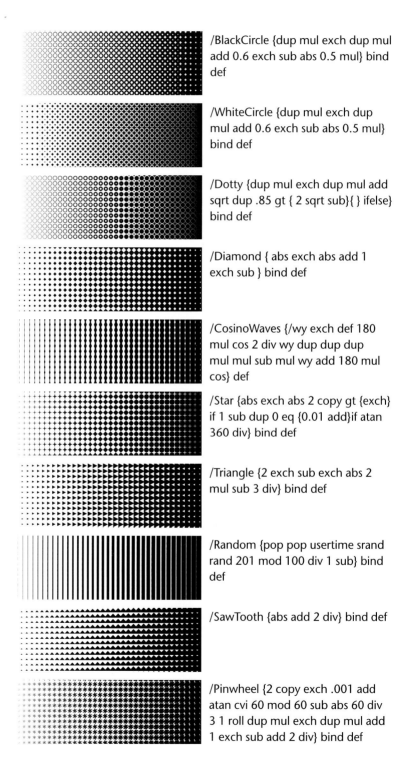

/BlackCircle {dup mul exch dup mul
add 0.6 exch sub abs 0.5 mul} bind
def

/WhiteCircle {dup mul exch dup
mul add 0.6 exch sub abs 0.5 mul}
bind def

/Dotty {dup mul exch dup mul add
sqrt dup .85 gt { 2 sqrt sub}{ } ifelse}
bind def

/Diamond { abs exch abs add 1
exch sub } bind def

/CosinoWaves {/wy exch def 180
mul cos 2 div wy dup dup dup
mul mul sub mul wy add 180 mul
cos} def

/Star {abs exch abs 2 copy gt {exch}
if 1 sub dup 0 eq {0.01 add}if atan
360 div} bind def

/Triangle {2 exch sub exch abs 2
mul sub 3 div} bind def

/Random {pop pop usertime srand
rand 201 mod 100 div 1 sub} bind
def

/SawTooth {abs add 2 div} bind def

/Pinwheel {2 copy exch .001 add
atan cvi 60 mod 60 sub abs 60 div
3 1 roll dup mul exch dup mul add
1 exch sub add 2 div} bind def

FIGURE 29-5
Some favorite
spot functions,
continued

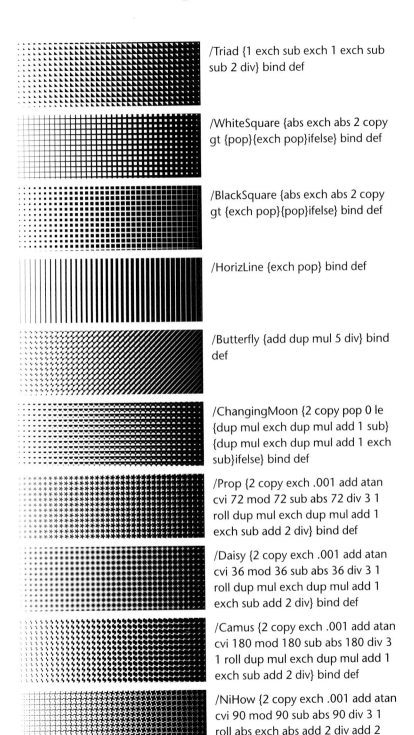

/Triad {1 exch sub exch 1 exch sub sub 2 div} bind def

/WhiteSquare {abs exch abs 2 copy gt {pop}{exch pop}ifelse} bind def

/BlackSquare {abs exch abs 2 copy gt {exch pop}{pop}ifelse} bind def

/HorizLine {exch pop} bind def

/Butterfly {add dup mul 5 div} bind def

/ChangingMoon {2 copy pop 0 le {dup mul exch dup mul add 1 sub} {dup mul exch dup mul add 1 exch sub}ifelse} bind def

/Prop {2 copy exch .001 add atan cvi 72 mod 72 sub abs 72 div 3 1 roll dup mul exch dup mul add 1 exch sub add 2 div} bind def

/Daisy {2 copy exch .001 add atan cvi 36 mod 36 sub abs 36 div 3 1 roll dup mul exch dup mul add 1 exch sub add 2 div} bind def

/Camus {2 copy exch .001 add atan cvi 180 mod 180 sub abs 180 div 3 1 roll dup mul exch dup mul add 1 exch sub add 2 div} bind def

/NiHow {2 copy exch .001 add atan cvi 90 mod 90 sub abs 90 div 3 1 roll abs exch abs add 2 div add 2 div} bind def

THE STRANGEST SPOT FUNCTIONS

As you can see, spot functions can be pretty strange. Typically, however, you'd never use the weird spot functions except for special effects. Even then, they're a little dodgy to use, and Adobe generally suggests you not use low-frequency custom-spot halftones for special effects. We think they're pretty cool, though.

When it comes to *really* strange spot functions, though, nothing beats these: custom pictures in a spot function. Figure 29-6 shows one of these. The code is too complex to include here, but we wanted to show you that it *can* be done.

FIGURE 29-6
Really strange
spot function

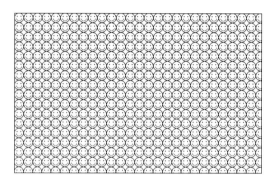

SPOT FUNCTIONS AND PAGE ORIENTATION

One final caveat about using strange spot functions for special effects: You can get messed up if you rotate a page on output. Since they're working with actual device pixels, halftone screens are by necessity working in *device space*. If you rotate *user space*—for instance, printing a page in transverse mode to an imagesetter—the orientation of the spots doesn't rotate with the page.

So if you're using triangle spots at a coarse screen frequency to point your reader's eye to the right, watch out when you rotate the page. The triangles will be pointing north or south, not east. The same problem arises with line screens, or any other orientation-dependent, asymmetrical spot function.

CACHING SPOTS

If you really want to understand PostScript's halftoning (and if you're still reading this chapter, you obviously do), you have to understand how it caches spots. When you use *setscreen*, the PostScript interpreter builds every possible spot for that frequency/ angle/spot function/resolution combination, and caches them all away. It builds a spot with one dot on, one with two dots on, one with three dots on, up to the total number of dots in the cell.

Then when it's time to actually image a halftone—a gray fill or a scanned image—the PostScript interpreter simply pulls the appropriate spots out of its cache. If it needs a 50-percent gray value, it grabs the spot with half the dots turned on, and plops it down. If it needs a 25-percent spot, it grabs the cached spot with one-quarter of the dots turned on.

There are a couple of implications to PostScript's spot-caching behavior. First, it's fast. Once it has built and cached all the spots, the interpreter just uses them; it doesn't have to recalculate the spot function for each individual spot. (This is why irrational screening—covered in Chapter 26, *Angle Strategies*—is so processor-intensive. Spots can't be cached; the interpreter must calculate, on the fly, each spot in an image.)

The second implication of spot caching is the impossibility of true random screening (for instance, a diffusion dither) using PostScript's standard spot-function-based screening. You can write a random spot function easily enough (*pop pop usertime srand rand 201 mod 100 div 1 sub*), and PostScript will build a spot with dots turned on randomly. But since PostScript builds all the spots once and caches them, all the 50-percent spots in an image are the same. And they're essentially the same as the 45-percent spots, but with more dots turned on.

If you print the job a second time, the spots will be different. But in each print job, all the spots of a given gray level are the same; and they're substantially the same as the other spots, but with greater or fewer dots turned on. The result is a patterned look that changes from print job to print job, but doesn't give you the randomized dither look you might be trying for.

ON THE SPOT

We're kind of weird this way, but we really like playing with spot functions. Strange spots are rarely useful for production work (but when you need 'em, you need 'em), and they can be problematic for special design effects, but they sure are fun to play with.

PART 3
APPLICATIONS

30 IMAGE APPLICATIONS

MESSING WITH BITMAPS

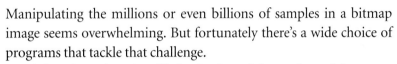

Manipulating the millions or even billions of samples in a bitmap image seems overwhelming. But fortunately there's a wide choice of programs that tackle that challenge.

Adobe Photoshop is still the leader of the pack, and has even spawned another version of itself: PhotoDeluxe, aimed at nonprofessionals who nonetheless want to have high-end tools for under $100. Meanwhile, Micrografx Picture Publisher, CorelPhoto-Paint, and Equilibrium DeBabelizer have continued their maturing process into higher and higher version numbers. And those of you who remember way back to Aldus days will remember Ulead Systems—which now produces PhotoImpact—as the folks who developed the now-defunct Aldus PhotoStyler.

Throughout this book, we've suggested techniques for doing the best correction and sharpening, and in this chapter we show you how to apply these lessons to other programs. We also talk about specific subjects, like importing Photo CD images, setting screen frequencies, and selecting halftone spot shapes.

PHOTOSHOP

Photoshop is *the* central tool for working with scanned images on the Mac and Windows desktop, and for that reason we've covered it in quite some detail throughout the book. (We've also used it to create the bulk of the illustrations.) In particular, we covered two of Photoshop's most important tools—Levels and the Unsharp Mask filter—in detail in Chapter 7, *Tonal Correction*, Chapter 8, *Color*, and Chapter 9, *A Sharper Image*.

We could write a whole book on Photoshop's other features—oh, wait, we already did! David and his colleague Bruce Fraser wrote *Real World Photoshop 4*, a book that covers the nitty-gritty issues of getting images beat into shape for a variety of purposes, including those we cover in this book. Think of a software manual as 1x magnification on the program, this book as 10x magnification, and *Real World Photoshop 4* as the 100x setting.

We also talk about Extensis Intellihance under the Photoshop heading, because we find it to be very close to the mythical Make Better button that Steve's been looking for since the dawn of DTP.

CONTROLLING SCREENING IN PHOTOSHOP

Photoshop provides better control over screening on output than any other program we've seen. Click the Screens button in the Page Setup dialog box, and up comes the Halftone Screen dialog box (see Figure 30-1).

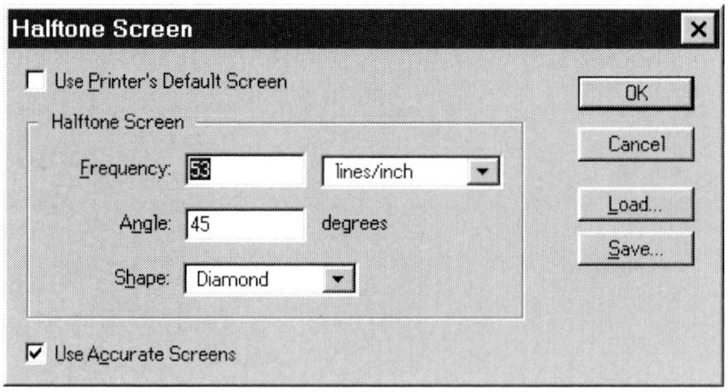

FIGURE 30-1
Photoshop's Halftone
Screen dialog box

When you specify frequency, angle, and spot shape in this dialog box, you get that halftone every time you print the image (until you change the settings). You can also include this screening information in a saved EPS version of the image by selecting Include Halftone Screen in the Save as EPS dialog box; see Figure 30-2. (For more on controlling screens in EPS files, see Chapter 27, *Controlling Halftone Screens.*)

FIGURE 30-2
EPS Format dialog box, which appears after selecting EPS and clicking Save in Photoshop

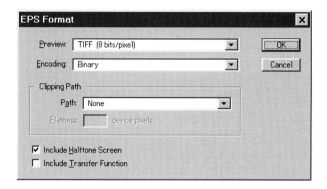

It's that easy. However, there are three items in the dialog box that deserve a little more discussion: the Shape popup menu, and the Use Accurate Screens and Use Printer's Default Screen checkboxes.

SHAPE. The Shape popup menu (see Figure 30-3) lets you specify what halftone spot function you want to use. You can choose among six canned spot functions, or define your own. The Ellipse spot function is especially interesting and relevant, because it generates the transforming elliptical spots that we described in Chapter 20, *The Glorious Spot.*

FIGURE 30-3
Custom spot shapes in Photoshop

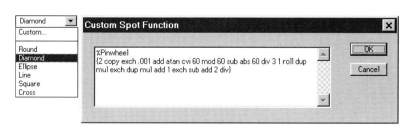

If you want to use a custom spot function, such as the ones we provide in Chapter 29, *Spot Functions,* choose Custom from the Shape popup menu. You can then type the PostScript code in the dialog box. Remember to include the curly braces { } on either side of the function. Note that custom halftone screens are rarely necessary except for low-frequency, special-effect screens.

USE ACCURATE SCREENS. The Use Accurate Screens checkbox causes imagesetters equipped with Adobe's Accurate Screens technology to use that technology, snapping requested frequencies and angles to ones that are included in the optimized screening sets. The thing is, no one we know really uses Accurate Screens. Most people use screening routines provided by the major imagesetter vendors: Agfa's Balanced Screens, Linotype-Hell's High-Quality Screens (HQS), or other built-in systems.

USE PRINTER'S DEFAULT SCREEN. Turn the Use Printer's Default Screen checkbox on if you want your image to print using the output device's default screen settings. Note that your service bureau may have changed its imagesetter's default settings, so the defaults you get may be different from what they were when the machine came from the factory. If you're placing this file inside a page-layout program, the defaults will come from that program, not the imagesetter; see Chapter 32, *Page-Layout Applications.*

HALFTONING WITHIN PHOTOSHOP

If Photoshop is remarkable in any way (and it's remarkable in many ways), it's because it can do many of the things that PostScript can. It can open Illustrator PostScript files and convert them to bitmaps, just like a PostScript interpreter. And it can convert any grayscale file to a black-and-white bitmap, halftoning it in the process.

To turn a grayscale image into a halftone, choose Bitmap (a.k.a. "bilevel bitmap") from the Mode menu. You'll see the dialog box in Figure 30-4. Choose Halftone Screen as the conversion option, and you get the Halftone Screen dialog box shown in Figure 30-5.

FIGURE 30-4
Photoshop's
Bitmap dialog box

FIGURE 30-5
Photoshop's
Halftone Screen
dialog box

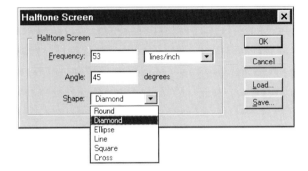

In the Halftone Screen dialog box, you can set the frequency and angle of the resulting halftone, and choose among Photoshop's built-in spot shapes. Unfortunately, you can't use a custom spot function in this dialog box. If you want a custom spot function, you might try creating it by selecting Custom Pattern in the Bitmap dialog box (you have to define a pattern first).

By the way, if you want to play around with your own version of stochastic, or frequency-modulated, screening—see Chapter 22, *Stochastic Screening*—try converting grayscale images to black-and-white bitmaps using the Diffusion Dither option. (Diffusion Dither isn't good enough for serious, high-resolution work; for that, you should use a professional stochastic program, like Icefields.)

PHOTO CD

Photoshop was one of the first programs to support Photo CD. Through the Kodak CMS system that ships with Photoshop 3 and later versions, you can open Photo CD images directly from the Open dialog box (see Figure 30-6). We suggest, however, using the

FIGURE 30-6
Photoshop's
Open dialog box
options for opening
Photo CD files

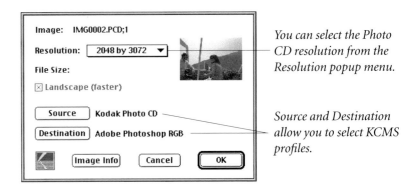

You can select the Photo CD resolution from the Resolution popup menu.

Source and Destination allow you to select KCMS profiles.

free Kodak Photoshop Acquire Module, which can be downloaded from the Kodak Web site, if you need to crop or do certain adjustments. The breakout on this plug-in is in Chapter 14, *Photo CD*.

INTELLIHANCE

Extensis Intellihance is a Photoshop plug-in that makes us cry with happiness. It has what feels like dozens of controls that you can use to tweak an image overall from a single set of menus. But better than that, a single button applies its best estimate of what will make the image better (see Figure 30-7). The average scan can just be run through Intellihance without much tweaking.

FIGURE 30-7
Intellihance's simple
"Make Better" button

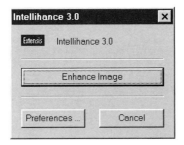

If you want to let your fingers do a bit more of the walking, there are two levels of refinement: Preferences and Fine Tuning. Preferences offers plain-English popup menus for each of the areas it controls: Descreen, Contrast, Brightness, Saturation, Cast, Sharpness, and Despeckle (see Figure 30-8). Note that the Contrast and Brightness adjustments are linear corrections, which we savaged back in

FIGURE 30-8
Intellihance's
Preferences view

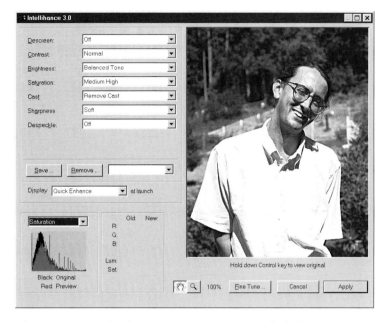

Chapter 7, *Tonal Adjustment.* To avoid this, click the Fine Tune button that appears under the preview image, and have access to a Tone tab instead, which provides nonlinear correction (see Figure 30-9). Fine Tune offers sliders for all of the values, instead of presets. We prefer to make these kinds of changes in Photoshop, however.

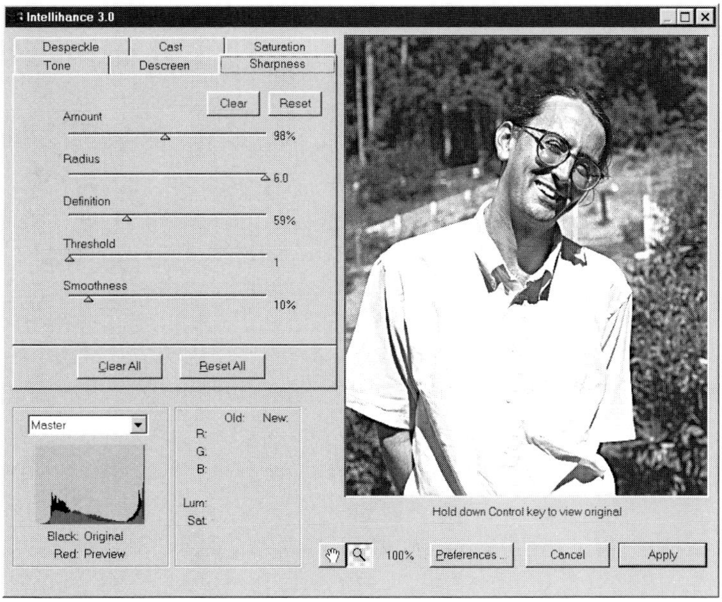

FIGURE 30-9
Intellihance's Fine
Tune settings

PICTURE PUBLISHER

Micrografx's Picture Publisher for Windows probably has the closest parity to Photoshop of any of the other image-editing applications. It actually exceeds a few of Photoshop's controls, but most of them work so similarly that we can just point out a few of the differences, rather than shortcomings.

TONAL CORRECTION

Picture Publisher uses the identical histogram metaphor for doing nonlinear tonal correction as Photoshop (see Figure 30-10). The Tone Balance dialog box has sliders labeled H, M, and S for highlights, midtones, and shadows. Unlike Photoshop, while you are dragging the sliders, you get a live preview of the changes; you don't need to release the mouse button to see changes.

FIGURE 30-10
Picture Publisher's
Tone Balance
dialog box (like Levels
in Photoshop)

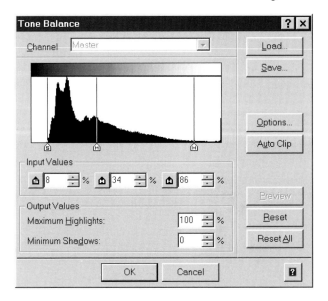

Below the histogram and sliders, you can see the percentages you've chosen for each slider. You can enter these manually instead of dragging the slider. Unlike Photoshop's separate display for output values, Picture Publisher lets you directly enter percentage values. The Auto Clip option makes a best guess at the right balance.

SHARPENING

Picture Publisher's unsharp masking controls (available via the Effects menu item) are very similar to Photoshop's, which we discussed in Chapter 9, *A Sharper Image.* The numbers in this dialog box work slightly differently, however. (See Figure 30-11.)

FIGURE 30-11
Picture Publisher's Unsharp Mask controls

The Radius setting works as follows: a setting of 1 yields blips on each side of a tonal shift that are one sample wide (two samples for the whole halo). A setting of 4 yields blips two samples wide (four samples for the whole halo). So to achieve halos ¹/₅₀ inch wide, as we suggest, divide the image resolution by 150, and add 1. Radius has to be specified in whole units, unlike Photoshop.

(Image resolution ÷ 150) + 1

Use the resulting value for your Radius setting.

The Strength setting is equivalent to Photoshop's Amount setting, except that it doesn't allow for values above 100 percent. We recommend leaving Strength set to the default of 100 percent—and even that isn't really enough. To compensate for this, you might try reducing Radius to 50 percent of what's recommended above, then running the filter twice. If it looks too extreme on the second pass, use the Undo command.

The Threshold setting works exactly like Photoshop's. Set it to 3 or 4 for most images.

SCREENING CONTROLS

Picture Publisher has only one place in which you can set the screen frequency, angles, and the shape of the halftone spot, and it's nested a bit deeply. You have to select Print from the File menu, then click the Properties button next to the printer selection, and finally click Setup Print Style to reach the Halftone tab (see Figure 30-12). Only three spot shapes are offered: circular, square, and elliptical.

FIGURE 30-12
Picture Publisher's Halftone tab in the Setup Print Style dialog box

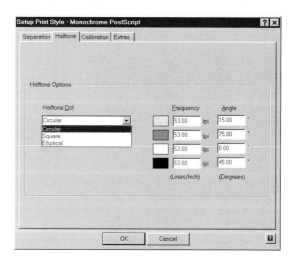

HALFTONING BITMAPS

You can't control the dither or halftone shape or size when converting an image to a black-and-white bitmap.

PHOTO CD

Some simple controls are available from the Open dialog box for cropping and importing a Photo CD image (see Figure 30-13). A Resolution popup menu lets you select the size to import, and a cropping rectangle allows direct selection in the preview. We described the Scene Balance Algorithm (SBA) in Chapter 14, *Photo CD*; the Open dialog checkbox allows you to turn off this correction.

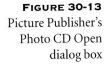

FIGURE 30-13
Picture Publisher's
Photo CD Open
dialog box

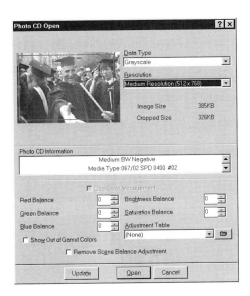

CORELPHOTO-PAINT

CorelPhoto-Paint is bundled with CorelDraw, and many folks may not be generally exposed to it. But it has a relatively powerful set of tools with controls that match Photoshop's in key areas.

TONAL CORRECTION

Photo-Paint has two methods of doing nonlinear tonal correction, although neither is quite to our specification. Both use histograms to visualize tonal balances. Sample/Target Balance lets you use eyedropper tools to target your ideal values (see Figure 30-14). This control doesn't let you specify output values, however, and it's visual in function rather than numeric. Level Equalization works much the way that Photoshop's Levels does, but it's missing an interative midtone-level slider, which would help you eyeball nonlinear correction (see Figure 30-15). It does offer a Gamma Adjustment, which affects the entire curve and effectively works the same way. And it also displays changes to the master and RGB channels as an overlay on the existing histogram as you make them.

FIGURE 30-14
Photo-Paint's
Sample/Target
Balance dialog box

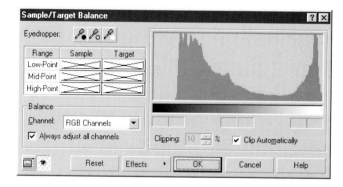

FIGURE 30-15
Photo-Paint's
Level Equalization
dialog box

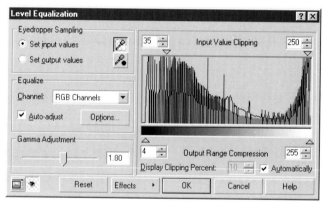

SHARPENING

Between versions 6 and 8 of Photo-Paint, Corel managed to make the unsharp masking controls substantially more powerful. You can control the same three variables that Photoshop offers, but the radius formula is different (see Figure 30-16). Radius corresponds exactly to the number of pixels on each side of a blip. So a radius of 1 means one pixel on each side; a radius of 2, two pixels; and so on. The formula we've provided earlier in this chapter for Picture Publisher works like this for CorelPhoto-Paint 8:

(Image resolution ÷ 200) + 1

Also, and this is funny, the Percentage setting is on a 0-to-500 scale—but 500 on that scale corresponds to 100 percent in Photoshop. Corel changed the scale from earlier versions without increasing amount's effect. They pulled a Spinal Tap: "Ours goes to 11!"

FIGURE 30-16

Photo-Paint's
Unsharp Mask
dialog box

SCREENING CONTROLS

Photo-Paint has rich controls for setting screens and spots that, in version 8, are identical to those in CorelDraw. Neither program derives frequency and angle information from the standard PPD file, but uses an odd combination of .ini files to create the popup list of possibilities. (In Chapter 31, *Illustration Applications*, we explain how to add values to this list by editing a few files.)

To set spot shape, frequency, resolution, and angles, select Print from the File menu and then click the Separations tab. Check the Print Separations box and the Use Advanced Settings box, or all is for naught—your settings are ignored otherwise. Finally, click the Advanced button. At long last, you can choose your screens, frequencies, and spot shapes (see Figure 30-17).

The Screening Technology popup menu lets you select both imagesetter and screening type—like a Linotronic 330 and HQS Screening. Whatever you select there affects the options available under the Resolution and Basic Screen popup menus.

FIGURE 30-17

Photo-Paint's
Advanced
Separations
dialog box

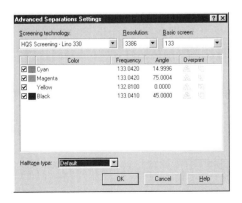

The Halftone Type popup menu offers 14 spot shapes, most of them special effects, like rhomboid or star. You can add your own custom spots functions; see CorelDraw in Chapter 31.

Changing an individual plate's screen frequency or angle is as simple as clicking on the value and typing in a new one. These values are picked up as well from the .ini files that we go into more for CorelDraw in Chapter 31, *Illustration Applications.*

Photo-Paint also provides a way to access advanced PostScript features through the Print dialog box's PostScript tab (see Figure 30-18). The tab allows you to choose JPEG compression to reduce the time it takes to transfer a file to a printer. This only works with Level 2 and PostScript 3 devices (see Chapter 10, *Compression*).

FIGURE 30-18
Photo-Paint's
PostScript tab in the
Print dialog box

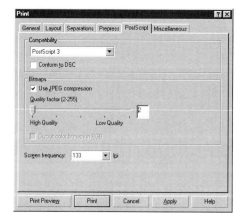

HALFTONING BITMAPS

Photo-Paint has a small cluster of spot shape options for converting grayscale images into halftoned black-and-white bitmaps when you select "Black-and-White (1 Bit)" from the Convert To menu (see Figure 30-19). The preview feature is simply—terrific!

PHOTO CD

The Photo CD controls in Photo-Paint are somewhat different from all the rest. After selecting a Photo CD image from the Open dialog box, you're presented with the Photo CD Image dialog box,

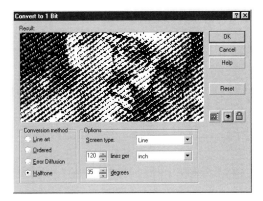

which has Image and Enhancement tabs (see Figure 30-20). The Image tab allows you select resolution from a popup menu.

The Enhancement tab has a variety of adjustment options, including the choice of various contrast corrections. Normally, we don't recommend using contrast adjustments. However, Photo CD stores 12 bits of luminosity or tonal information, and the contrast adjustment appears to work on the deeper data.

You also have checkboxes to show out-of-gamut colors, useful for prepress tasks. And you can turn the Scene Balance Algorithm (SBA) off; we discussed its uses in Chapter 14, *Photo CD*.

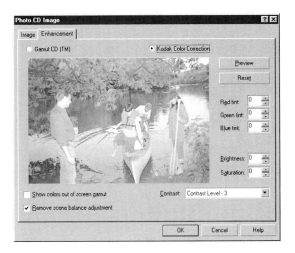

PHOTOIMPACT

In the olden days, there was just one image-editing program of note for Windows: Aldus PhotoStyler. The Aldus-Adobe merger put the kibosh on PhotoStyler, but the original developers, Ulead Systems, released an updated version as PhotoImpact. Tonal correction isn't very deep, and sharpening is a real problem. But it does have a few noteworthy features for PostScript output and Web file formats.

TONAL CORRECTION

Simple nonlinear correction appears in the Tone Map dialog box's Highlight Midtone Shadow tab (see Figure 30-21). The histogram scaling factor is unique; it lets you increase the magnification on the histogram levels to make slight differences more noticeable.

SHARPENING

The Unsharp Mask filter in PhotoImpact supports only Amount and Radius, which it calls Sharpen Factor and Aperture Radius (see Figure 30-22.) Use the Picture Publisher radius calculations. Unfortunately, PhotoImpact has a protection filter that applies USM only to the lighter side of an edge. We commend this in other programs, but only when it's a feature with options you can set.

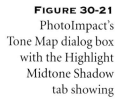

FIGURE 30-21
PhotoImpact's Tone Map dialog box with the Highlight Midtone Shadow tab showing

FIGURE 30-22
PhotoImpact's
Unsharp Mask
dialog box

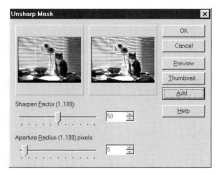

SCREENING CONTROLS

The Halftone tab in the Print Options dialog box offers choices almost identical to Photoshop's with a few more halftone spot shapes thrown in (see Figure 30-23). This version of Print Options shows up when you have an imagesetter or similar device selected.

If you select a laser printer, PhotoImpact provides you with a different dialog box, which contains a neat set of controls for PostScript Level 2 that's unique to it and CorelPhoto-Paint. When printing directly to a PostScript printer that uses Level 2, you can compress the images before sending by using either JPEG Compression (shown) or LZW Compression (see Figure 30-24).

HALFTONING BITMAPS

Selecting Black and White from the Data Type menu item converts an image into a black-and-white bitmap (see Figure 30-25). The halftoning options are similar to Photoshop's, but you don't have to be in grayscale mode to select it.

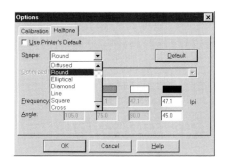

FIGURE 30-24
PhotoImpact's
PostScript Level 2
controls

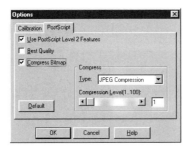

FIGURE 30-25
PhotoImpact's
bitmap conversion
dialog box

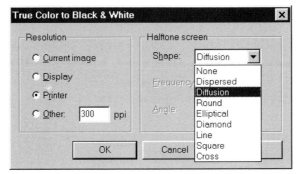

PHOTO CD

Photo CD support is minimal, allowing you to select resolution before opening the image (see Figure 30-26).

GIF AND JPEG CONVERSION

Before moving on, we want to point out well-done GIF and JPEG conversion tools, called SmartSavers, that come with PhotoImpact. They can be run separately from the program or accessed through the Web menu. The SmartSavers not only preview what the image will look like after conversion to GIF or JPEG, but also tell you file size, show you the indexed GIF palette, and allow you to make changes interactively and see how they affect all the other variables. The GIF SmartSaver even offers a few improvements over standard exporters (see Figure 30-27).

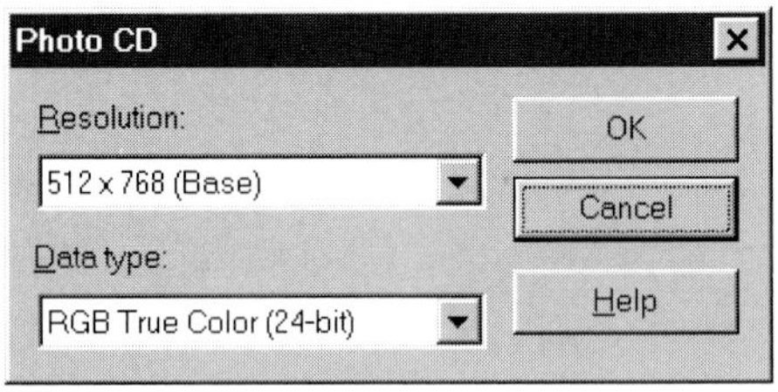

FIGURE 30-26
PhotoImpact's
Photo CD resolution
selection dialog box

DeBabelizer

DeBabelizer, now available on Macintosh and Windows 95/NT, is a dream come true for those who want to perform a lot of conversions on bitmapped graphics files. It allows automated batch processing with color, resolution, and palettes being preset, conditionally selected, or individually converted. Whew! It makes us tired just to look at its Open dialog box some days.

CONVERTING FORMATS

Whenever we get stuck and just can't open an image, or if we get a file in a format we've never heard of, we immediately open DeBabelizer—and it handles it. DeBabelizer can open every bitmapped graphic file format we've heard of, and it can write most of them back out, too. Combine this with batch processing, and, whoa, Nelly ! You've got a tool that just won't stop.

BATCH PROCESSING AND SCRIPTING

Almost every activity in DeBabelizer can be put into a script. It has its own scripting language that allows a combination of automatic actions, like converting files from one form to another, and batch processing to allow it to run through a folder or drive's worth of images. We've used scripting and batch processing in the past to take 500 images, open them, reduce the resolution to the same vertical pixels, convert to a common GIF indexed-color palette, and save with a new name in a new folder.

TONAL CORRECTION AND SHARPENING

DeBabelizer often baffles us with choices, requiring us to gain expertise because the program requires an expert hand. Tonal correction is no exception (see Figure 30-28). We don't always know what each of these settings does, partly because DeBabelizer gets used by folks doing video and multimedia more often than prepress. The CD-I settings in the tonal correction dialog box, for instance, are really only applicable to people authoring CD-Interactive disks for the Phillips players.

FIGURE 30-28
DeBabelizer's tonal correction dialog box

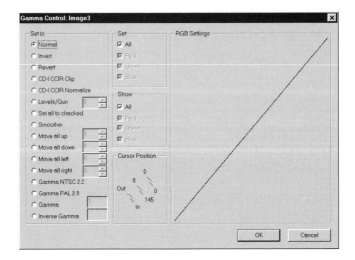

Sharpening doesn't exist. Although DeBabelizer can use Photoshop plug-ins, the unsharp masking controls in Photoshop are built-in, so DeBabelizer can't access them. We've wondered since 1993 why the folks at Equilibrium don't just write their own filter; it's our only real gripe with DeBabelizer.

SUPER PALETTES

GIF images use a small palette of 256 or fewer colors. These palettes can be saved as separate files and used to convert multiple images to the same super palette, as we discussed in Chapter 11, *Images for the Web*. DeBabelizer makes this process incredibly simple by offering a super palette option. You can batch-process images with the same palette, or point DeBabelizer to several images and have it generate the best set of common colors to a bit depth or number of colors you specify. The resulting palette becomes the template for converting images. (See Color Page L for the super palette dialog box.)

SLICK IMAGE

Don't be staggered by the number of options and controls you have. Typically, you only use a few and in tightly focused ways. The real trick is to learn the optimum values and apply those over and over again in a consistent manner.

In the next chapter, we move to an area that has a little less diversity—illustration applications.

31 ILLUSTRATION APPLICATIONS

DRAWING
PICTURES

Throughout this book we've talked about halftones and scans, and most of the talk and most of the illustrations have focused on natural, or scanned, images. But as we said way back in Chapter 16, *Frequency, Angle, and Spot Shape*, halftones aren't just for scans. You get a halftone anytime you print something with gray or a tint of a color.

So in this chapter we focus on illustration programs that create primarily synthetic, object-oriented artwork such as lines, boxes, circles, text, and so on. Although there are many of these programs, the primary ones (the ones you probably have on your computer) are Adobe Illustrator, Macromedia FreeHand, and CorelDraw.

ADOBE ILLUSTRATOR

For a program written by Adobe itself, Illustrator offers relatively few PostScript options to customize your vector illustrations. There are only two ways to control halftones: a limited method per file and a global method.

CONTROLLING SCREENS

Illustrator has two methods to control screens: the Separation Setup dialog box, which allows you to set frequencies and angles by color separation for each file; and the Riders plug-in, which allows you to make changes that are global, affecting every file printed or saved as EPS after the Riders changes are made.

SEPARATION SETUP. The Separation Setup dialog box has most of the functionality of what used to be the standalone Adobe Separator program. Separation Setup allows you to set individual screen frequencies and angles for each color separation, whether process or spot (see Figure 31-1). These changes are saved with the Illustrator file. The Halftone popup menu and the Frequency and Angle fields are populated in part by values from the PostScript Printer Description (PPD) file you choose.

RIDERS PLUG-IN. You can go beyond frequency and angle only with a bit of effort and only globally, for every file output or saved as EPS after you make the changes. To set this up, you need to quit Illustrator if you have it open and open the Utilities folder in the Illustrator folder. Inside there you'll find a Riders folder, which in turn contains a Riders plug-in (see Figure 31-2). Drag the plug-in to the Illustrator folder's plug-in folder. When you start up Illustrator again, there will now be an Other menu item under the Filter

FIGURE 31-1
Illustrator's
Separation Setup
dialog box

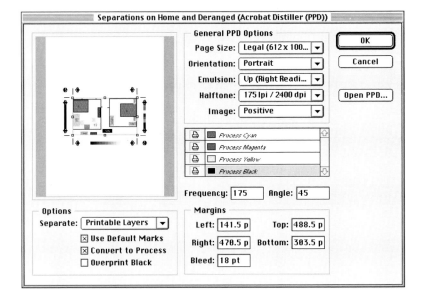

FIGURE 31-2
Where the Riders
plug-in and related
details live on the
Macintosh; Windows
users will find the
same nested
directories

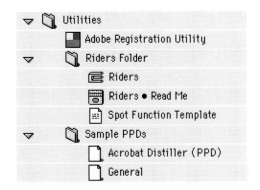

menu containing Make Riders and Delete Riders. (Windows users should substitute directory for folder, but you'll follow the same steps as above.)

The Make Riders option brings up a dialog box that allows you to set six variables (see Figure 31-3). These are global settings, although we have a workaround for you below.

Screen Frequency and Screen Angle are self-explanatory. Spot Function allows you to select a number of preset shapes or to import a spot function from a text file. A sample spot function file is located in the same directory or folder as the Riders plug-in. Essentially, it's just a text file with the spot function formatted correctly inside of it.

Flatness is a setting we described in detail back in "Encapsulated PostScript" in Chapter 4, *File Formats*. Setting Flatness above zero reduces the computation time for any curves in a file; we recommend a setting of 3 or 4, which is high enough to be useful without being noticeable.

FIGURE 31-3
Illustrator's Make
Riders dialog box

You can use Annotation to add text to the lower left of all output. You can insert up to 255 characters in this field.

The Error Handler popup option downloads some PostScript that will report on errors more thoroughly than the default printer options. If you're using a recent Adobe or Adobe-derived laser printer driver, like Apple's LaserWriter 8 driver, you can turn on error handling in the driver itself.

When you're done, you click Make, and Illustrator automatically drops in the filename "Adobe Illustrator EPSF Riders"; the Macintosh version even admonishes "Don't Change Name," which appears above the filename field. For Riders to work correctly, you must save it as that name in the Illustrator Plug-ins directory or folder. You can keep multiple different settings as long as you name them all differently. But to use each one, you have to rename it and drag it into place. Not the ideal solution, but it works.

The EPSF Riders file is just a text file containing PostScript instructions matching your choices. When you print or save a file after saving the EPSF Riders file in the right place, Illustrator inserts all the code in that file directly into the PostScript stream. This incorporates the riders information into an EPS you save or anything you print. (In older versions of Illustrator, you'd have to check a box to include this header information, but Illustrator now does it automatically as long as it's in the right directory location.)

If you use this method for saving files as EPS from Illustrator, be aware that the screen settings are hard-coded into the EPS. You won't be able to override them with your publication defaults (for instance, if you place the EPS file in PageMaker or QuarkXPress).

PLACING IMAGES

Although you can place EPS and bitmap files in Illustrator, you can't control any of them individually. If there's screening information in a placed EPS image, it is applied only to that picture; the rest of the Illustrator artwork is unaffected.

MACROMEDIA FREEHAND

It's gone through a few hands, from Aldus to Adobe to Altsys (its developer all along) to Macromedia, but it's still got a mean kick. When it comes to working with halftone screens, Macromedia FreeHand really gives you room to breathe. FreeHand lets you control screens when printing, control screens for individual objects within illustrations, and do some minor tonal adjustment on grayscale images. Let's look at each of these a little more closely.

CONTROLLING SCREENS

There are two places in FreeHand where you can control screens—in the Print Setup dialog box's Separations tab (this applies to the whole print job), and in the Halftone panel (this applies only to selected objects).

SEPARATIONS TAB. To get to the Print Setup dialog box's Separations tab (see Figure 31-4), choose Print from the File menu. Before going to Setup, you need to either select a printer or choose a PostScript Printer Description (PPD) file. Under Windows or with Desktop Printers on the Macintosh, you can choose the printer from a popup menu (old Mac printer drivers require that you go to the Chooser to switch). You can also choose a PPD file if you're targeting, say, an imagesetter. In either case, FreeHand looks in the PPD file for that printer; the file provides—among other things—a list of frequencies and resolution that appear in the Separations tab's Halftone Screen popup menu. Click on Setup and you're there. You can then select a dpi/lpi, or choose Other to type in your own combination. But beware: the default settings are the ideal ones.

You can control the halftone screen angle for a particular color by clicking on the separation angle. A dialog box appears with which you can alter the angle for any individual color (primarily useful for spot-color jobs). You can't alter frequency for individual colors, however.

FIGURE 31-4
FreeHand's Print
Setup dialog box

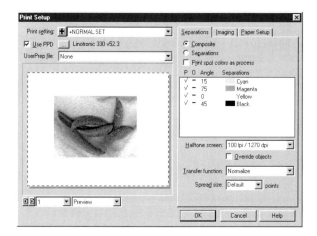

Note that the screens you specify in the Print Setup dialog box only apply when you're printing from FreeHand. They have no effect on exported EPS files.

HALFTONES PALETTE. To specify a special halftone screen for an individual element or group of elements within a FreeHand page, first display the Halftone palette by selecting it in the Panels menu item under the View menu (see Figure 31-5). Select the element(s) and then specify screen angle, screen frequency, and spot shape for the selected objects. Spot shape is under the Screen popup menu for reasons known best to Macromedia interface designers.

As we said back in Chapter 27, *Controlling Halftone Screens*, the object-specific values you set in the Halftone Screen dialog box

FIGURE 31-5
FreeHand's
Halftones panel

override the application settings in the Print Setup dialog box's Separations tab. These settings are also included when you export the file in EPS format.

This is just what you want if you're trying to create special effects for images, but beware if you apply it to a color object. When you specifically set the screen for an object, all the separations for that object print with the same angle and frequency—the one you specified. Document-level frequency/angle settings for individual colors are ignored for these objects.

You can control the spot shape for your FreeHand documents, however, without messing around with the frequency and angle. Just select everything on the page, and choose the spot shape you want from the Halftone Screen dialog box. Don't type anything in the Screen Angle or Screen Ruling fields. The spot shape you've chosen will apply to all the items in the document (even when you save it as an EPS), but frequency and angle aren't affected. They're still controlled by the printing application.

To alter the spot shapes in FreeHand's PPD files, see the section on PageMaker in the next chapter. Or, better yet, see the printing chapter of Olav Kvern's book *Real World FreeHand.*

TONAL ADJUSTMENTS

FreeHand also lets you make tonal adjustments of grayscale and black-and-white bitmaps via the Image dialog box. With an appropriate image selected, click on the Object Inspector tab in the Inspector palette and then click the Edit button to bring up the Image dialog box (see Figure 31-6).

Curiously enough, the Image dialog box looks remarkably similar to PageMaker's Image Control dialog box, although the two programs have diverged since the days when they were Aldus FreeHand and Aldus PageMaker. The tonal adjustments are hardly useful, but you might want to use them to screen back black-and-white images to gray, and other similarly simple adjustments. However, if you want real tonal adjustment for photographic images, look to your scanning or image-editing software (like Photoshop).

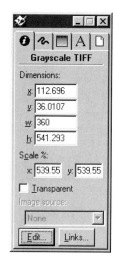

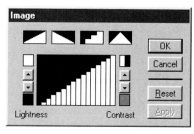

CORELDRAW

CorelDraw provides all the essential controls for handling halftone screens with especially impressive object-level controls (including a mind-bending array of built-in, special-effect spot functions). Because of its close integration with Photo-Paint, it's sometimes hard to see where CorelDraw ends and Photo-Paint begins.

IMPORTED BITMAPS

You can import bitmaps into CorelDraw in a variety of formats, but you can't do much with them aside from rotating and scaling them. You can, however, apply colors to bilevel bitmaps. Your best bet is to use an image-manipulation program for tonal correction and sharpening before importing images.

CONTROLLING SCREENS

CorelDraw uses the identical dialogs and settings as CorelPhoto-Paint, which we covered in some depth in Chapter 30, *Image Applications*. But as we noted in that chapter, Corel applications use their own files to set defaults for frequency and angle. It's not that difficult to edit or create your own; this is especially important and useful for process-color separations.

If you do the default installation, Corel installs version 8 in the C:\corel\graphics8 directory. If you look in the config directory there, you'll find a file called corelprn.ini. Open it up in a text editor and you'll find all the defaults for the printer and output settings. Under the section headed with "[PSScreenSets]", you'll find a list of files in the format:

FILENAME.INI=text describing the file

For instance,

AGFAD.INI=AGFA Balanced Screening - Dot

The files are stored in the programs\data directory, and are extremely simple to make. The format is

```
; comments start with a semicolon
[resolution]
lpi=cyan angle, magenta angle, yellow angle, black angle, cyan frequency,
magenta frequency, yellow frequency, black frequency
```

The frequencies are often the same as the menu item. So, for example, if you wanted to create a mythical Pregunta-brand Specksetter 1450, you'd first add to the corelprn.ini file:

PREG1450.INI=Pregunta Specksetter 1450

Then create a file in a text editor called PREG1450.INI and save it in the programs\data directory. That file should look like this:

```
; Pregunta Specksetter
[1200]
65=15,75,0,45,65,65,65,65
80=15,75,0,45,80,80,80,80
```

The next time you quit and run CorelDraw or Photo-Paint, the Pregunta imagesetter will appear just as you've specified. The corelprn.ini file also contains all the standard imagesetter resolutions. You can add or edit these by just editing the file in a text editor.

OBJECT-LEVEL SCREENING

CorelDraw has a slightly staggering number of patterns you can apply to any given object, and PostScript Textures is one of these options. The menu is reached by selecting an object or objects, and holding down the mouse button on the Fill button on the Tool palette. One of the options that appears is the PostScript Texture icon. Selecting this brings up a dialog box that lets you choose a custom PostScript fill (see Figure 31-7).

FIGURE 31-7
CorelDraw's
PostScript Texture
dialog box

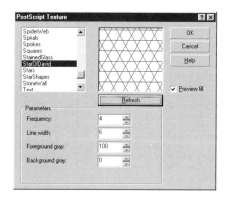

If you want to customize your fills with your own PostScript, go to the CorelDraw directory and edit the userproc.ps file in the Custom directory. This file has extraordinarily clear instructions on how to edit it to add or modify spot functions that appear in the Advanced Separations dialog box and the fills that show up in the PostScript Texture dialog box.

DRAW, PARDNER

We find ourselves using illustration applications in fits and starts. We've often forgotten everything we every learned about a program by the next time we have to use it. But the advances in each of these three applications have made it simpler for us to come back to them.

In the next chapter, we address putting all the pieces together in page-layout software, where images, type, and illustrations come together without—we hope—a resounding boom.

32 PAGE-LAYOUT APPLICATIONS

PUTTING IT ALL TOGETHER

Whenever someone calls PageMaker or QuarkXPress a "desktop-publishing program," we're quick to point out that these are actually *page-layout* applications. The difference is perhaps insignificant, but these programs are designed to lay out pages with text and graphics exactly the way you want. They are the core of desktop publishing, and as such, they provide a certain amount of control over scanned images and halftones.

In this chapter we discuss briefly the major issues of halftoning and scanning with PageMaker and QuarkXPress.

By the way, there are obviously other page-layout applications on the market, including CorelVentura and FrameMaker. We're covering only PageMaker and QuarkXPress here because, after almost 10 years, they are still the leaders in graphic arts production.

ADOBE PAGEMAKER

Adobe PageMaker, the granddaddy of desktop publishing programs, took a big leap forward in its control of screens way back in version 5.0, and it hasn't changed much since. Its Print dialog boxes, support for PPD files, and scan-related tools give you many of the tools you need to import scans and print them (and everything else) the way you want them.

CONTROLLING SCREENS

The main control for screen frequency and angle in PageMaker is in the Print Color dialog box (choose Print from the File menu, then click the Color button). To set the screen frequency and angle, select Custom from the Optimized Screen popup menu, and type the frequency and angle values you want in the appropriate fields (the default values for these fields are defined in the PPD file for the printer you have selected in the Print Document dialog box). If you choose Default from the popup menu, you get the output device's default screen settings (see Figure 32-1). (See Chapter 27, *Controlling Halftone Screens*, for information about defaults.)

COLOR SCREEN FREQUENCIES AND ANGLES. If you're printing color separations to an imagesetter, the screening controls change somewhat. The Optimized Screen popup menu presents you with a list of choices for different screen frequencies and resolutions (see Figure 32-2).

Select one of the optimized screens, then click on the different process colors in the Separations box. Notice that the angles and rulings are different for different colors, presenting options that are (presumably) the best choices for that screen frequency. Notice also that the frequencies aren't exactly the same as what's specified in the Optimized Screen popup menu.

As we mentioned in Chapter 26, *Angle Strategies*, it's often necessary to adjust screen frequencies for the four process colors to avoid

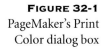

FIGURE 32-1
PageMaker's Print
Color dialog box

Print Color		
● Composite	☐ Mirror	**Style...**
● Grayscale	☐ Negative	**Cancel**
○ Print colors in black	☐ Preserve EPS colors	
○ Separations		**Document**
☐ Perform on printer	**CMS Setup...**	
Print Ink	*Print all inks*	**Paper**
✓ Process Cyan	*Print no inks*	**Options**
✓ Process Magenta	*All to process*	
✓ Process Yellow	*Remove unused*	*Color*
✓ Process Black		**Features**
☒ Print this ink	Frequency: 60.0 lpi	
Optimized screen:		**Reset**
Default	Angle: 45.0 °	

FIGURE 32-2

Optimized screens for
the Linotronic 330
with RIP 30

```
198 lpi / 3386 dpi
101 lpi / 2540 dpi
132 lpi / 2540 dpi
157 lpi / 2540 dpi
112 lpi / 2032 dpi
89 lpi / 1693 dpi
132 lpi / 1693 dpi
✓ 101 lpi / 1270 dpi
109 lpi / 1270 dpi
104 lpi / 3386 dpi / HQS
120 lpi / 3386 dpi / HQS
133 lpi / 3386 dpi / HQS
199 lpi / 3386 dpi / HQS
100 lpi / 2540 dpi / HQS
112 lpi / 2540 dpi / HQS
120 lpi / 2540 dpi / HQS
138 lpi / 2540 dpi / HQS
150 lpi / 2540 dpi / HQS
96 lpi / 2032 dpi / HQS
111 lpi / 2032 dpi / HQS
75 lpi / 1693 dpi / HQS
86 lpi / 1693 dpi / HQS
120 lpi / 1693 dpi / HQS
75 lpi / 1270 dpi / HQS
90 lpi / 1270 dpi / HQS
100 lpi / 1270 dpi / HQS
75 lpi / 846 dpi / HQS
```

moiré patterns. These are the best settings for a given frequency/
resolution combination, as determined by the imagesetter vendor.
You can change the screen values for each color plate individually,
but we only recommend it for spot-color jobs. For process-color
work, you're usually best off using the canned screen sets.

SCREEN SETTINGS FOR BITMAPS. You can specify the screen for
individual grayscale bitmaps within a PageMaker publication via the
Image Control dialog box (see Figure 32-3). Select a placed grayscale
image, then choose Image Control from the Element menu. Click
the Screened button, and type the frequency and angle you want in
the appropriate fields. You can also choose between a round spot or
line screen. These settings override the values in the Print Color dialog box, but only for the selected image.

FIGURE 32-3

PageMaker's Image
Control dialog box

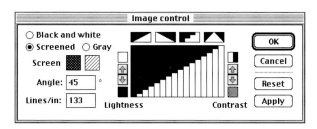

CONTROLLING SPOT SHAPE. Controlling the shape of your half-tone spots from PageMaker is a little trickier; you need to edit the PPD for the printer or imagesetter you're using. Using a word processor or the like, open the appropriate PPD. (If you're using Microsoft Word, select Show All Documents from the popup menu and select the PPD. Then, if you're given a formatting choice, select Text.) You should see a section like the following:

```
*% Halftone Information ===============
*ScreenFreq: "133.0"
*ScreenAngle: "45.0"
*DefaultScreenProc: Dot
*ScreenProc Dot: "
{abs exch abs 2 copy add 1 gt {1 sub dup mul exch 1 sub dup mul add 1
sub }{dup mul exch dup mul add 1 exch sub }ifelse }
"
*End
*ScreenProc Line: "{ pop }"
*ScreenProc Ellipse: "{ dup 5 mul 8 div mul exch dup mul exch add sqrt 1
exch sub }"
```

There are three spots defined in this code: Dot, Line, and Ellipse. You choose which one is used with the "*DefaultScreenProc:" keyword. Just type in the name of the spot function ("ScreenProc") you want to use. You can add additional spot functions ("*ScreenProc Propeller," for instance), or alter the existing ones. For instance, you might replace the code for "Dot" with code for a transforming elliptical spot, so images that have the round spot screen specified in Image Control actually print with elliptical spots. For more on halftone spots and PostScript spot functions, see Chapter 20, *The Glorious Spot*, and Chapter 29, *Spot Functions*.

BITMAP PRINTING OPTIONS

In the Print Options dialog box, you'll find four options under the Send Image Data popup menu: Normal, Optimized Subsampling, Low Resolution, and Omit Images. In the past, these options were limited to TIFFs; with the newer versions of PageMaker, the options apply to PCX and GIF files as well. Who's still using PCX? We have no idea.

NORMAL. This prints all the data in placed bitmaps—the full resolution of the source file.

OPTIMIZED SUBSAMPLING. This prints only as much data as is needed for the specified screen frequency—a resolution of two times frequency—downsampling the bitmap at print time. While we generally prefer to downsample in an image-editing application before placing in a page-layout program, this option is great when you're creating a document for high-res, high-frequency output, but proofing on a laser printer. Choose Optimized Subsampling for your proof output, and PageMaker sends only as much information as is necessary, greatly reducing transmission and print times. Switch back to Normal for final output.

LOW RESOLUTION. This option just prints the low-resolution screen rendition of a bitmap image. It's good for rough proofs.

OMIT IMAGES. This is when you want to go to the extreme. Selecting this option makes PageMaker print a box with an X in it instead of the bitmap. It's great when all you care about is proofing the text and general layout. It's also used to omit image files when you're working with OPI (Open Press Interface), and the low-res bitmap preview is replaced by a high-resolution image.

IMAGE CONTROL

We mentioned above that you can control screens for placed bitmaps in the Image Control dialog box. You can also adjust their tonal values by moving any of 16 bars in the dialog box. However, this tonal adjustment method is useless except for simple things like screening back black-and-white clip art. You can't see a histogram of the image, or control the shadow and highlight points explicitly.

And since sharpening should occur *after* tonal correction, and PageMaker doesn't provide sharpening, the tonal correction isn't much use. If you need image control, use your scanning or image manipulation software before placing the image in PageMaker.

COMPRESSING TIFFS

PageMaker can create compressed versions of TIFF files without leaving the program. Choose Place, select a TIFF file in the Place dialog box, and hold down the keys specified in Table 32-1 while clicking OK. PageMaker creates a new version of the file, in compressed form, with the filename extension specified in the table. For this to save any disk space, of course, you have to then go back and delete the uncompressed file.

Files have extensions added to them according to bit depth and platform. Windows files have an underscore and a single letter added, while Macintosh files add one to three letters in parentheses.

TABLE 32-1
PageMaker's compression options and renaming schemes on importing TIFF files

In the Place dialog box, select the TIFF file to compress/decompress, and press these keys while clicking the OK button.

TIFF compression	Keys to hold down for (M)ac and (W)indows
Medium	Command-Option (M) *or* Control-Alt (W)
Maximum	*Add Shift to Medium keys (M,W)*
Decompress	Command (M) *or* Control (W)

Bit Depth	Medium	Maximum	Decompressed
1-bit	_P *or* (P)	_L *or* (L)	_U *or* (U)
4- or 8-bit	_P *or* (P)	_L *or* (L)	_U *or* (U)
Grayscale or 24-bit	_D *or* (LD)	_M *or* (LD2)	_U *or* (U)

You have your choice of medium or maximum compression. Medium compression is faster to compress and decompress, but the files are larger than with maximum compression.

PHOTO CD

PageMaker's Photo CD Import Filter, which appears after you select a Photo CD file using the Place menu item, is much like Photoshop's advanced controls (see Figure 32-4). The filter allows you do some sophisticated things on import, such as aiming the output for the correct output device. And it even offers sharpening and some tonal balance tools. Generally, we recommend importing Photo CD files into Photoshop for correction, but some of our colleagues say these Filter adjustments are good enough for output.

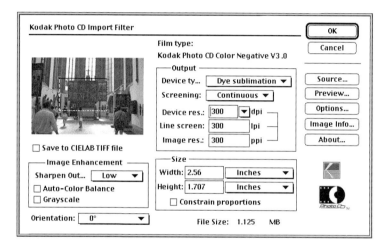

QUARKXPRESS

We've worked with QuarkXPress since the very beginning (this is evident if you've seen *The QuarkXPress Book*, now in its fifth edition), and have seen it transform from a minor player in the DTP arena to a major leaguer on everyone's to-buy list. Curiously in QuarkXPress, very little having to do with scanning and halftones has changed over the past six or seven years, at least on the surface.

(As we write these words, we've just taken QuarkXPress 4.0 out of its protective shrinkwrapping. We discovered that most PostScript output functions that used to require an XTension, such as QuarkPrint or PS Utilities, are now built inside QuarkXPress itself.)

CONTROLLING SCREENS

With QuarkXPress 4, all halftone functions are consolidated in the Print dialog box's Output tab (see Figure 32-5). The contents of this box are generated from the PPD file for the printer you've chosen in the Document tab. (Those of you who remember Quark's own Printer Description File will be happy to know they've adopted the industry-standard PPD.) The value in the Frequency field is applied to all bitmap images, and used as well for all tint values throughout your document—like tinted type, rules, background, and so on. You can override this value for bitmaps by using the Halftone feature (see below).

FIGURE 32-5
QuarkXPress's
Print dialog box's
Output tab

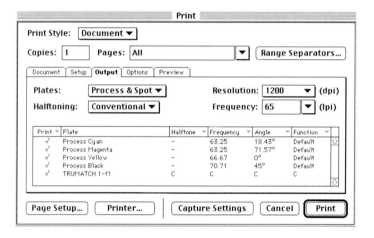

SEPARATIONS. If you've checked the Separations box in the Document tab, QuarkXPress uses the PPD file to drop in the "real" screen frequency and angle for each plate; if you don't know why the word real is in quotes, review Chapter 26, *Angle Strategies*. (In the example figure above, the values are dropped in for an Agfa ProSet 9600.)

To change frequency and angle for any given plate, or to choose a different spot shape, just click the line of text listing the plate, and popup menus are activated in the column headers for each row. QuarkXPress has five spot shapes: dot, line, ellipse, square, and tri-dot. The last of these is a special transforming spot shape.

SCREENING CONTROL. You can always override the screens of grayscale bitmaps (like TIFF) from within QuarkXPress by selecting the picture box with the Content tool and selecting Halftone from the Style menu (or just type Control- or Command-Shift-H; see Figure 32-6). The spot shapes available in the Picture Halftone dialog box are Dot, Line, Ellipse, Square, and Ordered Dither. The last of these generates a regular-pattern halftone (or a really non-random stochastic screen) for low-resolution output.

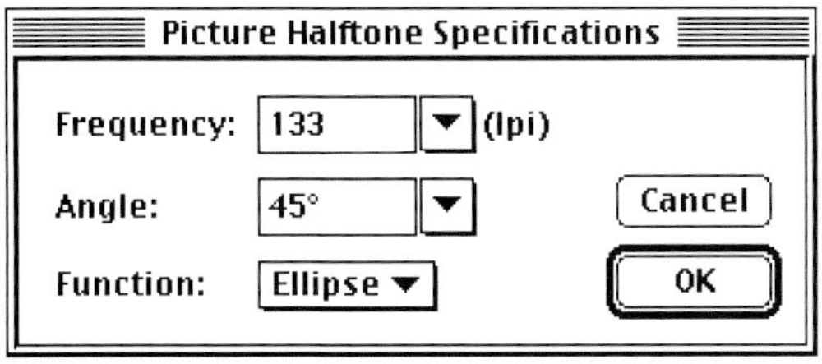

FIGURE 32-6
QuarkXPress's
Picture Halftone
dialog box

> **Picture Halftone Specifications**
>
> Frequency: 133 ▼ (lpi)
>
> Angle: 45° ▼   Cancel
>
> Function: Ellipse ▼   OK

PICTURE CONTRAST

Although QuarkXPress's ability to adjust tonal values in bitmap images is better than PageMaker's (see "Image Control," earlier in this chapter), it's still pretty pathetic when it comes to doing any real work. It does offer some good features such as posterization and pencil tools for manipulating the contrast curve (see Figure 32-7), but because you can't see a histogram or control any levels with precision, or sharpen an image after correcting it, we just can't recommend you do much with it other than screening back black-and-white artwork. Instead, use Photoshop or another image-manipulation program to prepare your images, then import them into your QuarkXPress documents.

FIGURE 32-7
QuarkXPress's
Picture Contrast
dialog box

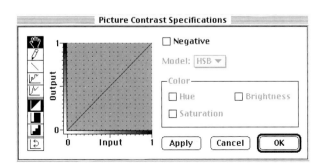

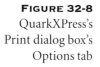

DOWNSAMPLING

Back in Chapter 6, *Choosing Resolution*, we said that you never, ever needed to have an image resolution above two times the screen frequency. QuarkXPress enforces this in a way by trying not to send more than that resolution to the printer. So, if you have a 300-spi grayscale image, and you're printing at 53 lpi (the standard for most desktop laser printers), QuarkXPress sends only 106 dpi of information. This is called downsampling, and because it never cuts off more than what you need, you'll almost never have a problem.

QuarkXPress also downsamples line-art TIFF images to the resolution of the printer itself. For example, if you print a 800-spi image to a 300-dpi laser printer, QuarkXPress sends only a 300-spi image. This saves a great deal of time, and sometimes money, too.

Note that downsampling only works for bitmaps. QuarkXPress has no control over what does or does not get sent in EPS images.

QuarkXPress 4 added a convenient checkbox in the Print dialog box's Options tab to override the downsampling. If you check Full Resolution TIFF Output, you'll output the full file with no downsampling (see Figure 32-8).

Why would you want to turn downsampling off? Because most applications' downsampling is pretty dumb. If you import a 200-spi image and scale it down to 25 percent, the final image is 800 spi. When you print that, QuarkXPress sends only a fraction of that to

FIGURE 32-8
QuarkXPress's
Print dialog box's
Options tab

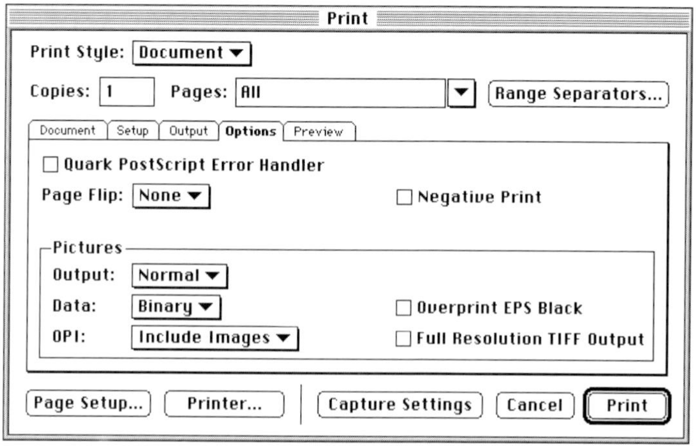

the imagesetter, right? Well, the fraction that it sends might not be the best possible choice and the image may appear mottled. The answer is really just to make sure your image is the proper resolution and size to begin with before you bring it into QuarkXPress.

PHOTO CD

The Photo CD XTension that comes with QuarkXPress lets you import Photo CD images directly into picture boxes, but we see lots of drawbacks to using it. The image gets imported as an RGB image—uncorrected and unseparated. You can't choose the resolution to acquire at; QuarkXPress figures this out at output time. And the image is linked to the file on disc, so you might have to juggle several Photo CDs when it's time to dump output.

We typically leave the Photo CD XTension alone or put it away someplace else. If we really have to use an image directly, we'll acquire it in Photoshop, or, if we're on a Macintosh, we'll import the PICT version (see Chapter 14, *Photo CD*).

PUTTING IT TOGETHER

Page layout is where it all comes together: the scans, the text, the illustrations, the design. Without a solid understanding of how your page-layout program handles scans and halftones, there's no telling what could happen in your final artwork.

33 SCANNING APPLICATIONS

SCANNING APPLICATIONS

Between the three of us, we've probably used a thousand software applications. But the ones we still find most baffling are the programs that ship with scanners. This is not to say they're not powerful and sophisticated and cool. But they are too often slightly batty: interface design is non-intuitive or too clever, program functions are masked by non-standard names, and important features are nested three dialog boxes deep. (To get out of that nesting you have to do what our colleague Steve Broback calls the Joe Pesci method: "ok, ok, ok, ok.") Too often, we're not given an option other than entering numbers we have to figure out in our head—and that's what a computer is supposed to help us with.

Throughout the rest of the book, we've discussed how to use tonal correction, unsharp masking, and other techniques to get the best possible scan. Although these techniques can be generalized to any scanner, we wanted to give you the necessary tweaks and tips on best using the major scanner brands' bundled software without losing your mind.

Most of this software has been around for three to six years, but we still hope for scanning packages that are as easy and straightforward to use as Photoshop. There are also a couple of general software bits to think about, notably TWAIN (a near standard) and ScanTastic, a third-party package available for three scanner models.

TWAIN AND PHOTOSHOP PLUG-INS

TWAIN is a scanner plug-in system that allows many programs to access scanners through a single, consistent interface. The TWAIN approach lets a scanner software developer write a single acquire module that works with any TWAIN-enabled program, from image editors to word processors.

A related approach has been to provide a Photoshop plug-in, because several programs competitive to Photoshop can use its plug-ins. This approach is most common on the Macintosh, where Photoshop and its closest competitors all use plug-ins. Under Windows, however, TWAIN has made huge inroads because of the variety of desktop-publishing applications that are available and that all support it.

TWAIN has also gotten a boost lately from Adobe PhotoDeluxe, a very simple entry-level image-editing application. We haven't covered it in this book because it lacks nonlinear tonal correction, unsharp masking, and halftone control. But it has become an almost de facto standard in bundled scanner software. If you're using a scanner not listed below, it's most likely shipping with PhotoDeluxe and a TWAIN module. We recommend that all you do in Photo-Deluxe is acquire an image and save it, and then use a full-featured image-editing application that has real tonal corrections and un-sharp masking to do the editing.

In our minds—and in our books—TWAIN has always stood for Technology Without An Important Name, but the TWAIN group claims TWAIN don't stand for nothin'. Either way, it's a great concept, and one carried out with some degree of success.

SCANNING SOFTWARE

The most popular scanners for serious desktop use come with software often found on much more expensive models. Agfa, Linotype-Hell, and Umax bundle an almost identical set of scanning modules and correction tools on their cheapest and most expensive scanners. This means that if you learn to use one well, you'll be able to transfer those skills to any other product in the same line-up. We've noted any differences in low-end and high-end versions of the software when we're found them, but they're few and far between.

AGFA FOTOLOOK

Agfa's FotoLook software, available for both Macintosh and Windows, provides every tool we could ask for in a scanner package. In many cases, you could perform most or all cropping, tonal correction, color manipulation, and sharpening before ever reaching the image-editing software. It's also the only package we tested that offered a 48-bit acquire option. Photoshop can handle 48-bit RGB data (16 bits per channel), but none of the other deep-bit scanners can transfer the data at this writing. (See Figure 33-1 for overview.)

SHARPENING. Clicking the Sharpen button in the acquire module's main screen brings up the Advanced Sharpening dialog box, which offers unsharp masking controls (see Figure 33-2). FotoLook uses different names but the same breakout of controls as Photoshop. Amount is the same and can be set up by entering a value.

FIGURE 33-1
Agfa FotoLook's main
acquire dialog box

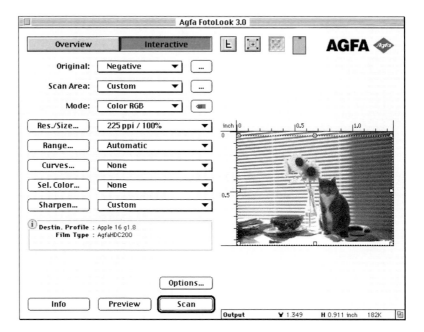

FIGURE 33-2
Agfa FotoLook's
Advanced Sharpness
dialog box

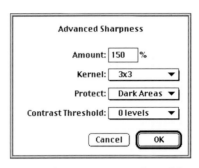

Radius becomes Kernel, and has presets for standard areas, such as 3 by 3 pixels. Contrast Threshold is a popup menu with a few choices of levels.

Protect offers you the option of applying the unsharp masking convolution on just one side or the other of an edge. If you set Protect to Dark Areas (or shadow detail), the lighter side of the edge is made lighter, but the darker side remains at its current level. This increases haloing if you choose values that are too high, but it can be a useful option to suppress unintentional enhancement of noise.

CORRECTION. A Photoshop Levels–like control called Range allows overall tonal balancing. It works for both color and grayscale images, and uses a histogram, value sliders, and eyedroppers to achieve nonlinear correction (see Figure 33-3). The color wheel can be used to choose a neutral gray value.

FIGURE 33-3
Agfa FotoLook's
Range control

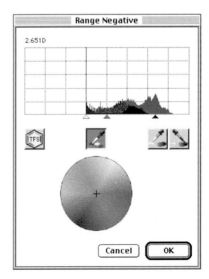

In the example in the figure, the software is adjusting a film negative; each input type (negative, positive, and reflective) has a slightly different set of controls. Density defines the histogram scale, so you can see exactly how good a dynamic range the scanner has captured.

FotoLook also allows adjustments through a standard set of curve-editing tools (see Figure 33-4).

FIGURE 33-4
Agfa FotoLook's
Curve Editor
dialog box

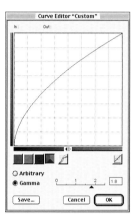

If you need to perform selective color changes, you can actually make these at the time of the scan using FotoLook's excellent tool (see Figure 33-5). You can select areas and define the extent of hue you're changing. Much of the tool is visual in nature, showing you source and target samples.

HEWLETT-PACKARD DESKSCAN II

It seems some things never change. The Hewlett-Packard DeskScan II software application is like a still point around which the rest of the scanning world rotates. The current version of this software, shipping in early 1998 with the HP 6100C, appears—to our eyes and minds—almost identical to the version shipped in 1991 with the DeskJet 3. It still lacks most useful correction and sharpening tools, but it's damn fast and simple, and we appreciate that.

FIGURE 33-5

Agfa FotoLook's
Selective Color
Correction
dialog box

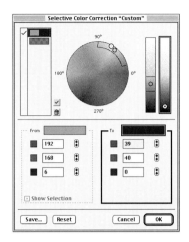

SCANNING. The main scanning window doesn't let you directly enter scanning resolution or image mode (see Figure 33-6). It relies on Type and Path settings, which are defined as separate entries. If you want to scan at 600 dpi, the top resolution of the 6100C model, you have to go into the Customize Print Path dialog box, enter new dpi settings for Photos, and enter a new setting name (see Figure 33-7). Once you set and select a print path, however, the enlargement percentage in the main scanning window corresponds directly to the resolution you've set up. So 100 percent means 600 dpi; 50 percent is 300 dpi, and so on. The Width and Height values are calculated based on this dpi, as well.

FIGURE 33-6

HP DeskScan II's
main acquire
dialog box

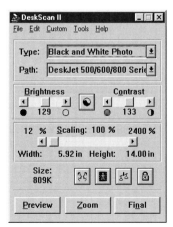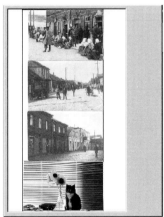

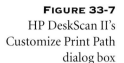

FIGURE 33-7
HP DeskScan II's
Customize Print Path
dialog box

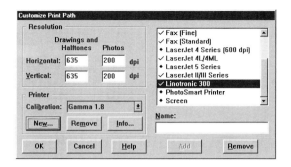

WARMING UP. You might recall that back in Chapter 2, *Scanning,* one of our tips for getting set up was to let the scanner's lighting element warm up before doing a scan. The DeskScan II software lets you set a preference to require this, and then gives you a status report as the lamp gets ready for its duty (see Figure 33-8).

FIGURE 33-8
HP DeskScan II's
Image Quality setting
and lamp warming
dialog box

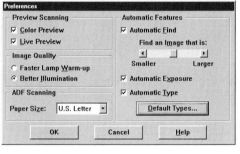

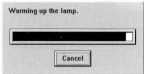

Setting Image Quality to Better Illumination gives the lamp a chance to heat up to the right temperature to perform a consistently high-quality scan.

SHARPENING. Sharpening control is virtually nonexistent. To set sharpening at all—or turn it off, if you're unintentionally using it— you have to venture into the Customize Image Type dialog box, and select a preset level of sharpening from a popup menu (see Figure 33-9). We recommend leaving this off in all cases.

CORRECTION. DeskScan II has the minimum possible tonal correction tools, including a relatively underpowered curves control

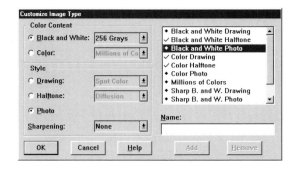

(called Emphasis), which sports just three control points and some preset choices from a popup menu (see Figure 33-10).

It's hard to figure out exactly what the Highlight and Shadow tool affects, but it appears to offer the equivalent of the highlight and shadow sliders in the Photoshop Levels dialog box (see Figure 33-11). The settings can be adjusted manually, or you can click on the eyedropper icon to the right of each setting and then sample directly from the image preview.

The Color Adjustment dialog box allows for coarse saturation, hue, and brightness adjustments (see Figure 33-12). Since these changes are applied before the scan is acquired, they can still be worthwhile on a 30-bit or deeper scanner.

FIGURE 33-10

HP DeskScan II's
Emphasis curve

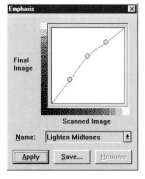

FIGURE 33-11

HP DeskScan II's
Highlight and
Shadow adjustment

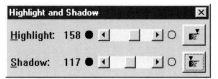

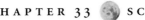

FIGURE 33-12
HP DeskScan II's
Color Adjustment
dialog box

MORE INFORMATION. If you'd like to devote yourself to more study of this odd little application/plug-in, consult Jerry Day's *Color Scanning Handbook*, out under the HP Professional Books series from Prentice-Hall. It's geared solely around HP ScanJets.

LINOTYPE-HELL LINOCOLOR

Linotype-Hell's line of scanners, from $500 to $40,000, uses almost the same LinoColor software package on the Macintosh. (Windows uses a package with similar controls but an entirely different interface; see Figure 33-13.)

SCANNING. Each scanner ships with a slightly different version of the Setup dialog box; we tested the Saphir model (see Figure 33-14). LinoColor organizes all of the tonal, color, and sharpening tools under categories in the Setup dialog box. Clicking on the ellipsis next to each popup menu (when that feature's available) brings up the first of what's usually a series of nested dialog boxes for more specific adjustment.

SHARPENING. We discovered one difference in the LinoColor software between high-end and low-end scanners: the software when bundled with the Saphir model (which sells for about $1,500) has LinoColor's superior sharpening settings disabled. Color guru Bruce Fraser calls LinoColor's sharpening the best of any of the scanner packages, but sadly, it's not available in the price range into which most professionals will be buying.

CORRECTION. Stand back! The developers were given free range in the correction arena. We can't detail every one of the what seems to

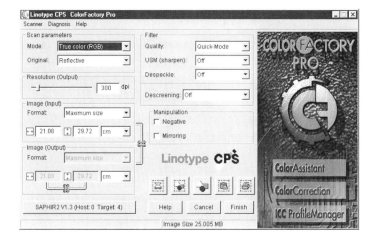

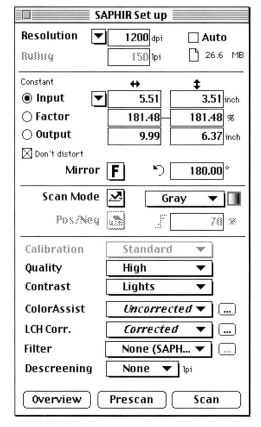

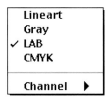

be dozens of nested correction tools. But we can discuss LinoColor's main approach. Each control is nested from the main Setup dialog box. For instance, clicking the ellipsis to the right of LCH Corr. in Setup takes you to the LCH Correction dialog box (see Figure 33-15. LCH stands for luminosity, chroma, and hue, and corresponds to brightness, saturation, and hue in the HSB model (see Chapter 8, *Color*).

LCH Correction lets you choose preset values for each of the settings—like dynamic range—or bring up yet another dialog box to modify the values with more refinement. Clicking the Dynamic Range ellipsis, for instance, brings up the dialog box in Figure 33-16. You can then modify the output curve by entering values for minimum and maximum L, C, and H.

FIGURE 30-15
LinoColor's LCH
Correction dialog box

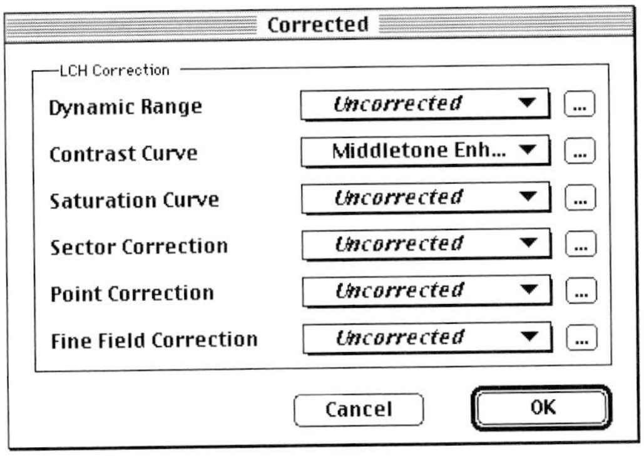

FIGURE 30-16
LinoColor's Dynamic
Range dialog box,
reached through
LCH Correction

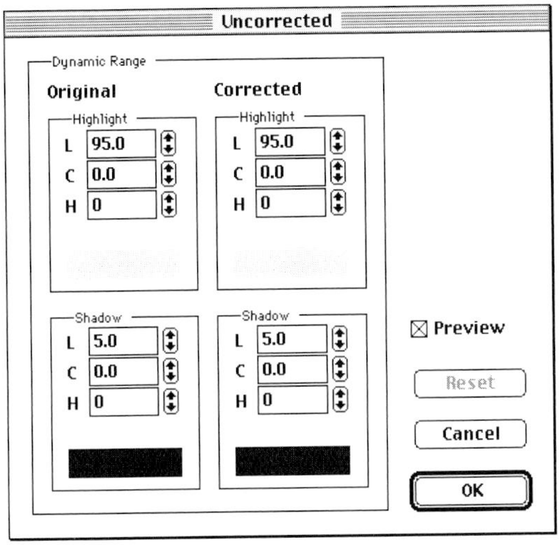

Of course, there's regular curve-based nonlinear correction, too, although LinoColor calls it Contrast. In Figure 33-17, we chose Middletone Enhancement from the Contrast Curve popup menu reached from the LCH Correction dialog box in Figure 33-15.

FIGURE 33-17
LinoColor's Contrast
Curve dialog box after
selecting Middletone
Enhancement

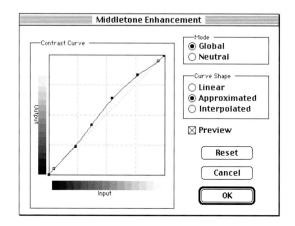

There are several kinds of tools for selectively changing different axes of the HSB model. A useful one is the Saturation Curve, again available from the main LCH Correction dialog box (see Figure 33-18). By adjusting this curve, you can control overall intensity of color throughout the image.

Sector Correction, on the other hand, lets you make color changes for any of the six primary and secondary colors (see Figure 33-19). You can move the entire chunk of the spectrum in any of the three axes of hue, saturation, and brightness (or H, C, and L).

FIGURE 33-18
LinoColor's
Saturation Curve
dialog box

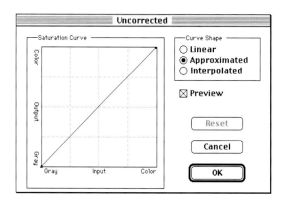

FIGURE 33-19
LinoColor's Sector
Correction dialog box

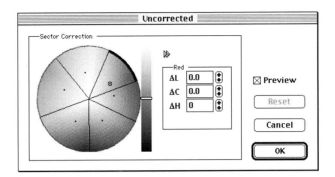

You can go even farther than this by using tools that allow you to specify areas in the image for correction. But suffice it to say, anything you can do in Photoshop to make specific corrections in hue, saturation, or brightness, you can accomplish with even finer gradations of control and selection in LinoColor.

SECOND GLANCE SOFTWARE SCANTASTIC

ScanTastic, from Second Glance Software, is available as a Photoshop plug-in on the Mac, with separate versions for Apple, Epson, and HP scanners. Each version sports the same set of features. We tested ScanTastic's HP-flavored version, and found it an enormous improvement over the DeskScan II software HP bundles (see our choice words on DeskScan II earlier in this chapter).

SCANNING. The main scanning window for Scantastic lets you set all the standard items (see Figure 33-20). A unique feature, however, is that the preview window shows a histogram. There's no way to use this elsewhere, but as you rescan with different values, the histogram updates to reflect it.

To access more advanced controls, check the Enhance box. ScanTastic tells you upfront which of these "enhancements" is done in the scanner hardware; that is, which are working on higher-bit-depth data rather than on 24-bit acquired images.

SHARPENING. Sharpening is, unfortunately, limited to a slider that affects all variables at once (see Figure 33-21). However, even with

FIGURE 33-20
ScanTastic's Control
dialog box, accessed
via the Photoshop
Import menu

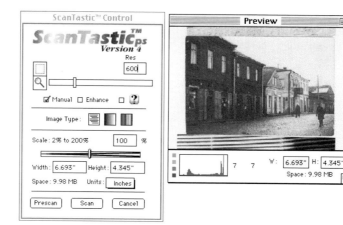

FIGURE 33-21
ScanTastic's
sharpening setting

this limited control, the final result isn't bad. With some experimentation you might choose to use it; more likely, you will want to wait until acquiring the image in Photoshop.

CORRECTION. ScanTastic has both tonal-curve and eyedropper adjustments, both of which show you swatches of the sample data or adjustments (see Figures 33-22 and 33-23). The curves setting, interestingly enough, is not done in hardware, while the eyedropper setting directly affects how the scan is made if you check the Perform In Hardware box.

The saturation setting lets you make changes for 14 points along the spectrum (see Figure 33-24).

FIGURE 33-22
ScanTastic's
curves setting

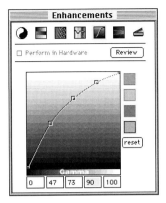

FIGURE 33-22
ScanTastic's
curves setting

FIGURE 33-23
ScanTastic's
eyedropper
sample setting

HALFTONING. If you set your scan type to bilevel—indicated by a little icon depicting rows of type—you can choose a halftoning method for the bitmap from within ScanTastic. For a sample of the line method, see Figure 33-25.

FIGURE 33-24
ScanTastic's
saturation setting

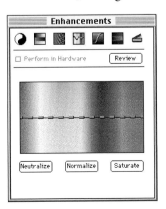

FIGURE 33-25
Halftoning in
ScanTastic

UMAX PHOTOPERFECT/MAGICSCAN

The Macintosh and Windows software bundled with most Umax scanners, including the PowerLook II, raises incomprehensibility to new heights. At first glance, the software appears simple. And it is, until you try to change something as simple as the level of sharpening being applied. This requires a multistep procedure into an Alice in Wonderland set of nested programs and dialog boxes.

The software package itself led us to distraction. To make a scan, you launch Binuscan PhotoPerfect. However, PhotoPerfect is just a processing and correction program that also handles batch processing. The actual scanning is done by a separate program called MagicScan. MagicScan doesn't offer any tools for correction or editing; it can barely make the scan sometimes. (The Windows version we tested consistently generated an error when launched as a TWAIN module from inside of Photoshop, but worked fine when launched as a standalone application.)

SCANNING. Setting up to scan is the most straightforward part of the process, with only a few settings that can be changed (see Figure 33-26). In the Scanner Control window, you can select the type of input data—reflective, or negative or positive transparency—and then set input resolution, color mode, and whether descreening should be applied.

You can select multiple areas on the preview and apply different settings, as long as you keep the kind of input data the same. Each area you add shows up in the Scan Job List window. You can rename these, but you cannot control where the files get saved. When you're ready to scan, you can do them one at a time or as a batch.

FIGURE 33-26
MagicScan's
somewhat confusing
set of windows for
performing a scan

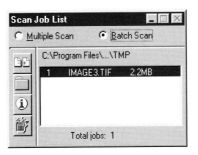

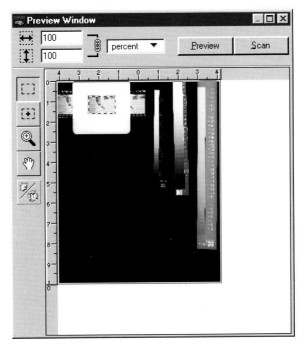

Here's where it gets confusing. Your scans are saved as raw, uncorrected data. These raw scans get saved (in Windows) in the "Data\tmp\" directory. This is important to know if you want to adjust how corrections are applied. The raw scans are taken by a part of PhotoPerfect (PhotoPerfect Image Manager or PIM), which runs in the background. It applies the correction settings against any images you scan and saves them in the "Done" directory.

CORRECTION. So what if you'd like to actually make corrections? Well, you can't on an image-by-image basis, but you can make changes to a settings file that affect all subsequent scans. The manual is a bit short on details on how to do this, but we've got it nailed.

To edit the settings file, you should first make a reference scan after quitting the PIM program. This reference scan gets stored in the tmp directory we note above. Next, quit the MagicScan program. This action, oddly enough, launches the PhotoPerfect application. Click on the settings icon, and you'll be taken to a dialog box that allows you to change settings for how images are saved and separated.

In that dialog box, the popup menu in the upper right lists the various settings files. What the manual doesn't explain is how to figure out which files work with your particular scanner and setting. Each scanner has a set of three files in the format "scanner_mode_type". The scanner is represented by four letters corresponding to the Umax model. For instance, PLII stands for PowerLook II. The mode is always C for color; and the type is either N for negative, R for reflective, or T for positive transparency.

After selecting the appropriate setting from the popup menu, an Edit button appears. Click on that and, at long last, the settings edit dialog box opens (see Figure 33-27). Click Load Image, and then open the uncorrected file from the tmp directory that you scanned as a reference image. You can then use this reference as you make

FIGURE 33-27
PhotoPerfect's
settings edit
dialog box

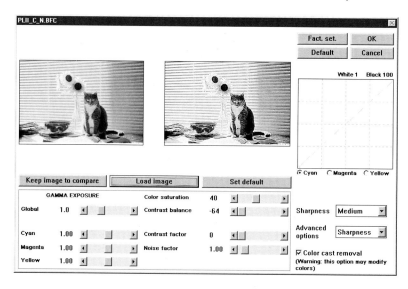

changes to the settings and see how they would be applied to an image of that type. The tools here are nonintuitive and, it would appear, not quite nonlinear. Your most profound tools are the Saturation and Contrast Balance bars, and the effect of these is pretty unpredictable, and not well explained in the manual.

Unfortunately, it appears that you cannot maintain multiple settings files, as the PIM software automatically selects the correct file for the scanner model, mode, and type, without the potential for a user to specify an alternative.

SHARPENING. The only way to turn automatic sharpening off is by visiting the dialog box shown in Figure 33-27. Select None from the Sharpness popup menu. If you've got the guts, you can attempt to wrestle sharpness controls to the ground by doing the very interface-rejecting act of selecting Sharpness from the Advanced Sharpness popup menu. Strangely, this brings up the Advanced Sharpness dialog box (see Figure 33-28). The values in this box are on an arbitrary scale from 1 to 9; the ratios listed at the top of each column correspond to the dpi:lpi ratio that you're scanning at. As we know from other parts of this book, the amount of sharpening you need is directly dependent on the resolution of the image compared to the output size. Our recommendation, as with all non-unsharp masking controls, is to turn this off and sharpen in an image-editing application that has the full range of USM settings.

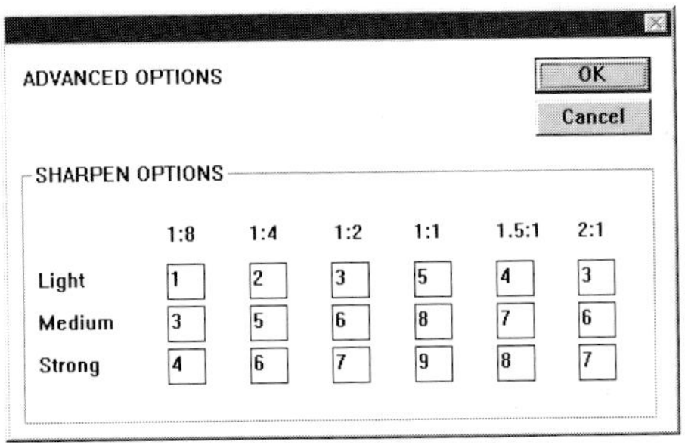

FIGURE 33-28
PhotoPerfect's
Advanced Sharpening
Options dialog box

ADVANCED OPTIONS   OK
                                   Cancel

SHARPEN OPTIONS

	1:8	1:4	1:2	1:1	1.5:1	2:1
Light	1	2	3	5	4	3
Medium	3	5	6	8	7	6
Strong	4	6	7	9	8	7

SCANNERIFIC AND HALFTONARAMA!

Two hundred years ago, no one used halftones. When they wanted to print a picture with grays or tints, they had someone etch it into wood or metal. Crosshatching was an art form, and the fine line art they created was so good that we still find it used today. In the subsequent years, the technology has progressed by leaps and bounds, but the concepts have held fast. Halftones—whether in illustrations or photographs—are subtle and can be beautiful. It's all in the hands of the creator: you.

We hope you've enjoyed this waltz through the process of creating scans and halftones. We have no doubt that with all this information under your belt, in no time you'll be roaring through the desktop-publishing jungles, scanner in one hand, imagesetter in the other—a true DTP professional.

INDEX

C

PERMISSIONS

Photographs of the Earth and moon used for the part, chapter, and other opening pages of the book, courtesy National Aeronautics and Space Administration.

The following images are reprinted with permission from the Special Collections Division, University of Washington Libraries.

Figures 16-2, 16-4, 24-5, pages 208, 210, 283, Photo #659

Figures 17-1, 7-4, 7-5, 7-6, pages 214, 94, 95, 96,
Photo #80.A.W&S

Figure 18-1, page 222, Photo by A. Curtis, Negative #30744.

Figures 20-2 through 20-9, pages 243, 245, 246, 247, 248, 249,
251, 252, Photo by Farquharson, Negative #11.

Figure 9-1, page 125, Photo by Goetzman Photo

Figure 9-6, page 128, Photo by Clifford Photo,
Negative #UW9685

Figure 9-7, page 129, Photo by Todd, Negative #UW neg 10511

Figure 9-9, pages 134–137, Photo by Lee, Negative #20056

Illustrations used as Figures 15-2, 16-1, and 16-3, pages 202, 208, and 209, © 1993 Steve Stankiewicz.

Illustration used as Figure 3-4, page 38, courtesy Simon Tuckett.

Udaipur in Figure 7-2, pages 90–91 courtesy of Carol Thuman.

Figure 9-5, page 127 courtesy PhotoDisc.

Images on Color Page F, G, H, I, J, and K, courtesy PhotoDisc, Inc., from *The Signature Series: 4, The Painted Table* and *8, Study of Form and Color*; and their regular series, volume 6, *Nature, Wildlife and the Environment.*

Cookie monster food styling appearing on Color Pages B and P by Lynn D. Warner.

STAY IN TOUCH

As we said way back at the beginning of the book, it took us over five years to finally get around to writing this book and another four to write the second edition. In that time, it seems like the whole world of scanning and halftones from the desktop has changed a thousand percent. And there's no sign that the changes will slow down in the future. One way that we'll keep up with all of the new tools, techniques, and tribulations (so we can roll them into the third edition) is by keeping up with all of you. If you find techniques that you find helpful, if you've learned anything particularly good from this book, or if you find something that you think is just plain wrong, let us know. Here's how to get in touch.

Email	\<authors@rwsh.com\>
Web site	\<http://www.rwsh.com\>
Mailing address	1619 8th Ave. N, Seattle, WA 98109-3007
Fax	(206) 285-0308

COLOPHON

SOFTWARE

We certainly used a lot of software in testing concepts and creating this book. We mention it throughout, but here's a comprehensive list of software and version numbers we tested and used. For details on the software and links to the manufacturers' Web sites, see the *Real World Scanning and Halftones* Web site at http://www.rwsh.com.

Adobe Systems:
      Photoshop 4, Illustrator 7, PageMaker 6.5, and
      Acrobat 3 (including Capture)
Beale St. Exposure Pro (Macintosh only)
Caere Corporation OmniPage Professional 7 for Mac
Equilibrium DeBabelizer 4 and 4.5 for Windows 95/NT
Extensis Intellihance and PhotoTools
HyperSnap (Windows only)
Macromedia FreeHand 7
Microsoft Word 6.0.1
QuarkXPress 3.3 and 4.0
Corel Corporation CorelDraw 8 and CorelPhoto-Paint 8
Micrografx Picture Publisher 7
Ulead PhotoImpact

HOW WE MADE THIS BOOK

This book was put together on several machines over several months.

TYPEFACES. The body copy and running heads are set in Roger Slimbach's Minion (Adobe Systems); and the headings, chapter, and part openings are set in Copperplate Gothic 33bc.

ILLUSTRATION,   DESIGN,   TESTING,   AND   PRODUCTION. Illustrations were created and manipulated using Adobe Photoshop 2.5 and 4.0, Macromedia FreeHand 3.1 and 7.0, LaserTalk 1.3, and Adobe Illustrator 5 and 7.0. The book was designed and produced by Glenn Fleishman using an Apple PowerBook 3400c with 80Mb of RAM in QuarkXpress 3.3 and 4.0.

Glenn tested Macintosh and PC software and hardware using the PowerBook running both Mac OS 8.0 and Windows 95 OSR2 (through Connectix Virtual PC 1.0.1); and running Windows 95 with a non-brand-name 166 Mhz Pentium MMX with a Jaz Jet Ultra Wide SCSI card, and a Diamond Stealth S220 4MB 3D video card. He used both a Motorola BitSURFR Pro EZ (ISDN) and a Motorola ModemSURFR 33.6 fax/modem ISA card for 'Net connectivity. David and Steve were 'Netted via a Farallon Netopia running ISDN.

We used a lot of scanning and output equipment for the second edition: a Hewlett-Packard PhotoSmart Photo Scanner, PhotoSmart Photo Printer, and 6100C color scanner; Umax PowerLook II; Linotype-Hell Saphir; and Agfa Arcus II.

To create screen captures, we used The Beale Street Group's Exposure Pro for the Macintosh and HyperSnap for Windows 95.

IMAGES. Images of the earth were scanned from 35 mm color reversal film directly into Photo CD format. Most of the images throughout the book were scanned on a Hewlett-Packard ScanJet IIc flatbed scanner (for the first edition) and any of the four scanners mentioned above for the second edition. The scans for the color pages were all created using the Agfa Arcus II and FotoLook scanning software.

COVER. The cover illustration was designed by Cary Norsworthy, using a Linotype-Hell Jade scanner, Photoshop 3.0, and Illustrator 6.0. Cary worked on a Power Mac 7200/90 with 72 Mb of RAM and an ixMicro Twin Turbo graphics card.

OUTPUT. The black-and-white portions of the book were output CTP (computer to plate) by R. R. Donnelley using an LF3244 Creo platesetter at 2,540 dpi. Color pages were output at 2,400 dpi on an Agfa ProSet 9600 by LithoTech Canada in Vancouver. (thanks to Ernst Vegt). R. R. Donnelley printed this book on an OA-4BK-1600 narrow web offset using 70 pound Sterling Web Dull paper.